SEAN DENNIS CASHMAN

African-Americans and the Quest for Civil Rights, 1900–1990

NEW YORK UNIVERSITY PRESS
NEW YORK AND LONDON

Library of Congress Cataloging-in-Publication Data
Cashman, Sean Dennis.
African-Americans and the quest for civil rights, 1900–1990 / Sean
Dennis Cashman.
p. cm.
Includes bibliographical references and index.
ISBN 0-8147-1440-4 (cloth)
1. Afro-Americans—Civil rights. 2. Civil rights movements—
United States—History—20th century. 3. United States—Race
relations. 4. Racism—United States—History—20th century.
5. Civil rights workers—United States—Biography. I. Title.
E185.61.C292 1991
323.1'196073'009—dc20 90-28841
CIP

New York University Press books are printed on acid-free paper,
and their binding materials are chosen for strength and durability.

Book design by Ken Venezio

For Donald and Basha Baerman, whose friendship has sustained me over many years and whose experiences have sharpened my own vigil of American society.

Contents

vii

Illustrations

ILLUSTRATIONS

Preface and Acknowledgments

This short book charts in outline the progress of African-Americans in their quest for civil rights in the United States from 1900 to 1990. Primarily a political and social history, it is not a history of achievements on the part of African-American artists, musicians, and performers, often outstanding though these have been. However, some chapters do contain summaries of the work of African-American historians and novelists, especially where these have emphasized black consciousness or made people more keenly aware of the political, intellectual, and artistic contributions of African-Americans to American culture.

The book came to be written as a result of very particular circumstances. In the 1980s I wrote four interdisciplinary histories of the United States for New York University Press covering in sum the period 1865–1945. Having concluded the fourth book with the Japanese surrender at the end of World War II in 1945 and the onset of the Cold War, I found myself poised to begin writing about modern America as the United States moved toward the close of the twentieth century. Not only does the modern period seem remarkable for the part the United States has played and for its commitment to economic, political, and military involvement across the globe; for being an affluent society despite poverty amid plenty; and for its continuing revolutions in communications and transportation; but also for the emergence of protest for and by African-Americans at the fore of the political stage and its later shift in emphasis from civil rights to black power. Indeed, in the recent past the story of protest by African-Americans carries a principle key to the evolving history of the United States.

The book was drafted in 1988 and 1989. However, it grew out of the many years I had previously spent in the Department of American Studies at the University of Manchester, England, several of them teaching interdisciplinary courses with my versatile colleague Godfrey Kearns. I owe a particular debt to Chris Harries, former graduate student, who had undertaken a thorough review of African-American history since slavery. He allowed me to draw from what he had written and also identified various articles and other materials for me to study. He was especially perceptive about the roots of the civil rights movement; debates over Washington, Garvey, and Du Bois; the early protests of African-Americans against Jim Crow racism in the South; and the latent political power of the African-American church. The early chapters of the book owe much to his contribution. Like many readers, I have been moved by the profound novels of Richard Wright, Ralph Ellison, and their heirs. I have also been much influenced by, and have drawn from, the works of historians and analysts Godfrey Hodgson, Manning Marable, James T. Patterson, and William Julius Wilson.

The book begins and ends with broad strokes, covering the history of African-Americans before and after the zenith of the great civil rights movement of the 1950s and 1960s in only four chapters. By comparison, the intense activity and significant achievements of civil rights at flood tide are discussed in greater detail in five chapters. Thus the book moves from long shot to close-up and back again. It borrows directly from one of its companion volumes in American history for New York University Press. This is particularly true of the first and second chapters, which are drawn from *America in the Twenties and Thirties* with some additional material from its sequel, *America, Roosevelt, and World War II*. The rest of the book, however, is new.

During the period covered in this history the preferred descriptive name for American citizens descended from both Africa and the United States has moved from Negro to colored in mid-century to black from the late 1960s to the 1980s and then, as we come to the close of the twentieth century, to African-American. We have chosen to use African-American throughout while respecting whatever term is used in the various books and articles that are quoted directly in the text.

Colin Jones, director of New York University Press, responded courageously to the idea of a short history about African-Americans and the quest for civil rights and offered helpful advice. The manuscript was typed by Mrs. Eileen Grimes of the University of Manchester and by Mrs. Lee Plaut, Mrs. Dorothy Kreppein, and Mrs. Maureen Boerner of Adelphi University. Ms. Mary Ison, Ms. Maja Felaco, and Mr. Jerry Kearns of the Library of Congress, Washington, D.C., were most helpful in the selection of illustrations, as was Ms. Terri Geeskin of the Museum of Modern Art, New York.

PART ONE

Before

1

Southern Efficiency and Northern Charm

The story of African-Americans and their quest for civil rights in the twentieth century, the subject of this book, is a story with deep resonances. It is about nothing less than the transformation of African-American citizens' place in American society—constitutional, social, and cultural—and it tells us something of the transformations white society had to ask of itself.

In a century where one of the primary themes of art has been the relationship of the individual and society, the continuously shifting fortunes of African-American citizens in American society have proved fertile subjects for argument and discussion. Moreover, the experience of African-Americans makes a stark comment on a central paradox of American history—how a nation composed of such diverse ethnic groups and beliefs could endure and survive. Thus novelist James Baldwin declared, "The story of the Negro in America is the story of America, or, more precisely, it is the story of Americans." His most fundamental point seems to have been that, as the African-American experience moved from slavery and incarceration to freedom and citizenship, African-Americans were, ironically enough, especially privileged to articulate the problems and preoccupations of men and women in modern society.

The history of the nineteenth and twentieth centuries has included various national struggles for liberation, mass migrations, and both freedom of political expression and the lack thereof. The fragmentation of society and the alienation of the individual from society and from himself or herself are also important cultural phenomena. Because of their experiences, African-Americans have been deeply involved in and have become identified with these things. They have expressed their responses in words, in music, and in their political struggle for recognition and rights. They benefitted from their double alienation from Africa and from American society at a time when America was responding to them and becoming ready to meet them, at least culturally, on their own terms.

What is meant by civil rights? For the generations who witnessed the apogee of the drama in the Second Reconstruction of the 1950s and 1960s, civil rights had a very precise meaning: they were the political, social, and economic rights of African-American citizens to vote and to enjoy equality of opportunity in education, employment, and housing. This also entailed free access to places of public accommodation such as parks, bars, cafes and restaurants, and public transport. The essential means of the loose coalition we call the civil rights movement to address its ends were litigation and demonstration, whether by rallies and marches, economic boycotts, or debate in the mass media. However, such a precise definition of civil rights and of the tactics of the civil rights movement must also take into account the social and cultural condition of African-Americans—their location and dispersal following the Great Migration and their work, economic prospects, and play.

The original circumstances for the development of a civil rights movement to restore their due dignity to African-American citizens had not been promising at the turn of the century and for several decades thereafter. Of the total American population of 76,094,000 in 1900, 8,833,000 were African-Americans—about 11.5 percent of the whole. Over 85 percent of them lived in the South—the eleven states of the old Confederacy and five others, Oklahoma and Kentucky to the west and Delaware, Maryland, West Virginia, and the District of Columbia to the north. Of the total population of 24,524,000 of this "Census South," 7,923,000 were African-American. Thus, whereas the ratio of African-Americans to whites across the country as a whole was, approximately, one in nine, in the South it was one in three. In two states, Mississippi and South Carolina, they predominated.

The abolition of slavery and the destruction of the rebel Confederacy

Although the crowding throng waiting for a bus at the Greyhound Bus Terminal in Memphis, Tennessee, in September 1943, mixes white and African-American citizens, the waiting room in the bus station is clearly designated for whites only. In a century that witnessed several remarkable revolutions in transportation, it was the continuing presence of segregation in interstate transport facilities that reminded the United States that the deep South had barely entered the twentieth century with appropriate social values. As public pressure upon transportation resources increased, it was inevitable that segregation of interstate transportation facilities would be among the first targets of the civil rights movement. (Photograph taken for the Office of War Information by Esther Bubley; Library of Congress.)

in the Civil War (1861–1865) had led to the granting of equal social and political rights to African-Americans in the period of Reconstruction (1865–1877). The Thirteenth Amendment (1865) proscribed slavery. The first section of the Fourteenth Amendment (1866) defined American citizens as all those born or naturalized in the United States. It enjoined states from abridging their rights to life, liberty, property, and process of law. The second section of the amendment threatened to reduce proportionately the representation in Congress of any state denying the suffrage to adult males. Congress determined to protect African-American suffrage in the South by the Fifteenth Amendment (1869–1870), according to which the right to vote was not to be denied "on account of race, color, or previous condition of servitude." Yet forty years later these rights had been assailed or eroded by white racists. The abject position of African-Americans was such that historian Rayford Logan in *The Betrayal of the Negro* (1954; 1969) described the turn of the century as "the nadir" of African-American history, notwithstanding the existence of slavery up to 1865.

The Tyrant Custom—Race Relations at Their Nadir

The regular intimacy of contact under slavery was being superseded by a caste system with next to no sustained contact, which resulted in an inexorable gulf between African-Americans and whites. Although African-Americans were the largest of America's ethnic minorities, they were segregated in schooling, housing, and places of public accommodation, such as parks, theaters, hospitals, schools, libraries, courts, and even cemeteries. The variety and fluidity of access of the late nineteenth century were abandoned as state after state adopted rigid segregation in a series of so-called Jim Crow laws. ("Jim Crow" was the title of a minstrel song of 1830 that presented African-Americans as childlike and inferior.)

In *The Strange Career of Jim Crow* (1955; 1974) historian C. Vann Woodward argues that cast-iron segregation was a product of the late nineteenth and early twentieth centuries and that the avalanche of Jim Crow laws began when poor white farmers came to power. Moreover, a new generation of African-Americans had grown up who had never known slavery. Previously, aristocratic southerners had shown a paternalistic attitude to African-Americans, protecting them from some overt racist attacks by poor whites. They knew that they did not need segregation laws to confirm their own privileged social position. Nevertheless, none of the states passed a single comprehensive segregation law. Instead, they proceeded piecemeal over a period of thirty to fifty years. Thus South Carolina segregated the races in successive stages, beginning with trains (1898) and moving to streetcars (1905), train depots and restaurants (1906), textile plants (1915 and 1916), circuses (1917), pool halls (1924), and beaches and recreation centers (1934). Georgia began with railroads and prisons (1891) and moved to sleeping cars (1899) and, finally, pool halls (1925), but refused to segregate places of public accommodation until 1954.

Another factor in turning the tide of white resentment was the move of African-Americans to new mining and industrial communities where, for the first time, white hillbillies were not only thrown into daily contact with them but also into competition for the same low-caste jobs at rockbottom wages. For low-class whites, social segregation was a means of asserting their superiority. As C. Vann Woodward puts it in his *The Origins of the New South* (1951), "It took a lot of ritual and Jim Crow to bolster the creed of white supremacy in the bosom of a white man working for a black man's wages." The South had made sure that African-Americans were socially and academically inferior by denying them a decent education. Southern legislatures starved African-American schools of adequate funds, thereby making it impossible for them to approach anywhere near the same standards. In 1910 the eleven southern states spent an average of $9.45 on each white pupil but only $2.90 on each African-American pupil.

The South reacted against the natural tide of resentment by African-Americans to its new restrictive policies with more repression. Mississippi was the first state effectively to disfranchise African-American citizens by a constitutional convention in 1890. It was followed by South Carolina in 1895, Louisiana in 1898, North Carolina (by an amendment) in 1900, Alabama in 1901, Virginia in 1901 and 1902, Georgia (by amendment) in 1908, and the new state of Oklahoma in 1910. Four more states achieved the same ends without amending their constitutions: Tennessee, Florida, Arkansas, and Texas. Three pernicious and sophistical arguments were advanced by the proponents of disfranchisement. The removal of the African-American vote, they said, would end corruption at elections. It would prevent African-Americans from holding the balance of power in contests between rival factions of whites. Moreover, it would oblige African-Americans to abandon their false hopes of betterment and, instead, make them accept their true social place. As a result, race relations would steadily improve.

The Mississippi Constitution of 1890 set the pattern. It required a poll tax of two dollars from prospective voters at registration. Those who intended to vote at elections had to present their receipt at the polls. Thus anyone who mislaid his receipt forfeited his vote. More insidious was the requirement that, in order to register, prospective voters had to be "able to read the Constitution, or to understand the Constitution when read." It also excluded those convicted of bribery, burglary, theft, and bigamy. Racist officials used the various ordinances to discriminate in favor of poor, illiterate whites and against African-Americans.

The ruling elites in other states approved of the new Mississippi plan and several states borrowed from one another. In so doing they improved on previous attempts to disfranchise African-Americans. For example, Louisiana believed that the understanding clause was so obviously suspect that it could be invalidated in a court case. Thus it hit on the grandfather clause as being, legally, more secure. Only those who had had a grandfather on the electoral roll of 1867 could vote.

These devices were nothing if not effective. In Louisiana 130,344 African-Americans were registered to vote in 1890; in 1900 there were 5,320. In 1909 there were only 1,342. In Alabama there were 181,000 African-American voters in 1890; in 1900 there were three thousand. In the South as a whole African-American participation fell by 62 percent. In 1900 Ben ("Pitchfork") Tillman of South Carolina boasted on the floor of the Senate, "We have done our best. We have scratched our heads to find out how we could eliminate the last one of them. We stuffed ballot boxes. We shot them. We are not ashamed of it." Despite concessions to poor whites, white participation in elections also declined —by 26 percent. Thus while, on average, 73 percent of men voted in the 1890s, only 30 percent did so in the early 1900s. Opposition parties dwindled away and the Democrats were left undisputed champions of the South.

Social segregation was also upheld by the Supreme Court. Its most notorious decision came in *Plessy* v. *Ferguson* in 1896. Louisiana state law required "separate but equal" accommodations for African-American and white passengers on public carriers and provided a penalty for passengers sitting in the wrong car. Homer Plessy was an octoroon so pale that he usually passed for white, but when he sat in a white car he was arrested. He argued that the state law of Louisiana violated the

The Georgia Capitol in Atlanta rises above nearby slums in the block between Fair and Hunter Streets at the corner of Fraser Street. Buildings to the left are white dwellings; those in the center are occupied by African-Americans. (Photograph taken for the Federal Public Housing Authority, October 1938, by Oliver; Library of Congress.)

Fourteenth and Fifteenth Amendments. Justice John Marshall Harlan of Kentucky agreed with him, maintaining, "Our constitution is color-blind and neither knows nor tolerates classes among citizens." Moreover, "What can more certainly arouse race hate, what more certainly create and perpetuate a feeling of distrust between these races, than state enactments which in fact proceed on the ground that colored citizens are so inferior and degraded that they cannot be allowed to sit in public coaches occupied by white citizens?" However, he was overruled by the other eight justices, who approved of the doctrine of "separate but equal." Justice Henry Billings Brown of Michigan, speaking for the majority on May 18, 1896, ruled with corrosive racial candor, "If one race be inferior to the other socially, the Constitution of the United

States cannot put them upon the same plane." In *Williams* v. *Mississippi* on April 25, 1898, the Court went further and approved the Mississippi plan for disfranchising African-Americans. The Court unanimously upheld the opinion of Justice Joseph McKenna that "a state does not violate the equal protection clause of the fourteenth amendment when it requires eligible voters to be able to read, write, interpret, or understand any part of the Constitution."

Edgar Gardner Murphy, a humanitarian journalist, reported in *The Basis of Ascendancy* (1909) how extremists had moved "from an undiscriminating attack upon the Negro's ballot to a like attack upon his schools, his labor, his life—from the contention that no Negro shall vote to the contention that no Negro shall learn, that no Negro shall labor, and [by implication] that no Negro shall live." The result was an "all-absorbing autocracy of race," an "absolute identification of the stronger race with the very being of the state." In 1903 analyst Charles W. Chestnutt said that "the rights of the Negroes are at a lower ebb than at any time during the thirty-five years of their freedom, and the race prejudice more intense and uncompromising."

Racist scientists tried to prove that African-Americans were inferior to whites. In 1929 Lawrence Fick in the *South African Journal of Science* declared that Africans showed "a marked inferiority" to European whites and that the number who could benefit from education was limited. Americans measured intelligence on the basis of a test first developed by Frenchman Alfred Binet in 1905 and based on the skills expected of, and acquired by, educated children from the middle class. Not surprisingly, such a test found undereducated children, whether poor white, immigrant, or African-American, less intelligent. The final, conclusive "proof" of the inferiority of African-Americans came when African-American soldiers scored worse than whites in intelligence tests given in World War I. Subsequent investigation showed that African-Americans from the North scored higher than southern whites. Here was disturbing proof of the inferiority of southern education as a whole.

The Early Contours of Civil Rights

The response by African-Americans to raw oppression was confused. The most rigorous leaders struggled to obtain equal rights for African-Americans. But, as they were trapped half in and half out of American society, this struggle alternated between a desire for assimilation with white society and a desire to assert independence for African-Americans. W. E. B. Du Bois described the dilemma of African-Americans in *The Souls of Black Folk* (1903): "One feels his twoness, an American, a Negro, two souls, two thoughts, two unreconciled strivings in one dark body." Novelist James Baldwin observed years later how the African-American was often "gloomily referred to as that shadow that lies athwart our national life." That shadow began to take shape and impose its will on American society despite the considerable obstacles in the way.

As far as the quest for civil rights is concerned, we can interpret the period 1900–1945 as a journey over a giant suspension bridge across a turbulent river, the dark waters of racism. On near and far sides, the bridge is suspended between the poles of two very different Supreme Court decisions. The first is the notorious "separate but equal" ruling in *Plessy* v. *Ferguson* of 1896, symbol of the heinous institutional racism of the period 1890–1910; the second is the ruling that separate is unequal in *Brown* v. *Board of Education* of 1954, the most momentous post-World War II court decision yet and a mighty symbol of the victories of the great civil rights movement of the 1950s and 1960s. The outlying buttresses of the bridge are provided by the enduring civil rights or separatist groups that were formed in the period: in 1910 the National Association for the Advancement of Colored People (NAACP); in 1911 the Urban League; in 1931 the Nation of Islam; and in 1943 the Committee, later the Congress, for Racial Equality (CORE). The apex of the suspension bridge is provided by the great flowering of cultural talent of the 1920s, known variously as the "Black" or "Negro" or "Harlem Renaissance." During these years four charismatic leaders guided their followers across a bridge, albeit to different destinations beyond the river: Booker T. Washington, W. E. B. Du Bois, Marcus Garvey, and Asa Philip Randolph.

Although there were specific political organizations that focused their attention upon the quest of African-Americans for civil rights in the period 1900–1945, there was no mass civil rights movement. What existed from the variety of groups—the NAACP, UNIA, the Nation of Islam, and others—was the potential for one. Thus the story of the preface to the civil rights movement is composed of a tissue of factors. These include not only the latent political power of African-American people but also the power of their arts to raise national consciousness about the contribution of African-Americans to the social fabric and provide poignant expressions of their dilemmas.

Moreover, certain of the phenomena that account for the way civil rights moved to the center of the political stage in the 1950s and then shifted emphasis to black power in the course of the 1960s were already present early in the century. These include the Great Migration of African-Americans from countryside to city and from the South to the North, making African-American problems known to the North and transforming African-Americans into a potentially potent political force to be courted by both main parties and by radical groups; increasing literacy among African-Americans and their awareness of the discrepancy between the ideals of the American Constitution and the blatant practice of racism, most notably in World War II; the development of nonviolent tactics to protest discrimination, initially by religious groups; and various Supreme Court and lesser court hearings that provided forums for such eloquent African-American attorneys as Moorfield Storey, Walter F. White, and Thurgood Marshall to press for rulings on racial equality that exposed discrimination, established the legal principle of equality before the law, and legitimized the civil rights movement. Furthermore, the later tension between civil rights and black power was anticipated in the 1920s by the controversy between W. E. B. Du Bois and A. Philip Randolph on one side and Marcus Garvey and his short-lived United Negro Improvement Association (UNIA) organization (1914) on the other.

Before 1900, protest by African-Americans existed only in local groups, apart from a series of conventions summoned to endorse presidential candidates. Nevertheless, state and local conventions debated the new laws on public accommodation and disfranchisement. Their protests were handicapped by poverty, illiteracy, and fragmentation. Leaders found it almost impossible to develop consciousness among African-Americans and unity on a scale to combat the considerable white forces arrayed against them, notably the adverse political climate, the indifference of the Supreme Court, and white intimidation and violence. Their political voice was silenced. There was no African-American congressman for twenty-seven years, between 1901, when George H. White of North Carolina left Congress, and 1928, when Oscar De Priest was elected for Chicago.

Booker T. Washington and W. E. B. Du Bois

Since African-Americans were being displaced from their traditional trades and confined to menial jobs in the towns, those who did succeed in entering the worlds of business and the professions were obliged by white society to adopt its attitudes in order to retain their hard-won position. Their undeclared leader was Booker T. Washington, head of Tuskegee Industrial Institute, Alabama.

Booker Taliaferro Washington was born at Hale's Ford, Franklin County, Virginia, in 1856, the son of a white father and an African-American mother who was enslaved. At the end of the Civil War he worked in a coal mine and salt furnace at Malden, West Virginia, while he attended school. From 1872 to 1875 he studied at Hampton Institute, the Negro vocational school in Virginia, where he earned his keep by working as a janitor. He also taught school at Malden (1875–1877) and subsequently studied at Wayland Seminary, Washington, D.C. In 1879 he returned to Hampton Institute, where he was in charge of the Indian dormitory and night school. In 1881 he was selected to organize an African-American normal school at Tuskegee chartered by the Alabama legislature.

Thereafter, his name was practically synonymous with African-American education. In fact, Booker T. Washington created three major institutions: the Normal and Industrial Institute for Negroes, the college in rural Alabama devoted primarily to agricultural and technical education; the Tuskegee Machine, a lobby of African-American intellectuals, politicos, and educators and white philanthropists who supported Washington's political and economic aims; and the National Negro Business League, committed to establishing and consolidating a system of African-American entrepreneurs within the existing framework of white capitalism. Washington believed that the optimum strategy for the rural masses of African-Americans was to concentrate as much as possible on economic independence by thrift and the acquisition of property. For the time being they were to disregard disfranchisement and Jim Crow social segregation. The encouragement Washington and his school of thought gave to a new generation of African-American entrepreneurs and their clients to "buy black" and to think in terms of black nationalism allowed them to rise commercially at the expense of a different group of artisans, caterers, and porters who were essentially integrationists and who had had the lion's share of the market among African-Americans in the 1870s and 1880s.

Washington was as well known as a propagandist and polemicist as he was as an educational leader. He was invited to speak at the opening of the Cotton States and International Exposition in Atlanta on September 18, 1895, by businessmen who recognized his remarkable powers of expression. His address was one of the most effective political speeches of the Gilded Age, a model fusion of substance and style.

In what was later called the Atlanta Compromise he abandoned the postwar ideal of racial equality in favor of increased economic opportunity for African-Americans. "The wisest among my race understand that the agitation of questions of social equality is the extremest folly and that progress in the enjoyment of all the privileges that will come to us must be the result of severe and constant struggle rather than of artificial forcing." He preached patience, proposed submission, and emphasized material progress. Those African-Americans who rejected the Atlanta Compromise, such as rising activist W. E. B. Du Bois, considered his stance a capitulation to blatant racism. But Washington was telling white society exactly what it wanted to hear—that African-Americans accepted the Protestant work ethic. His most widely reported remark was a subtle metaphor about racial harmony: "In all things social we can be as separate as the fingers, yet one as the hand in all things essential to mutual progress."

Washington's emphasis on racial pride, economic progress, and industrial education encouraged white politicians and businessmen, such as steel tycoon Andrew Carnegie, to subsidize the institutions for African-Americans that he recommended. Through his close connections with business he was able to raise the funds necessary to create the National Negro Business League in 1900. Moreover, he used money not to advance acquiescence by African-Americans but to fight segregation. Others sought a more open insistence on racial pride. In 1890 T. Thomas Fortune, a journalist of New York, persuaded forty African-American protection leagues in cities across the country to join in a national body, the Afro-American League. Historian C. Vann Woodward assesses Washington's work thus: "Washington's life mission was to find a pragmatic compromise that would resolve the antagonisms, suspicions, and aspirations of 'all three classes directly concerned—the Southern white man, the northern white man, and the Negro.' It proved, he admitted 'a difficult and at times a puzzling task.' But he moved with consummate

One of the most controversial of all African-American leaders, Booker T. Washington, the wizard of Tuskegee, not only created an agricultural and technical institute to educate and train African-Americans to achieve economic self-sufficiency but also created an effective bloc of political and financial backers. (Library of Congress.)

diplomacy, trading renunciation for concession and playing sentiment against interest."

Five weeks into his presidency (1901–1909), Theodore Roosevelt invited Booker T. Washington to the White House on October 18, 1901. Roosevelt was also committed to trying to reconcile the South to the Republican party. His invitation was intended as a symbolic gesture to African-Americans and was widely interpreted as such. There was terrible logic in the subsequent outrage of racist southerners when the story broke. The New Orleans *Times-Democrat* thought Roosevelt's action mischievous: "When Mr. Roosevelt sits down to dinner with a negro, he declares that the negro is the social equal of the White Man." Senator Benjamin ("Pitchfork") Tillman declared, "The action of President Roosevelt in entertaining that nigger will necessitate our killing a thousand niggers in the South before they will learn their place again."

Despite Washington's insistence on patience, some African-Americans began to agitate for desegregation on trains, a prime target of the protest movement that was the forerunner of civil rights. They reckoned that railroads would realize that it was more expensive to have segregated seating and would thus yield, if only for the sake of economy. In 1898 the Afro-American League called for a boycott of trains in protest of Jim Crow laws. In 1904 the Maryland Suffrage League began campaigning against the new Jim Crow law there and financed a successful lawsuit against segregated travel in 1905. Also in 1905, the Georgia Equal Rights League declared that African-Americans should be able "to travel in comfort and decency and receive a just equivalent for our money, and yet we are the victims of the most unreasonable sort of caste legislation." In 1909 the National Negro Conference denounced segregation and the oppression of African-Americans. Whites were taken aback by the effectiveness of boycotts when African-Americans either simply stopped using white-owned transport or established small companies of their own. White streetcar companies either ended segregation or went out of business, such as the streetcar company in Richmond, Virginia. However, the wave of protests was short lived.

Washington's approach of so-called gradualism could be justified as a necessary complement to the fearful atmosphere of prejudice and violence in the South. However, African-American intellectuals in the North grew impatient with his time-serving and ambiguity. William Trotter, son of Cleveland's recorder of deeds and a graduate of Harvard, founded

The Niagara Conference of 1905 drew together African-American and white activists to promote the due civil rights of African-Americans and led in 1910 to the founding of the National Association for the Advancement of Colored People (NAACP), the most venerable of all civil rights organizations. In this historic photograph taken in a studio before a backdrop of Niagara Falls, W. E. B. Du Bois is seated in the middle row second from the right. (Library of Congress.)

the most vehemently critical paper, the *Boston Guardian,* in 1901, and roundly abused Washington for his association with Roosevelt, calling him a "self seeker" and a "skulking coward." Trotter criticized Washington at the 1903 annual convention of the Afro-American Council and created uproar at a meeting of the Boston Business League later the same year when he heckled Washington as he tried to speak. The uproar resulted in "the Boston riot" that ended with the imprisonment of

Trotter for thirty days for having disturbed the peace. Nevertheless, Trotter and his creations were radical, vocal forces in the struggle for civil rights.

The publication of *The Souls of Black Folk* by W. E. B. Du Bois in 1903 solidified protest around a new spokesman. William Edward Burghardt Du Bois was born in Great Barrington, Massachusetts, in 1868, graduated from Fisk and Harvard, and attended the University of Berlin. After returning to America in 1894, he taught at Wilberforce University, Ohio, and Pennsylvania University before becoming professor of sociology at Atlanta. A handsome and invariably immaculately dressed man, Du Bois was also a creative writer who produced two novels, *The Quest of the Silver Fleece* (1911) and *The Dark Princess* (1928), and two volumes of essays and poems, *Dark Water* (1920) and *The Gift of Black Folk* (1924). One of Du Bois's early supporters, James Weldon Johnson, said of *The Souls of Black Folk* that "it had a greater effect upon and within the Negro race than any single book published in the country since *Uncle Tom's Cabin*." One of the essays was a withering attack on what Du Bois considered Washington's acceptance of the heinous doctrine of racial inferiority. Du Bois insisted on an end to accommodation: "By every civilized and peaceful method we must strive for the rights which the world accords to men."

Deeply angered by Washington's counterrevolutionary tactics and intensely hostile to the strategy of accommodation, Du Bois invited likeminded activists to a national conference at Fort Erie in July 1905 that established the Niagara Movement. This was an elite cadre of about four hundred college-educated professional people. The Niagara Movement committed itself to continuing vocal protest against "the abridgment of political and civil rights and against inequality of educational opportunity." Du Bois and others published the *Moon* and, later, the *Horizon* as unofficial journals of the movement. Nevertheless, the Niagara Movement failed to establish itself as a distinctive national voice.

Moreover, it was becoming obvious to increasing numbers of African-Americans and sympathetic whites that a policy of accommodation was futile in the face of outright racist hostility. Despite Washington's supposed influence with Roosevelt, the president arbitrarily discharged three companies of African-Americans of the Twenty-fifth Regiment on an unproven charge of rioting in Brownsville, Texas, on August 14, 1906, after some soldiers had retaliated against racial insults. For their part, Roosevelt and his successor, William Howard Taft (1909–1913), had to hold together a diverse coalition of Republicans that included a section of gross racial bigots, the lily-whites, who wanted to establish an all-white Republican party in the South. To appease this faction both presidents limited the number of federal appointments of African-Americans, thereby contributing to racial prejudice.

Jack Johnson and the Great White Hope

White southerners came to accept without question the racist orthodoxy of such men as educator Thomas Pearce Bailey, as expressed in his article "Race Orthodoxy in the South" for *Neale's Monthly Magazine* (1903). He set forth a creed of fifteen points, including such statements as "the white race must dominate"; "The Teutonic peoples stand for race purity"; "The Negro is inferior and will remain so"; "Let there be such industrial education of the Negro as will best fit him to serve the white man"; and "Let the lowest white man count for more than the highest Negro." Even environmentalists who argued that nurture, rather than nature, determined human behavior were reluctant to challenge popular stereotypes. Progressive intellectual John R. Commons expressed the dominant reformist view in 1907. He claimed that African-Americans had opportunities "not only on equal terms, but actually on terms of preference over the whites." Their failure to rise "is recognized even by their partisans as something that was inevitable in the nature of the race at that stage of its development."

However, arguments about genetic inferiority were silenced when boxer Jack Johnson, an African-American and former stevedore from Galveston, Texas, won the world heavyweight boxing title from Canadian Tommy Burns in Sydney, Australia, on Boxing Day, December 26, 1908. Johnson's victory aroused deep consternation throughout the white community. Racists in Congress were so disturbed by the defeat of a white man by an African-American that they proposed, and had passed, a law forbidding the interstate transportation of motion picture films showing prize fights. Immediately after Johnson's sensational victory, former world champion James J. Jefferies, then living in retirement on a farm in California, was urged to come out of retirement to regain the title for the white race. He was eventually persuaded to do so and was defeated in a fifteen-round match at Reno, Nevada, on July 4, 1912.

Johnson was the greatest heavyweight of his time, standing over six feet tall and weighing over two hundred pounds. He moved with the swiftness and grace of a panther. He was widely known for his good nature, his "golden smile," which revealed numerous crowned teeth, and his badinage while in the ring. During the bout with Jefferies, Johnson stopped briefly to lean on the shoulders of his weary opponent and jeered at another, former fighter, Jim Corbett, at the ringside, saying, "Jim, this big bum can't fight any better than you could." However, when a blow reached Johnson that really told, his veneer of good nature vanished and his killer instinct surfaced. He gloried in adulation and enjoyed provoking his numerous white critics. Johnson's prowess was a symbol of strength to African-Americans and his success could make him a rallying point for solidarity among them. In fact, he was inaugurating a mighty tradition of powerful African-American heavyweight champions extending through Joe Louis in the 1930s to Muhammad Ali in the 1960s and 1970s and then to Mike Tyson in the 1980s.

In the 1910s Jack Johnson's numerous white enemies determined to find a white challenger who could defeat him and restore the myth of white supremacy. The great white hope turned out to be Jess Willard of Kansas, a former cowpuncher who was known for feats of strength such as bending a silver dollar between his fingers. However, he was a mediocre fighter. Eventually Johnson, sated with European night life and adulation, became homesick and was keen to accept the suggestion of promoters that he should return and fight Willard. The venue would be Havana, Cuba. When Johnson arrived in poor condition, he disappointed his backers by doing next to no training and spending his days driving about the city with his white wife. The fight was held on April 5, 1915, with soldiers surrounding the stadium in order to prevent racial violence. The first twenty-two rounds were dull but in the twenty-third Johnson sank to the floor—though whether from a blow by Willard or from sunstroke, opinions differ. Thus fell the first of the great African-American stars of the worlds of entertainment and sports. Johnson returned to Chicago, attended subsequent boxing contests in which champions won millions, and in the 1930s became conductor of his own jazz orchestra.

The NAACP and the Early Civil Rights Movement

Not surprisingly, given the prevailing atmosphere of hysteria stoked by institutional racism and the pseudoscientific jargon of prejudiced scientists, African-Americans became helpless victims of race riots instigated

The Great White Hope. Director and playwright Howard Sackler developed the legend of the first African-American heavyweight champion, Jack Johnson, an African-American colossus, into a stunning play about black lives and white lies in a fictional version about a character named Jack Jefferson. It drew a thundering virtuoso performance on stage (1968) and screen (1970) from James Earl Jones, loyally supported by his boxing coach and his white wife (Jane Alexander). Jefferson is brought down because of white fears of African-American prowess and sexuality and white need to have white powers affirmed in a white champion. (Museum of Modern Art Film Stills Archive.)

by malicious, scared whites, such as the one in Atlanta, Georgia, in 1906, in which ten African-Americans were killed before martial law restored order. In 1908, after a white woman claimed she had been raped, whites invaded the African-American section of Springfield, Illinois, lynched two African-Americans, and flogged several others. The white assailants escaped without punishment. However, on this occasion the North was influenced by an article denouncing the outrage, "Race War in the North," written by a southern socialist, William English Walling. Together with settlement workers Mary White Ovington and Dr. Henry Moskowitz, Walling persuaded Oswald Garrison Villard, editor of the *New York Evening Post* and grandson of the abolitionist leader, to call a conference on race in 1909, the centenary of the birth of Abraham Lincoln.

At a meeting in New York on May 31 and June 1, 1909, African-American and white American radicals proposed a new national organization to protect the rights of African-Americans and a similar conference in 1910 established the National Association for the Advancement of Colored People (NAACP), with its declared goal of "equal rights and opportunities for all." Under its first president, Moorfield Storey, the NAACP formed several hundred branches. Under the editorship of W. E. B. Du Bois, the NAACP journal, the *Crisis,* reached a circulation of one hundred thousand. Du Bois's own column, "As the Crow Flies," attacked white racism. Together with the *Chicago Defender,* the *Pittsburgh Courier,* and the *Baltimore African-American,* the *Crisis* made an ever-increasing spectrum of literate African-Americans aware of their national responsibilities and what the nation owed them.

The NAACP's distinctive strategy was litigation to challenge racist laws. For example, in 1917 the NAACP challenged a statute of Louisville, Kentucky, requiring "the use of separate blocks for residence, places of abode, and places of assembly by white and colored people respectively." Moorfield Storey took the case to the Supreme Court at a time when it was, in the terms of analyst Richard Kluger, peopled by men of Paleolithic perspective, notably Justices Willis van Devanter and James Clark McReynolds. Nevertheless, in the case of *Buchanan* v. *Warley* the Court unanimously, and surprisingly, decided on November 5, 1917, that "all citizens of the United States shall have the same right in every state and territory, as is enjoyed by white citizens thereof, to inherit, purchase, lease, sell, hold and convey real and personal property." However, the *Buchanan* decision resulted in a spate of private restrictive covenants under which residents agreed to sell or rent their property to individuals of one race only. The Court subsequently upheld this pernicious practice in *Corrigan* v. *Buckley* in 1926, maintaining that civil rights were not protected against discrimination by individuals.

Another sequence of NAACP cases tested the constitutionality of disfranchisement. In 1910 Oklahoma introduced its own grandfather clause to prevent African-Americans from voting. Two of its election officials, Guinn and Beal, were prosecuted by the NAACP for carrying out the new state law. When the officials were found guilty of violating the Fifteenth Amendment by a district court, they appealed to the Supreme Court. However, in the case of *Guinn* v. *United States* (1915), the Court unanimously declared that the grandfather clause was "an unconstitutional evasion of the 15th Amendment guarantee that states would not deny citizens the right to vote because of their race." On the same day the Court ruled by seven votes to one in the case of *United States* v. *Mosley* that it "upheld congressional power to relegate elections tainted with fraud and corruption." It seemed the law was on the side of civil rights for African-Americans.

Oklahoma reacted quickly. It passed a new election law, providing permanent registration for those entitled to vote according to the unconstitutional law and allowing African-Americans only twelve days to register or be disqualified from voting for life. The new law was not contested in the Supreme Court for another twenty-two years.

The second oldest surviving organization on behalf of African-Americans, the Urban League, was founded in New York in 1911. It was primarily a social welfare organization assisting migrants in finding work and accommodation and trying to relieve the worst excesses of African-American urban poverty. It, too, had a journal, *Opportunity*, founded in 1923. In the 1930s, the extreme circumstances of the depression allowed the organization the occasion for special pleas against economic, as well as political, oppression of African-Americans. Of these first concerted attempts at association by African-Americans, Harvard Sitkoff concludes in *A New Deal for Blacks* (1978), "The civil rights organizations of the early twentieth century lacked adequate finances, political leverage, the support of most blacks, influential white allies, and access to the major institutions shaping public opinion and policy."

Another possible avenue of political protest for African-Americans would have been through some third party or labor union. However, because 85 percent of African-Americans lived in the South, three-quarters of them in rural areas, they were largely removed from industrial unions. Moreover, the American Federation of Labor (AFL) bluntly excluded African-Americans. The dominant creed of racial superiority had poisoned the attitudes of many radicals to African-Americans. Thus Socialists, Communists, and other left-wing activists had nothing to offer the African-American cause until the 1930s.

Nevertheless, W. E. B. Du Bois believed socialism provided the optimum solution for racial discrimination. He reasoned that in a truly socialist society, racial prejudice would disappear. In his article "Socialism and the Negro Problem" for the *New Review* of February 1, 1913, he asserted, "The Negro problem . . . is the great test of the American socialist." It was a test that many Socialists failed to pass.

The founding convention of the United Socialist Party of America acknowledged the "peculiar position" of African-Americans in the working class but failed to declare opposition to lynching or segregation and the entire subject was omitted from future conventions. Du Bois eventually left the Socialist party because of its antiquated attitude to race relations. One of his biographers, Elliott M. Rudwick, has described Du Bois as "the off-again-on-again Socialist."

African-American Writing

At the close of her novel *Iola Leroy* (1892), Frances Harper regretted that the African-American race "has not had very long to straighten its hands from the hoe, to grasp the pen and wield it as a power for good and to erect above the ruined auction block and slave-pen institutions of learning." Yet there were various sustained and systematic attempts to inform Americans of both races of the serious contribution of African-Americans to the United States. They included the Banneker Institute of the 1850s and the Negro Historical Society, formed in 1892, both in Philadelphia. There were, also, the American Negro Academy in Washington, D.C. (1897), and the Negro Society for Historical Research (1911) in New York. In 1915 Carter A. Woodson and others formed the Association for the Study of Afro-American (initially Negro) Life and History (ASALH) in order to encourage the development of historians who could teach and write African-American history in a thorough, appropriate, and dignified manner. Indeed, the ASALH became the principle organization for stimulating interest in African-American history. It did this in a variety of ways: by creating the *Journal of Negro History* in 1916; by publishing the *Negro History Bulletin* in 1933; by creating Negro History Week in 1924; and by sponsoring various monographs. All of these efforts had a revisionist basis. They were intended to show, as Carter G. Woodson said in the first edition of his *The Negro in Our History* (1922), "how the Negro has been influenced by contact with the Caucasian and to emphasize what the former has contributed to civilization."

It was W. E. B. Du Bois who came closest to redefining this history in his *Gift of Black Folk* (1924), retelling the cultural and spiritual achievements of African-Americans and foretelling the liberation of women.

Earlier generations of African-American historians before and after the turn of the century had two fundamental objectives. They wanted to convince white readers that African-Americans had a worthy past sufficient in dignity that they should be treated equally in American society. At the same time they wanted to inspire African-Americans, to give them confidence in their past and in their right to equality. Writer Lucy Delaney remarked in a preface to her memoirs of 1891, "Although we are each but atoms, it must be remembered that we assist in making the grand total of human history."

Despite the adverse political climate of renewed white repression of African-Americans, a younger generation of African-American women, including Anna John Cooper and Anne Burton, proved themselves highly courageous and most articulate in propounding African-American rights in the 1890s and 1900s. In general these women authors laid foundations for the flowering of African-American creative talent in the Harlem Renaissance.

The Great Migration

The way racist whites openly flouted the basic rights of African-American citizens was now so flagrant as to be scarcely credible in a society moving through a phase of self-styled progressivism. For African-Americans, the notion of progressive reform was a joke in very bad taste. Ironically, the African-American community, like the white, was stronger economically than ever. In 1913 African-Americans owned 550,000 houses, worked 937 farms, ran forty thousand businesses, and attended forty thousand African-American churches. There were thirty-five thousand African-American teachers, and 1.7 million African-American students attended public schools.

The accession of Woodrow Wilson to the presidency (1913–1921) resulted in the most racist administration since the Civil War. Southern Democrats were dominant in Congress, the White House, and the Supreme Court. African-American needs were peripheral to Wilson's interests. Inasmuch as he had views on the subject, they were in the tradition of southern paternalism. As a result, and spurred on by his first wife, Ellen Axson Wilson, he acquiesced in the unrest of segregation. His postmaster general, Albert S. Burleson, introduced the subject of segregation at an early cabinet meeting, suggesting separation to reduce friction between white and African-American railway clerks. Convinced by this argument, Wilson and the cabinet allowed systematic segregation in government offices, shops, rest rooms, and lunchrooms. African-Americans were even removed from appointments they had previously held. The sum total of the Wilson policies was that only eight African-Americans out of thirty working for the federal government in Washington retained their appointments.

Emboldened, racists began to demand that Congress legislate for segregation throughout the civil service, forbid interracial marriages, and even repeal the Fourteenth and Fifteenth Amendments. The South extended its segregation to public transport. Thus, African-Americans were prevented from using taxis reserved for whites in the state of Mississippi in 1922 and in the cities of Jacksonville in 1929 and Birmingham in 1930.

Such discrimination, important in itself, had more momentous consequences because of the contemporary exodus of African-Americans from the South to the North. For the 1910s and 1920s were also the years of the Great Migration. The immediate reason for the exodus was the industrial requirements of World War I. Whites were being drawn increasingly into the armed services and newly created war industries. However, the war prevented European immigrants from coming to America and taking their place as laborers. Thus, in 1915 agents for northern employers began recruiting African-American labor from the South. However, at least four times as many African-Americans went north on word of mouth than did so at the prompting of labor agents. The exodus was mainly spontaneous and largely unorganized; whatever the personal motives for individual moves, the collective motive was bad treatment in the South. The Great Migration was facilitated by railroad transportation and continued after the war was over. In sum, the South lost 323,000 African-Americans in the 1910s and 615,000 in the 1920s —about 8.2 percent of its African-American population. At the outset white attitudes in both the North and the South to the migration were somewhat ambivalent. As time went on, they became alarmist: northerners resented another ethnic disruption following in the wake of the new immigration; southerners did not want to lose their ready supply of cheap labor. Some southern communities passed laws to prevent African-Americans from leaving. This happened in Montgomery, Savannah, Greenville, and elsewhere. Charleston editor William Watts Ball commented ruefully in 1925, "We have plenty of Southerners whose disposition is identical with that of the ancient Egyptians—they would chase the Negroes to the Red Sea to bring them back." However, nothing could reverse the tide.

Whereas the Great Migration is often interpreted as part of the inevitable progress of African-Americans to full citizenship because they were less likely to encounter political disfranchisement in the North than the South, some, such as playwright August Wilson, believe that it represented an incorrect cultural choice for African-Americans intent on capturing their legacy. In April 1990 he told the *New York Times,* "We were land-based agrarian people from Africa. We were uprooted from Africa, and we spent over 200 years developing our culture as Black Americans. Then we left the South. We uprooted ourselves and attempted to transplant this culture to the pavements of the industrialized North. And it was a transplant that did not take. I think if we had stayed in the South, we would have been a stronger people. And because the connection between the South of the '20s, '30s and '40s has been broken, it's very difficult to understand who we are."

World War I and After

The war to make the world safe for democracy was not intended to free society from racism. During World War I (1914–1918), the armed services were completely segregated and able African-American soldiers humiliated. For instance, Colonel Charles Young, the highest-ranking African-American officer, was retired on June 30, 1917, supposedly because of high blood pressure but more probably because he was close to promotion to the rank of brigadier general and the system of accelerated wartime promotion would have soon advanced his rank even further. In April 1917 the army had four African-American regiments of enlisted men. Colonel William Hayward of the 369th Regiment was told that his unit could not accompany the Rainbow Division to France because "black was not one of the colors of the rainbow." All told, about forty-two thousand of a total of 380,000 African-American troops were assigned to combat duty. The others were placed in labor and stevedore battalions; some were not even given military training. In the Navy, African-Americans were employed only as messboys. The convenient explanation for such discrimination was that African-Americans lacked the necessary attributes for combat.

To compound these humiliations, the War Department acted unjustly over a series of racial incidents. When African-American troops of the

Fifteenth New York Infantry threatened to retaliate against whites in Spartanburg, South Carolina, who had beaten up an African-American soldier, the War Department suddenly had the regiment shipped overseas. When African-American troops took the law into their own hands after being provoked by white violence in Houston, an ugly incident developed in which sixteen people died. Thirteen African-Americans were condemned to death following convictions for mutiny and murder. They were hanged swiftly before any review of the sentences could be carried out. Several others were sentenced to life imprisonment.

African-American leaders at home felt ambivalent toward American intervention. W. E. B. Du Bois initially opposed the war effort but as of June 1918 began to support it on the assumption that an Allied victory would yield African-Americans the right to vote, work, and live without continuous harassment. Other activists disagreed. These included A. Philip Randolph and Chandler Owens, editors of the *Messenger,* a journal they had founded in 1915 as part of a strategy to recruit African-American hotel workers into a labor union.

A. Philip Randolph (1889–1979), born in Crescent City, Florida, was to emerge as one of the most significant African-American leaders of the twentieth century. In a very long life, his participation in various civil rights activities spanned a period of over fifty years. The son of James Randolph, an African Methodist Episcopal Church preacher, A. Philip moved to New York and joined the Socialist party in 1911. He was fired from successive jobs as an elevator operator, maintenance man, and waiter for having tried to start unions with his fellow workers. Roi Ottley describes him in *Black Odyssey* as "unique among Negro leaders in that he was neither preacher, educator, nor rabble-rousing politician, but a labor organizer. Tall, dark, and brooding, Randolph impressed Negroes as being all soul." Along with fellow socialist Chandler Owens, Randolph condemned the war in the *Messenger* and traversed the country making speeches in opposition to it. He declared in the *Messenger,* "Lynching, Jim Crow, segregation, and discrimination in the armed forces and out, disfranchisement of millions of black souls in the South —all these things make your cry of making the world safe for democracy a sham, a mockery, a rape of decency, and travesty of common justice." After an antiwar meeting in Cleveland in 1918 Randolph was arrested and jailed for a few days. In the antiradical hysteria following the war, the *Messenger* was banned from federal mails.

In the North, African-American migrants were condemned by circum-

Open faces, openly arrived at. For its second mass march down Pennsylvania Avenue, Washington, D.C., in 1928, the by-now declining ranks of the Ku Klux Klan doffed the masks from their cowl-like hoods to brazen out their open defiance of the civil rights of new immigrants and African-Americans, as if to parody Woodrow Wilson's Fourteen Points of "open covenants, openly arrived at." (Library of Congress.)

stances to a life in squalid tenement ghettos. They faced resentment and hostility from white workers who feared for their livelihood. In 1917 there were race riots in towns and on army bases. In July 1917 a savage race riot in East St. Louis killed between forty and two hundred blacks and drove almost six thousand from their homes. The first year of peace, 1919, was the most violent in African-American history since Reconstruction: there were twenty-five race riots across the country.

The notorious Red Summer began in July 1919 when whites entered the African-American area of Longview, Texas. They were looking for a schoolteacher who had accused a white woman of sleeping with an African-American. They burned shops and houses and ran African-Americans out of town. In Washington, gangs of whites and African-Americans fought pitched battles on the streets for four days following unsubstantiated press accounts of assaults by African-Americans on white women. Six people were killed and 150 wounded. Order was only restored by federal troops and after driving rain that had cleared the streets. Thirty-eight people were killed and 537 injured in a horrific riot in Chicago on July 27, 1919.

The worst riot of all was in Phillips County, Arkansas, in October. To protect themselves against abuse from exploitive landlords, African-American tenant farmers formed a union, the Progressive Farmers and Household Union of America. They threatened to withhold their cotton crop and charge landlords with peonage. Their stand roused whites in Arkansas, Tennessee, and Mississippi who came in droves with arms to quell a supposed insurrection by African-Americans. At least five whites and twenty-five African-Americans were killed. Governor Charles H. Brough intervened. He used federal troops to round up African-American dissidents and confine them in a stockade. White planters justified their unprovoked aggression by claiming that the union of African-American tenants was "established for the purpose of banding Negroes together for the killing of white people." Governor Brough described the affair as a "damned rebellion." An independent view was put forward by U. S. Bratton, former postmaster of Little Rock. He told an African-American paper he could find "no basis for the belief that a massacre was planned by the Negroes and, in point of fact, it was the Negroes who were massacred." Far from being an insurrection by African-Americans, the disorder was part of a preconceived plan by whites "to put a stop to the Negro ever asking for a settlement."

Nevertheless, within the month sixty-five African-Americans were indicted and tried for rebellion. Twelve were sentenced to death and fifty-four were given prison sentences ranging from one to eleven years. Of those sentenced to death, six were released in 1923 by the state supreme court on the grounds of irregularities during the trial. The other six were allowed a retrial by the Supreme Court. In the case of *Moore* v. *Dempsey* on February 29, 1923, it ruled by six votes to two that mob hysteria and inadequate counsel had prevented them from having a fair trial in the first place. In January 1924 Governor Hugh McRae had them released. The NAACP victory belonged to Walter White, whose persuasive evidence had moved the Supreme Court and established his reputation as a champion of civil rights.

The final full scale riot of the early postwar years happened in Tulsa, Oklahoma, in 1921. A white mob gathered at the jail to lynch an African-American prisoner but was opposed by a crowd of African-Americans. The whites drove the African-Americans into their own quarter and they looted and razed forty-four blocks.

Southerners ascribed the general cause of the riots to improved, but mistaken, treatment meted out to African-Americans in the North. In particular, they thought that service by African-Americans in the war had given them ideas above their station. According to the Houston *Chronicle,* army uniforms had afforded African-Americans "an unprecedented degree of protection and consideration while huge wages and allotments have tended to make them shiftless and irresponsible."

White southerners also blamed the African-American press. In August 1919 Congressman James F. Byrnes of South Carolina called on the Department of Justice to prosecute the editors of the *Crisis,* the Chicago *Messenger,* and other African-American papers under terms of the Espionage Act. The *New York Times* of November 23, 1919, reported how the Department of Justice deemed the work of African-American editors as "a well concerted movement . . . to constitute themselves a determined and persistent source of radical opposition to the Government, and to the established rule of law and order." In reply, the editor of the Oklahoma City *Black Dispatch* of October 10, 1919, denied that radical politics were mixed with African-American politics. "It does not take an IWW to clinch the arguments that the majority of Negroes in the United States cannot vote. . . . It does not take a Bolshevist to inform us that . . . a separate status as citizens is designed for the black man." The Atlanta *Independent* of October 18, 1919, went further. Resistance by African-Americans to white racism was inevitable. There would be no harmony "until all classes and conditions of men shall have equal opportunities in the race for life, liberty and the pursuit of happiness." Reviewing the terrible scenes of 1919, poet Claude McKay revised the famous lines of Rupert Brooke about England—"If I should die think only this of me"—to read

> If we must die, let it not be like hogs,
> Hunted and penned in an inglorious spot

While round us bark the mad and hungry dogs,
Making their mock of our accursed lot.
If we must die, O let us nobly die.

With the death of prominent spokesman Booker T. Washington in 1915 the initiative in the political movement among African-Americans passed to the NAACP. Within ten years W. E. B. Du Bois, editor of the NAACP journal, the *Crisis,* had made himself the leading spokesman for African-Americans. The NAACP's base was in the North but its principle officers were natives of the South—William Pickens, Robert W. Bagnall, Walter White, and James Weldon Johnson. Johnson had graduated from Atlanta University and was a distinguished novelist and poet who had served the State Department in Nicaragua and Venezuela. As secretary he expanded the NAACP's activities. In 1919 the association had 88,448 members distributed among three hundred branches, of which 155 were in the South. This rapid increase in size since 1913 (when there had been only fourteen branches) laid the NAACP open to racist criticism that it had fueled postwar riots. This was ironic. The NAACP was an elite organization committed to legal protest against injustice. Nevertheless, it was determined that African-Americans should be made aware of their due civil rights.

Du Bois was also the founder of the Pan-African movement with its belief in special cultural and political links between African-Americans and Africa. Thus the NAACP supported the Pan-African Congress in Paris in 1919 and lobbied statesmen at the peace conference for self-determination for African colonies. It was Du Bois who recognized the connection between the struggles by African blacks for national independence from Europe and by African-Americans for civil rights in the United States.

Southern senators such as Walter F. George, John Sharp Williams, and James F. Byrnes were utterly complacent in their faith that white supremacy was inviolable. On the surface, it seemed that statistical evidence was on their side. In the South only 21.1 percent of African-Americans worked outside of agriculture. Only 7 percent of African-Americans in towns had professional, managerial, or clerical occupations. Furthermore, African-Americans were still being systematically disfranchised. In the South the real contest was not in the election itself but in the Democratic nomination; the Democratic party prevented its African-American members from voting in primaries. It did this by state laws in eight states and by county or city laws in three others.

Texas was one of the states that decided to use the device of excluding African-Americans from Democratic primaries. However, Dr. A. L. Nixon, an African-American of El Paso supported by the NAACP, challenged the racist law in the case of *Nixon* v. *Herndon,* in which he was represented by Moorfield Storey, then aged eighty-two. The case reached the Supreme Court, which ruled on March 7, 1927, that the Texas law violated the Fourteenth Amendment. The Texas state legislature decided to undermine the ruling by investing the state executive committees of the political parties with the authority to decide who could and could not vote. Thus the Democratic party committee restricted voting in primaries to "all white Democrats who are qualified under the constitution and laws of Texas." Dr. Nixon continued to press his, and the NAACP's, case. He was now represented by attorney Nathan Margold, author of a report recommending the NAACP to oblige states to make educational facilities for African-Americans equal to those for whites. In the case of *Nixon* v. *Condon* the Supreme Court decided by five votes to four on May 2, 1932, that the power of executive committees to exclude African-Americans from primaries was a form of state power and, therefore, unconstitutional.

Within weeks the devious Texas Democrats had convened a state convention that declared that all white citizens could vote in primaries but African-Americans could not. When African-American William Grovey of Texas tried to get a ballot for the Democratic primary election of July 1934, he was refused. Supported by African-American lawyers Carter Wesley and J. Alston Atkins, he fought the test case of *Grovey* v. *Townsend* to the Supreme Court, which on April 1, 1935, unanimously ruled that the Texas Democratic party was within its rights because it was a private organization and not subject to the Fourteenth Amendment.

Sometimes African-Americans were allowed to vote in municipal elections, especially in Texas and Virginia. They played a decisive part in local elections in Louisville in 1920, Nashville in 1921, and Savannah in 1923. In Atlanta in 1921 the NAACP mobilized African-American voters to ensure the passage of a $4 million school bond, of which $1 million was pledged to African-American schools. Some urban bosses elicited support from African-Americans and repaid it in kind. In San Antonio, Texas, Charles Bellinger had a regular supply of African-American votes. Thus he controlled city elections in San Antonio from 1918 until 1935. In return, he provided African-Americans with schools and parks, a library and an auditorium, as well as paved streets and sewers.

The Insolent Foe and the Tragedy of Lynching

Not content with holding African-Americans in social chains, vicious whites sometimes sought their lives. Many African-Americans were victims of lynch law, especially in the South, where the trees of small towns bore strange fruit about once in every generation. The common charge was that African-American victims of white lynch mobs had tried to rape white women. According to surveys on their behalf, there were over a thousand lynchings between 1900 and 1915. Moreover, as historian Harvard Sitkoff observes, "Petty brutality, lynchings, and pogroms against the Negro sections of towns occurred so frequently in the first decade of the twentieth century that they appeared commonplace, hardly newsworthy." American intervention in the war and its vicious propaganda to smash the Hun released a new tide of savagery. Between 1918 and 1927, according to NAACP officer Walter F. White in his *Rope and Faggot* (1929), 456 people were victims of lynch mobs. Of this number, 416 were African-American, eleven were women, and three of them were pregnant. Forty-two of the victims were burned alive, sixteen were cremated after death, and eight were either beaten to death or dismembered and cut to pieces.

Racist Winfield H. Collins defended such barbarities in a scurrilous book of 1918, *The Truth about Lynching*: "The white man in lynching a Negro does it as an indirect act of self-defence against the Negro criminal as a race." The practice of lynching was necessary "in order to hold in check the Negro in the South." Congressman James F. Byrnes agreed. He told Congress that lynching was the surest way of defending white women from rape. Perversely turning the burden of guilt to the victims of lynching, he declared that "rape is responsible directly and indirectly for most of the lynching in America."

For some communities the act of lynching became what historian George Brown Tindall has called in *The Emergence of the New South* (1967) "a twentieth century auto-da-fe." It was an event for white men, women, and children to attend in order to relieve the boredom of small-town life. They wanted entertainment, and prolonging the torture of a hapless victim and taking bizarre photographs of the cruel scene gave them sadistic pleasure. A contributory factor in the epidemic of lynching was the depressed provincialism of isolated southern communities. According to historian James H. Chadbourn in *Lynching and the Law* (1933), a county given to lynching was "characterized in general by social and economic decadence." Its family incomes were well below average and 75 percent of its inhabitants were likely to belong to Southern Methodist and Baptist churches.

The NAACP assumed that if it publicized lynchings and other outrages, mass public indignation would demand reform. Thus it organized public meetings, lobbied public officials, and stimulated press investigation. Walter F. White of Atlanta could pass for white. Thus he gained access to public officials in the South who held records of lynchings. Those officials who discovered he was an African-American were more antagonized by his methods than they were by his disclosures.

The NAACP published its research findings as *Thirty Years of Lynching, 1889–1918.* The report was published to coincide with a national conference on the subject held in New York in May 1919. The review challenged popular stereotypes about lynching. In particular, it showed that fewer than one in six victims of lynching had even been accused of rape by their assailants. The conference called for a federal law against lynching.

In 1921 the NAACP established an office in Washington. Its aim was to lobby Congress in support of Congressman L. C. Dyer of St. Louis, who had introduced an antilynching bill in 1919. The Dyer bill proposed to eliminate lynching by making counties in which the offense occurred responsible. If they failed to protect citizens or prisoners from mob rule and a lynching took place, then the county would be fined. The Dyer bill passed the House by 230 votes to 119 in 1922. However, it was defeated in the Senate because of a southern filibuster.

Although the Dyer bill failed in Congress, the publicity it earned helped reduce the extent of the evil. The South grew ashamed of lynching. Southern papers asserted that southern courts could handle the problem and punish aggressors without needing a federal law to show them how. According to the *Negro Year Book* (1932), whereas the total number of lynchings was eighty-three in 1919, by 1924 it had fallen to sixteen. It rose to thirty in 1926 and then declined further to eleven in 1928. The NAACP did not work alone. In 1929 reporter Louis I. Jaffe of the *Virginian Pilot* won an editorial prize for his campaign against lynching.

Another disturbing expression of primitive racist fear was found in the revival of the Ku Klux Klan. This subversive organization operated both inside and outside the regular political and economic framework of the various states. At its height in 1924 it may have had two, three, or even five million members. Its size alone indicates how formidable were the massed obstacles in the path of civil rights. A historian of the Klan, Charles C. Alexander, explains that there were actually three Klans. The first was the original Ku Klux Klan founded in Pulaski, Tennessee, in 1867. Its aim was to disrupt so-called Radical Reconstruction. It proscribed and terrorized freedmen and their few white allies. The second Klan lasted from 1915 to 1944. This was the "Invisible Empire, Knights of the Ku Klux Klan, Inc." It was as secret, violent, and subversive as its predecessor. However, unlike the Reconstruction Klan, it was ultrapatriotic, nativistic, and moralistic. The third Klan was made up of several racist societies, each determined to prevent African-American citizens from exercising their civil rights after World War II.

In contrast, an association working for improved race relations in the 1920s was the Commission on Interracial Cooperation (CIC). It was founded on April 9, 1919, by a group of African-Americans and whites in Atlanta who were disturbed by the events of 1919. They gave priority to the special social needs of African-American soldiers and their families in the process of demobilization. The commission secured a grant from the National War Work Council and organized conferences to advise white and African-American social workers. The strategy was to persuade one white and one African-American social worker to act as liaison officers in each southern community. Their aim was to reduce social tensions. In 1920 there were five hundred interracial committees and by 1923 there were about eight hundred. The CIC was well aware of the extent of the problem as it uncovered "vast areas of interracial injustice and neglect that could not be cleared up in a few months or a few years."

After the first two years, the CIC began to receive funds regularly from various Protestant churches and public foundations, and it instituted a campaign to redress the grievances of African-Americans. By this time, Will W. Alexander, a former Methodist minister and YMCA worker from Nashville, had emerged as leader of the commission. His strategy was to get African-Americans and whites to cooperate with one another by sharing a common task of welfare. The CIC was supported by the NAACP, the African-American press, and the Methodist church and

Langston Hughes, unofficial poet laureate of black America, photographed by Carl Van Vechten. (Library of Congress.)

governors in seven states. It persuaded Governor Hugh M. Dorsey of Georgia to publish an account on April 22, 1921, of 135 atrocities against African-Americans in the previous two years. However, the CIC, fearing loss of funds from its white sponsors, failed to take a stand on the issue of desegregation.

The Garvey Movement

During the course of the 1920s feelings of alienation, outright rage, and, above all, despair among African-Americans encouraged extremism and division. One logical expression of this was emigration to Africa, or repatriation, for African-Americans, as first proposed by sea captain Paul Cuffee in the 1810s and Haitian leader Toussaint L'Ouverture in the 1820s.

It was now Marcus Garvey who provided African-Americans with an avenue of escape from the Americas. Born in Jamaica in 1887, Marcus Moziah Garvey emigrated to London and worked there for several years as a printer. After his return to Jamaica, he led an unsuccessful printers' strike and lost his job. However, he was inspired by Booker T. Washington's autobiography *Up from Slavery* (1901) to organize the Universal Negro Improvement and Conservation Association (later known as the UNIA) in August 1914. The aims of the new organization were to establish a universal cofraternity of African-Americans, civilize tribes in Africa, encourage race pride, and develop a "conscientious Christianity." Having been encouraged by Washington to visit Tuskegee, he arrived after Washington's death. Undeterred, he established the UNIA in Harlem, initially among other West Indian immigrants. The organization reached its peak of membership in 1921 with between, perhaps, one million and four million supporters.

Garvey's leadership of a particular faction in the embryonic civil rights movement was significant not least because it suggested a fissure that would eventually become a schism between two schools of thought —political, economic, and social improvement for African-Americans leading either to integration or separatism. The former route was advocated by W. E. B. Du Bois while the latter route was advocated by Marcus Garvey and the Black Muslims. Garvey was a commanding and charismatic speaker who promoted the slogan "Africa for Africans at home and abroad" (a variant on a phrase first coined by Martin R. Delany in 1860) and exhorted his followers with "up you mighty race, you can accomplish what you will." The UNIA established the Black Star Steamship Line to carry migrants across the Atlantic. It also petitioned the League of Nations to transfer the former German colonies in Africa, South West Africa and German East Africa, held as mandates by South Africa and Britain, respectively, to Garvey's control. In 1922 Garvey designated himself president of a new African republic. He organized a militia and created dukes of the Nile among his lieutenants. The panoply of grand titles and imperial uniforms soon seemed foolish. However, the UNIA was the first truly mass movement of African-Americans, a predecessor of later African-American organizations, especially those advocating black power and black pride.

However, because Garvey criticized the lighter-skinned integrationists and middle-class African-Americans of the NAACP for being ashamed of their ancestry, he himself drew withering attacks from such as A. Philip Randolph, Chandler Owens, and W. E. B. Du Bois. Randolph and Owens abused Garvey for concentrating on the issue of race and ignoring what they considered to be more important, the issue of class. The mutual attacks and recriminations were venomous in the extreme.

Du Bois described Garvey as "a little fat black man, ugly but with intelligent eyes and a big head." Garvey retorted, calling Du Bois a racial monstrosity on account of his mixed African, French, and Dutch ancestry. He was a "lazy dependent mulatto." Du Bois published his most virulent attack on Garvey in the editorial "A Lunatic or a Traitor" in the *Crisis* of May 1924, saying Garvey had convicted himself by his own "swaggering monkey shines." "Marcus Garvey is, without doubt, the most dangerous enemy of the Negro race in America and in the world. He is either a lunatic or a traitor."

In *Race First* (1976) Tony Martin comments,

What was most fascinating about the Garvey-Du Bois struggle was that it was in a most real sense a continuation of the Washington-Du Bois debate. The ideological questions raised were largely the same. Furthermore, Garvey was very self-consciously a disciple of Washington. Along with his admiration for Washington, Garvey had early imbibed a dislike for Du Bois. He therefore saw himself as the heir to Washington's fight against Du Bois and never missed an opportunity to compare the two, to the detriment of Du Bois.

Garvey realized that Washington had accommodated himself to white racism but preferred to believe that, had he lived longer, Washington would have shifted emphasis from gradualism to black nationalism. He shared Washington's opposition to social equality, which he interpreted as free and unhindered social intercourse between the races. Moreover, unlike Du Bois, Washington had preached and practiced self-reliance and had formed a power base independent of white influence.

Hostility between integrationists and separatists was so great as to split the UNIA convention in Harlem in 1922. James W. H. Eason, a Philadelphia minister and prominent member of the UNIA, quarreled violently with Garvey on the platform. He withdrew from the UNIA and set up a rival organization, the Universal Negro Alliance, pledged to concentrate on the problems of African-Americans in the United States. He was also due to testify against Garvey over various irregularities in the Black Star finances but was shot at a speaking engagement in New Orleans in January 1923. Two Jamaicans were indicted for attempted murder, Garvey's chief of police, William Shakespeare, and a patrolman, F. W. Dyer. However, Eason died before he could identify them and they were released. Outraged by this bizarre murder, a Committee of Eight, a group of African-American leaders, sent a letter to Attorney General Harry M. Daugherty, protesting about the length of time it was taking to bring Garvey to trial for irregularities in the funding of the Black Star Steamship Line. He was arrested on a charge of using the federal mails to defraud the public, convicted in 1923, and, after his appeal failed, imprisoned in Atlanta in 1925. In December 1927 he was deported to Jamaica and died in obscurity in London in 1940. Premature reports of his death had already been circulated and he had the misfortune to die reading his own obituaries in the press.

The collapse of the Garvey movement allowed advocates of integration among the African-American community to reassert themselves. In the 1930s, 1940s, and 1950s both the NAACP and the Urban League served as counsel for moderation as desired by their conservative supporters among African-American professional classes, such as teachers, clerics, and employees of the federal government. While their stance against inequality, segregation, and general racism was consistent and honorable, their emphasis was social and political rather than economic. W. E. B. Du Bois commented in *Dusk of Dawn* (1940) how "the prosperous Negro professional men, merchants and investors, cling to the older ideas of property, ownership, and profits even more firmly than the whites." The educated and highly articulate elite among African-Americans was shorn of political and economic power by being separated from the masses on account of superiority of caste and education. The elite included proponents of integration and of separatism. The early proponents of black nationalism were profoundly critical of American society and deeply afraid of the potential loss of the special cultural identity of African-Americans, drawn from Africa and from the United States and developed in African-American social institutions.

The Garvey movement had represented a new black consciousness in which millions of African-American citizens could sublimate their de-

Versatile athlete, actor, and singer Paul Robeson (1898–1976) in one of the roles that established him as a prominent artist: the Pullman porter who rises and falls as ostracized dictator of an African state in the film version of Eugene O'Neill's expressionist play *The Emperor Jones* (1933). While paying full attention to appropriate nightmare effects of a dark jungle, the film also emphasized different ways of seeing oneself in various reflections —whether windows, mirrors, or pools. Moreover, situations and costuming in the film emphasized various associations within the drama of the tragedy of Marcus Garvey and his ill-fated Back to Africa movement, which anticipated Paul Robeson's own (and others') later cry of "Black Power." (Museum of Modern Art Film Stills Archive.)

spair and disillusionment in the promise of a better and more fulfilled future. Most significantly, Garvey had also convinced African-Americans that it was white racism and not failings or inadequacy among African-Americans that was responsible for their poverty and sense of powerlessness. James Weldon Johnson of the NAACP commented how Garvey collected more money "than any other Negro organization had ever dreamed of." In a most prophetic statement, the *Amsterdam News* of November 30, 1927, declared how "Marcus Garvey made black people proud of their race. In a world where black is despised he taught them that black is beautiful."

The Witchcraft I Have Used—The Harlem Renaissance

During the 1920s the cultural consciousness of African-Americans in the North was being nourished by the Harlem Renaissance. Hitherto, even substantive achievements in literature, such as *The Litany of Atlanta* that Du Bois wrote to commemorate the Atlanta Riot of 1906, were sporadic, hardly part of a movement. In contrast, the 1920s produced a wealth of artistic and literary talent among African-Americans that paralleled similar achievements by whites. Both expressed the conflict of values in society between countryside and town, following World War I, and also artists' alienation from small- town bourgeois society.

African-American versatility in the arts received extensive patronage from wealthy whites. The Great Migration that had swelled the African-American community of Harlem had also made it prosperous. Since New York was the artistic capital of the United States, it was in the interests of producers, publishers, and agents there to promote good art from those ethnic groups who could make a distinctive contribution. While novelist Norman Mailer's perceptive and prophetic remarks of 1957 on the "hipsters" and "white Negro" were still far into the future, the seeds of African-American influence upon white fashions, customs, and articulation were already being sown. As writer Langston Hughes commented, "It was the period when the Negro was in vogue." In his *From Slavery to Freedom* (1947; 1967) historian John Hope Franklin explains how the writers of the Harlem Renaissance expressed the social and economic grievances of African-Americans:

Despite his intense feelings of hate and hurt, [the African-American writer] possessed sufficient restraint and objectivity to use his materials artistically, but no less effectively. He was sufficiently in touch with the main currents of American literary development to adapt the accepted forms of his own materials, and therefore gain a wider acceptance. These two factors, the keener realization of injustice and the improvement of the capacity for expression, produced a crop of Negro writers who constituted the "Harlem Renaissance."

The pivotal figure was NAACP leader James Weldon Johnson (1871–1938), who both took part in and recorded the history of the Harlem Renaissance. Johnson produced his *Fifty Years and Other Poems* (1917), following it with a collection of others' work, *The Book of Negro Poetry* (1922), two books of Negro spirituals (1925 and 1926), a book of African-American sermons in verse, *God's Trombones* (1927), and an indictment of discrimination against African-American Gold Star mothers, entitled *Saint Peter Relates an Incident of the Resurrection Day* (1930). Johnson's considerable achievement was capped by the reissue of his 1912 *Autobiography of an Ex-Colored Man* (1927) and by two works that told the story of the Harlem Renaissance, *Black Manhattan* (1930) and *Along This Way* (1933).

Alain Locke (1886–1954) of Philadelphia, who took a Ph.D. at Harvard and was the first African-American Rhodes scholar, wrote articles, essays, stories, and poems, first published in the *Survey Graphic*. His preface expressed boundless optimism about the future of African-Americans. He believed that "the vital inner grip of prejudice has been broken" and that "in the very process of being transported, the Negro is becoming transformed." "We are witnessing the resurrection of a people," a "rise from social disillusion to race pride."

The first writer to capture a wide readership was Claude McKay, who emigrated from the West Indies when he was twenty-one. After attending Tuskegee and the University of Kansas, McKay settled in Harlem and published poems in such magazines as the *Seven Arts*, the *Liberator*, and the *Messenger*. However, it was his *Harlem Shadows* (1922) that placed him in the forefront of American poets with the plangent defiance of poems like "The Lynching," "If We Must Die," and "To the White Fiends." Thereafter, he turned increasingly to prose, producing a novel of life among African-Americans in New York, *Harlem: Negro Metropolis*.

The most cosmopolitan and prolific writer, Langston Hughes (1902–1967), was also the most wide ranging and rebellious in terms of content and form. Thus he earned the nickname "Shakespeare in Harlem." He called himself the first African-American "literary sharecropper" who was dedicated to writing about African-Americans. He created a body of writing that drew on traditions established by Walt Whitman, Carl Sandburg, and Vachel Lindsay, but imposed upon their forms his own genial irony laced with caustic humor. He could move from the passionate, defensive pride of race in *The Negro Speaks of Rivers* to the mix of noble expression and low-life settings in *Brass Spittoons*. His achievements in *Weary Blues* (1926) and *Fine Clothes to the Jew* (1927) were crowned by a novel, *Not without Laughter* (1930), *The Ways of White Folks* (1934), and his autobiography, *The Big Sea* (1940). His plays included *Mulatto* (1936) and *The Prodigal Son* (1964) and he also wrote libretti for opera, lyrics for musicals, and a cantata, *The Ballad of the Brown King*.

Other leading writers in the Harlem Renaissance included Jean Toomer, Countee Cullen, Jessie Redmond Fauset, and Nella Larsen. NAACP antilynching campaigner Walter White was also an accomplished novelist who wrote *Fire in the Flint* (1924), a fast-moving tragedy of African-Americans in the South, and *Flight* (1926), about a woman light enough to pass as white. In 1929 he wrote *Rope and Faggot: A Biography of Judge Lynch,* an acute summary of his research into the problem.

From 1910 onward African-American actors began to disappear from plays presented downtown and there soon developed an African-American theater in Harlem in which African-American actors appeared before African-American audiences in both African-American and white roles. In April 1917 a group sponsored by Emily Hapgood appeared in three one-act plays by Ridgely Torrence at the Garden Theater, Madison Square Garden, that were widely reviewed by the white press. However, press concentration on America's formal entry into World War I immediately afterward obscured the achievement. In 1919 the noted African-American actor Charles Gilpin played Rev. William Custis in *Abraham Lincoln* by John Drinkwater and his performance reminded critics of the wealth of acting talent among African-Americans.

Now white artists, writers, musicians, and dramatists began to draw on the experience of African-Americans to explore the themes of root-lessness, restlessness, and alienation. One such was playwright Eugene O'Neill (1888–1953), who was, like poet T. S. Eliot, greatly influenced by European expressionism and used modern psychology to analyze biblical and classical myths. In 1920 O'Neill's *The Emperor Jones* was produced in New York with Charles Gilpin as the deposed and ostracized dictator of an African island who declines through persecution to a sense of paranoia, all to the accompaniment of accelerating drums and within sets that symbolize his fears. Gilpin found the strain of having to use the word *nigger* again and again every night intense and he began to amend the text onstage and to drink heavily off it. Eventually, he was replaced by Paul Robeson. In *All God's Chillun Got Wings* (1924) O'Neill examined a marriage between a black husband and a white wife. The scene at the close when the white actress must kiss the hand of the African-American actor caused a storm of protest when the play was published and led to threats against O'Neill.

In 1927 *Porgy,* a folk play by Dorothy and DuBose Heyward, adapted from Dubose Heyward's novel about the African-American community in Charleston, was presented by the Theater Guild with Rose Mc-Clendon and Frank Wilson. George and Ira Gershwin would later mold this material into the basis for their opera, *Porgy and Bess* (1935). The greatest commercial success of the African-American legitimate theater was *The Green Pastures* (1930) by Marc Connelly. It retold the story of the Old Testament as if the playwright were Uncle Tom and with Richard B. Harrison playing de Lawd.

African-American artists had scored special success as dancers, comedians, and singers in a variety of musical shows ever since Bert Williams and George Walker had brought their vaudeville act to New York in 1896. African-American music, whether jazz, blues, spirituals, or soul, has been among the most influential of all twentieth-century art forms across the world. These forms also shaped African-American music and its performers onstage in theaters. The writer-producer team of F. E. Miller, Aubrey Lyle, Eubie Blake, and Noble Sissle mounted the revue *Shuffle Along* (1920), considered by most the most brilliant by any company to that time, with its string of popular songs, including "I'm Just Wild about Harry" and "Love Will Find a Way." It established a vogue for reviews by African-Americans, such as Irving Miller's *'Lisa,* Miller and Lyle's *Runnin' Wild,* and Blake and Sissle's *Chocolate Dandies,* which introduced Josephine Baker (all 1923), as well as *Dixie to Broadway* (1924), which starred Florence Mills, "the little black mosquito," who also appeared in *Blackbirds* (1926).

Among white artists who painted African-American subjects were Mexican-born Miguel Covarrubias and Winold Reiss, who illustrated Alain Locke's *The New Negro.* Black artist Henry Ossawa Tanner enjoyed a reputation at the turn of the century that remained unsurpassed by his successors—Laura Wheeler Waring, who painted scenes from the lives of affluent African-Americans, and Edward A. Harleston, who concentrated on artisans.

With the coming of the depression, the initial flame that had fueled the Renaissance in Harlem began to flicker and the New York wits carried their torches to different parts of the country and to Europe. Some new talents began to emerge to keep the spirit of the Renaissance alive until its second flowering at the end of the decade. Among these transitional writers was the anthropologist Zora Neale Hurston, a student of Franz Boaz at Barnard College, who collected a mass of folklore in the United States and from the Caribbean on which she would base scholarly articles and novels between 1931 and 1943.

2

Not in the Mood

The Onset of the Great Depression

Following the Wall Street crash of the great bull market on the New York stock exchange in autumn 1929, America entered a devastating and extended economic depression that lasted for a decade.

The Great Depression was an even worse catastrophe for the African-American community than for the white. Of the total population of 123,077,000 in 1930, 12,518,000 were African-Americans or nonwhite. Of the population of 37,858,000 of the Census South, 9,362,000 were African-American. Thus, whereas the ratio of African-Americans to whites across the country as a whole was about one in ten, in the South it was one in four. In an article, "Negroes out of Work," of April 22, 1931, the *Nation* showed that unemployment among African-Americans was four to six times as high as among whites, particularly in industrial towns. In specially created jobs in public works there was positive discrimination against African-Americans.

For those African-Americans who had a job, the average income during the depression in the South was only $634 in cities and $566 in the countryside. Sociologist Kelly Miller described the African-American in 1932 as "the surplus man, the last to be hired and the first to be fired." By 1933, 50 percent of urban African-Americans could not find jobs of any kind and most rural African-Americans could not sell their crops at a price that would repay their costs. In the cities unemployed whites contested for menial work they would once have thought beneath them and thus "negro jobs" disappeared as domestic service and garbage collection became white occupations. African-American communities across the country were threatened by privation, malnutrition, and even starvation. Not only did southern states provide the lowest levels of unemployment benefit and relief but white officials also openly discriminated against African-Americans in administering them. Thus in Mississippi, where over half the population was African-American, less than 9 percent of African-Americans received any relief in 1932, compared with 14 percent of whites.

The Great Migration slowed down. African-Americans were just as keen to move from the South to the North as previously, not because they thought they could find work more easily but because they heard that relief was distributed more equitably in northern cities and that the schools were better than in the South. However, the costs of transportation were beyond what most African-Americans could afford. Thus only 347,000 came north in the course of the 1930s.

At first, the depression had a crippling effect on civil rights organizations, reducing financial contributions from industry and charitable foundations. At one point the *Crisis,* starved of funds and subscriptions, was almost forced to close down. Faced with the possibility of extinction, the NAACP, the Urban League, the CIC, and other such groups agreed to pool their resources and share the cost of lobbying operations. They formed a Joint Committee on National Recovery to supervise and coordinate various programs. In the process the Urban League was transformed from an organization responsible for a broad range of social services into a protest and lobbying group. However, the NAACP expanded its activities to include cooperating with the Congress of Industrial Organizations (CIO), lobbying Congress, and participating in a small number of court cases, led by Charles Houston, dean of Harvard Law School, William H. Hastie, and Thurgood Marshall. Rather than challenge Jim Crow outright, Houston began a painstaking assault on inequity in public accommodation.

The Great Depression also exacerbated racial tensions. The number of lynchings provides a barometer of race relations, rising from seven in 1921 to twenty-one in 1930 and twenty-eight in 1933. However, the NAACP campaign against lynching attracted widespread support, although southern senators repeatedly secured the defeat of antilynching bills. Lynching united the opposition of liberals, both African-American

The dreary and unending routine of rigorous labor. A stevedore with a sack of oysters in Olga, Louisiana. (Photograph taken for the Farm Security Administration, September 1938, by Russell Lee; Library of Congress.)

and white, thereby swelling support for civil rights. The notorious murder of Claude Neal in Florida on October 23, 1934, was widely publicized in the NAACP pamphlet by Howard Kester, who recounted how the mob vivisected its victim and hung his mutilated limbs from a tree outside a court house.

A bill proposed by Senators Edward Costigan of Colorado and Robert Wagner of New York called for the fining or jailing of state or local officials found delinquent, either in protecting both African-Americans and white Americans from lynch mobs or in arresting and prosecuting violators of the law. Furthermore, it provided for a fine of ten thousand dollars to be levied against the county in which the lynching took place. It was supported by governors of twelve states, including David Scholtz of Florida, where Claude Neal had been murdered. Nevertheless, the Costigan bill was rejected in April 1935 after a filibuster of southern senators that lasted six days. However, many southern newspapers had changed their minds and now favored legislation. Congressman Joseph A. Gavagan of New York proposed a new bill that passed the House in

April 1937 by 277 votes to 120 after a terrible incident at Duck Hill, Mississippi, where a mob killed two African-Americans with a blow-torch. However, it was abandoned in the Senate on February 21, 1938, after a filibuster led by Senators Tom Connally of Texas and Theodore Bilbo of Mississippi.

The NAACP campaign had, as usual, been conducted by Walter White, who had become its executive secretary in 1930. White won nationwide recognition for his efforts, including the title of "Man of the Year" by *Time* magazine in January 1939. Perhaps because of all the adverse publicity, the number of lynchings gradually began to fall— from eighteen in 1935 to two in 1939.

A Trick to Put Me from My Suit—New Deal or Cold Deck?

The impact of the New Deal, the reform program of President Franklin D. Roosevelt (1933–1945), on the African-American community as a whole was, at best, indirect. The first major code of the National Recovery Administration (NRA) for cotton textiles provided neither fewer hours nor higher pay for unskilled work, work normally performed by African-Americans, and this differential treatment set a precedent for other textile codes. NRA codes in other industries, such as steel and tobacco, specifically allowed lower wages for African-Americans than for whites. Where there was no legal discrimination, employers could still hire whites rather than African-Americans. In general, the shortcomings of the NRA toward blacks led to some calling the NRA "Negroes Ruined Again."

Moreover, the administration of relief in the New Deal programs was decentralized and this allowed local and party officials to exercise their prejudices against African-Americans. Of over ten thousand WPA supervisors in the South, only eleven were African-American. Not surprisingly, public assistance for African-Americans in the South was meager and difficult to obtain. White planters and landlords took advantage of the total or partial illiteracy of African-Americans and of their economic dependence on them to prevent their Agricultural Adjustment Administration (AAA) reduction checks from reaching them. When AAA procedure was changed to allow direct payments to tenants, certain landlords decided to dispense with tenants, evicting them and collecting the crop reduction bonuses themselves. Such dishonesty fueled discontent among

Jack Delano's photograph of severe gully erosion on a farm in Greene County, northwest Georgia, in October 1941 suggests an excavation, as if the land had been mined, and emphasizes the severe nature of problems in the agricultural depression that dispossessed many African-Americans as well as whites of their livelihood. (Farm Security Administration; Library of Congress.)

both African-American and white sharecroppers, who united in the biracial Southern Tenant Farmers Union. Later, the Farm Security Administration (FSA) encouraged African-American farmers to buy their own land.

However, by the time of the 1936 election, a series of factors combined to aid the cause of civil rights. In 1935 Arthur Mitchell of Chicago became the first African-American Democratic congressman, having defeated the Republican Oscar De Priest. By 1936 the African-American vote in the North was sizable enough to merit serious consideration by both major parties. The Republicans tried to present their presidential candidate, Alf Landon, as a defender of African-American rights in the party of Lincoln. In fact, he had openly favored a law against lynching.

Striking changes now occurred in the Democratic party: for the first time thirty African-American delegates attended the Democratic convention. Roosevelt chose an African-American minister to open the convention and had Arthur Mitchell deliver the first address, much to the disgust of southern representatives. Historian William Manchester comments ruefully, "In that year the black vote was still to be had for a prayer." Yet *Time* magazine accurately reported how, for the first time, the Democrats were making a serious bid for the African-American vote. Indeed, no other voting section shifted its allegiance so markedly. A Gallup poll disclosed that 76 percent of African-Americans in the North voted for FDR. The Roosevelt coalition of farmers, workers, labor, intellectuals, and African-Americans was decisive in his landslide victory of 60.8 percent of the popular vote. Various African-American leaders interpreted this as the start of a new phase of African-American influence in politics. Earl Brown, a political analyst who was African-American, considered that the African-American vote was now a key sector of the northern electorate. If the Democrats were to maintain, or the Republicans to recapture, the African-American vote, they would have to offer African-Americans more in the industrial states.

Although southerners occupied half the chairs of congressional committees in every Congress throughout the New Deal, several leading administrators began to show an unprecedented concern for civil rights. One of the most notable was Secretary of the Interior Harold Ickes, who was also a former head of a Chicago chapter of the NAACP. However, it was FDR's wife, Eleanor Roosevelt, who was the most conspicuous New Dealer to demonstrate this new humanitarianism by her visits to Harlem and to African-American schools and projects and by her readiness to speak at African-American functions. She made the president accessible to African-American leaders, notably Walter White of the NAACP and Mary McLeod Bethune (1875–1955), president of the National Council of Negro Women, who were allowed interviews with FDR from 1936 onward—something that would have been unthinkable even three years earlier.

Roosevelt's personality and the extraordinary way he had overcome the disadvantages of his poliomyelitis were likely to make him an attractive candidate to African-American voters. The warmth of his voice, the charisma of his style, and his uncanny ability to identify himself with human exploitation encouraged African-Americans, somewhat ironically, to think that here was their stoutest champion since Lincoln.

Unlike previous presidents who had simply sought unofficial advice

In this painting by the Swedish artist Gilbrand Sether, Franklin D. Roosevelt is captain, steering the ship of state forward with Roosevelt and away from the hazardous waters of the Great Depression. In attendance are his wife Eleanor (*extreme right*), whose sympathy for the rights of the dispossessed and of African-American citizens was decisive in moving the New Deal to the left, and Secretary of Labor Frances Perkins (*left*), while the mortarboard caps of academics in the background suggest the contribution of the brain trust in planning New Deal legislation. More ominous, on the horizon loom the ships and planes of war. (Library of Congress.)

from African-Americans, Roosevelt employed more African-Americans in office. Thus Mary McLeod Bethune became director of the Division of Negro Affairs in the NYA; William H. Hastie, dean of Howard University Law School, became, first, assistant solicitor in the Department of the Interior, and, later, the first African-American federal judge; Robert C. Weaver also worked in the Interior and, later, in the Federal Housing Authority; Eugene K. Jones of the Urban League served as adviser on Negro Affairs in the Department of Commerce; Edgar Brown had a similar post in the CCC; and veteran social worker Lawrence A. Oxley was in charge of the Department of Labor's Division of Negro Labor. These and other such appointments were sufficiently numerous to earn the collective title of "Black Cabinet."

Furthermore, the expansion of the executive branch during the New Deal opened additional career opportunities for African-Americans, as for white Americans. Whereas in 1932 the Civil Service employed fewer than fifty thousand African-Americans, by 1941 it employed three times as many. The NYA under the liberal Aubrey Williams of Mississippi pursued a policy of appointing African-American state and local supervisors in those areas with a sizable population of African-Americans. The NYA provided young African-Americans with funds to attend school, from grammar schools to graduate schools.

These things stimulated greater political consciousness in African-American communities, especially in the South. Although only 5 percent of adult African-Americans voted in the South in 1940, others were forming a number of new voting organizations to try to persuade African-Americans to register to vote. For example, the Negro Voters League was formed in Raleigh, North Carolina, in 1931 and Committees on Negro Affairs were established in Charlotte, Durham, Greensboro, and Winston-Salem that together held a pro-Roosevelt rally in 1936.

Thus, as the political consciousness of African-Americans was being developed, they turned increasingly to the Democratic party. Toward the end of the 1930s Democratic candidates received as much as 85 percent of the vote in such areas of traditional settlement by African-Americans as Harlem in New York and the South Side of Chicago.

This phenomenon was to prove a decisive factor in Roosevelt's three campaigns for reelection. Of fifteen major African-American wards in nine cities, Roosevelt had carried only four in 1932. In 1936 he carried nine and in 1940 all fifteen wards elected him by large majorities. The marginal Democratic victory of 1944 was supplied by votes by African-

Americans in several states. For instance, in Michigan, which the Republicans had carried in 1940, the Democratic plurality of only 22,500 votes in the state as a whole was more than accounted for by the African-American Democratic vote in Detroit alone. In New Jersey African-American voters in five major cities provided Roosevelt with a plurality of almost twenty-nine thousand in a state that went Democratic by only 26,500.

However, the notorious poll tax, white primaries, and the maze of regulations about registration still thwarted African-American voting campaigns. In 1939 eight states used a poll tax of between one dollar and twenty-five dollars to disfranchise African-Americans (Alabama, Arkansas, Georgia, Mississippi, South Carolina, Tennessee, Texas, and Virginia). Moreover, four of these states (Alabama, Georgia, Mississippi, and Virginia) also enforced an annual liability (or fine) on every voter who failed to pay. All but South Carolina enforced payment for primary voting as well. Liberals joined forces with civil rights leaders to try and get such practices outlawed. Democratic Congressman Lee E. Geyer of California introduced a bill against poll taxes that passed the House in October 1941 but was blocked by southern senators in the upper house. The House voted various forms of anti-poll tax legislation in 1943, 1945, 1947, and 1949, only to see them all buried in Senate committees or blocked by filibusters.

Gradualism and Litigation

There were also advances in litigation for African-Americans. A series of constructive decisions by the Supreme Court during the 1930s paved the way for major civil rights decisions in the postwar period. As the Supreme Court moved to the left, it changed the criteria for decisions on civil rights, showing decreased interest in the rights of property and increased interest in the rights of the individual. This shift, too, stemmed from the upheaval of the New Deal. When the Supreme Court greatly expanded the powers of the national government, it reduced the principle of states' rights and, by implication, began to undermine the validity of political and social discrimination preserved by state governments.

In June 1935 Lloyd Lionel Gaines, a graduate of Lincoln University, the state-supported African-American college of Missouri, applied for a place at the law school of the University of Missouri, which was then all-white. Although he was duly qualified, the university refused him admission and advised him either to apply to Lincoln (which had no law school) or to apply out of state. Gaines took legal action and the test case of *Missouri ex rel. Gaines* v. *Canada* was decided by the Supreme Court on December 12, 1938. By seven votes to two the Court ruled against the state. In the words of Chief Justice Charles Evans Hughes, "A state denies equal protection of the laws to a black student when it refuses him admission to its all-white law school, even though it volunteers to pay his tuition at any law school in an adjacent state. By providing a law school for whites but not for blacks the state has created a privilege which one race can enjoy but the other cannot." Equally significant was the Supreme Court's repudiation of southern subterfuges to deny the vote to African-Americans. In the case of *Love* v. *Wilson,* on May 22, 1939, the Court finally ruled against the Oklahoma law replacing the grandfather clause the Court had nullified in *Guinn* v. *United States* (1915). It declared the replacement law as "a violation of the Fifteenth Amendment ban on racial discrimination in voting."

A series of cases provided unequivocal evidence that the absence of African-Americans from state juries was prima facie evidence of the denial of due process of law to African-Americans. Furthermore, in *Brown* v. *Mississippi* the Court ruled on February 17, 1936, that use of torture to extract confessions from defendants was clear denial of due process of law.

When Harlan Stone succeeded conservative Charles Evans Hughes as chief justice in 1941, NAACP attorney Thurgood Marshall became more optimistic about the outcome of civil rights cases. Stone's accession marked an even more decisive liberal shift in the court. It was also true that other recently appointed justices—Hugo Black (appointed 1937), Stanley Reed (1938), Frank Murphy (1940), and Robert Jackson (1941) —had all served the New Deal and appreciated the significance of the African-American vote for the Democratic party.

On May 26, 1941, in *United States* v. *Classic* (a case arising out of corruption in white primaries in Louisiana and brought by white voters), the Court, by five votes to three, awarded Congress power to regulate primary elections, thereby reversing earlier decisions. This ruling gave NAACP attorneys William Hastie and Thurgood Marshall the confidence to use the *Classic* opinion as a basis for contesting all-white primaries in *Smith* v. *Allwright*. Thurgood Marshall declared, "We must not be delayed by people who say, 'The time is not ripe,' nor should we proceed with caution for fear of destroying the status quo. People who deny us our civil rights should be brought to justice now." The Court decided on the *Smith* case on April 3, 1944, and ruled by eight votes to one that actions by a political party to prevent African-Americans from voting in primaries were subject to the Fourteenth and Fifteenth Amendments, thereby reversing the infamous decisions of *Grovey* v. *Townsend* in 1935. Whereas the impact of the Court's decisions on southern practices was negligible, its influence on the criteria for postwar decisions was vital.

The Nation of Islam

A number of movements favoring black nationalism emerged during the 1930s, including the National Movement for the Establishment of a Forty-Ninth State, founded in Chicago in 1934 by Oscar Brown, Sr., and Bindley C. Cyrus. The most famous of such organizations was the Nation of Islam, popularly called the Black Muslims, founded in Detroit circa 1931 by Wallace D. Fard (or Farrod Mohammed or Wali Forrod), a peddler of silks and raincoats who was of obscure origins—possibly black, possibly part Arab. The Black Muslims represented the most extreme reaction of African-Americans to white racism.

Basing their beliefs on the Muslim religion and a version of the Koran, Black Muslims taught that all whites were devils, perverse creations of an evil scientist, Yakub, and that only blacks were the true children of Allah. Absurd? Well, both the Jewish Torah and Christian Bible allow the book of Genesis not one but two different stories of the creation of the world and neither is consistent with subsequent scientific interpretations. Religions are conceived by men of faith rather than men of science and they enshrine myths, imaginative stories that help us understand the mysteries of human existence. The myth of the evil Yakub expresses a profound truth about the systematic exploitation of African-Americans by white society, notably in human slavery, and also about the ways society finds to justify and institutionalize white racism. Moreover, in the 1930s the myth became terrible prophecy. In Germany the Nazis set out to perfect a master race of Aryans and to exterminate the Jews, and also dabbled in terrible sexual and scientific experiments on their victims in concentration camps. In the United States, scientists chose to study the degeneration of African-American sufferers of venereal disease by allowing them to survive but deteriorate without remedial treatment in the "Bad Blood" experiment at Tuskegee, chronicled by James Jones.

The subjects were simply told they suffered from bad blood. Here in the 1930s were two instances of white science fulfilling the worst contemporary fears among African-Americans.

By 1933 the Black Muslims had established a temple, created a ritual, founded a University of Islam, and formed the Fruit of Islam, a bodyguard. The sect drew followers from other similar organizations, notably the Moorish Science Temple in Newark, New Jersey. This sect had been first founded in 1913 by Timothy Drew of North Carolina, who subsequently opened temples in New York, Chicago, Detroit, and other major cities that were attended by an aggregate congregation of between twenty and thirty thousand people.

By 1933 Fard had established a hierarchy in the Nation of Islam, notably his minister, Robert Poole of Georgia, known as Elijah Muhammad. When Fard disappeared mysteriously in 1934, Elijah Muhammad assumed control, moving headquarters from Detroit to Chicago. During the 1930s membership stabilized at around ten thousand but was damaged by the onset of World War II. Elijah Muhammad and some others were convicted of draft evasion and he was imprisoned from 1942 to 1946. During the war membership fell to below one thousand, with four temples in Detroit, Chicago, Milwaukee, and Washington, D.C. An obscure religious sect for almost thirty years, the Nation of Islam gained wide publicity in the 1950s with the rise of its most charismatic leader, Malcolm X.

The cult of separatism had repercussions in the NAACP. In 1934 Du Bois broke with the NAACP over his ideas for developing a separate state for African-Americans, a "Nation within a Nation." He averred that "if the economic and cultural salvation of the American Negro calls for an increase in segregation and prejudice, then that must come." Du Bois was to return to the NAACP in 1944 and leave it once again four years later over another policy dispute. In the meantime, he had become a consultant to the United Nations and was more involved in the activities of the Communist party.

The Scottsboro Case

Some African-Americans were attracted to communism because of its emphasis on economic and racial equality and its strategy of working-class solidarity. Radical interest in racial matters was furthered by white Communists, including James S. Allen, Herbert Aptheker, and Philip S.

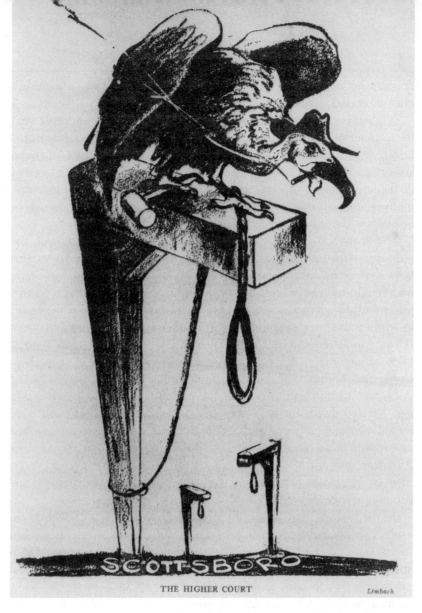

THE HIGHER COURT

Límbach

Socialists and other radical groups exploited the sensational case of the Scottsboro boys, unjustly convicted of rape in Alabama, to expose the injustice of southern racism, as in this cartoon by Limbach for the *New Masses* of October 16, 1934, in which a sharp-beaked vulture, replete with wide-brimmed hat and cigar, represents the "Higher Court." (Library of Congress.)

Foner, who wrote about black culture and argued that racial prejudice must be erased.

While it is true that African-Americans were potentially a fertile field for communism and perhaps twenty-five hundred African-Americans belonged to the Communist party in the mid-1930s, African-American radicalism was essentially indigenous to the United States, uninterested in theory, especially foreign ideologies, and suspicious of Communist motives at home and abroad. The verdict of many was, "It's enough to be black without being red, as well."

The Scottsboro incident of 1931 provided the Communists with the opportunity to rally support among African-Americans. The Scottsboro boys were nine African-American youths falsely accused of multiple rape on a freight train near Scottsboro, Alabama, on March 25, 1931, by two foul-mouthed white women, Victoria Price and Ruby Bates, who needed to explain their presence among the youths. The youths, aged between thirteen and twenty, were Charlie Weems, Ozie Powell, Clarence Norris, Olen Montgomery, Willie Roberson, Haywood Patterson, Eugene Williams, and Andrew and Leroy Wright. Willie Roberson was suffering from syphilis and gonorrhea and Olen Montgomery was blind in one eye. Viewed dispassionately, the allegations that intercourse had been forced were none too plausible. However, this sensational case touched an exposed nerve of race relations—sexual intercourse between African-American men and white American women. The metaphor or imprisonment of white over black was here made physical with the unjust incarceration of innocent men.

At the first trial of Clarence Norris and Charlie Weems on March 30, 1931, two doctors gave medical evidence that the girls were not injured in any way consistent with rape. Nevertheless, in the hysterical atmosphere of Alabama in the 1930s all-white juries doubtless felt they had no option but to convict African-Americans accused of raping white women, and the only possible penalty was death. The sentence of electrocution was cheered by the crowd. At trials held later that week the other defendants were found guilty and also sentenced to death.

The publicity generated by the case, the speed of the trial, and the savage nature of the sentences reached all parts of the country and led the Communist party to convene protests in Cleveland and New York. The International Labor Defense (ILD), a committee with close ties to the Communists, hired George W. Chamlee, a famous southern lawyer, to defend the youths. The way the Communists appropriated the case antagonized the NAACP and divided potential sources of support for the defense. Nevertheless such organizations as the American Civil Liberties Union (ACLU) and the Southern Commission on Interracial Cooperation (SCIC) sustained the defendants and helped save their lives through a long series of appeals before the state supreme court and the U.S. Supreme Court.

On March 24, 1932, the case reached the Alabama Supreme Court, which sustained all the convictions but commuted the death penalty for Leroy Wright to imprisonment on account of his extreme youth. However, on November 7, 1932, the Supreme Court ruled in *Powell* v. *Alabama* that there must be a retrial on the basis that the prejudice of the all-white juries had denied the defendants due process of law as guaranteed by the Fourteenth Amendment.

At the first retrial (of Haywood Patterson), held at Decatur, Alabama, fifty miles west of Scottsboro, on March 27, 1933, ILD defense attorney Samuel Leibowitz failed to get any African-Americans elected to the jury. However, he had already persuaded star witness Ruby Bates to appear for the defense and repudiate her earlier allegations of rape. The jury was obdurate and impervious to the new weight of evidence, again finding Haywood Patterson guilty and recommending the death penalty. The other defendants were also found guilty at their second trials and the Alabama Supreme Court set the date for their execution as August 31, 1934. Once again, the defense appealed to the Supreme Court. On April 1, 1935, in *Norris* v. *Alabama,* the court duly and unanimously ruled that the exclusion of African-Americans from juries and grand juries was contrary to the Fourteenth Amendment.

The defense now drew its conflicting forces together and the ILD, NAACP, ACLU, and the League for Industrial Democracy created a special Scottsboro Defense Committee on December 19, 1935. However, for its part, the prosecution began to fall apart, ready to compromise with prison sentences for all but Norris. President Franklin D. Roosevelt tried to persuade Governor "Bibb" Graves of Alabama to parole the Scottsboro boys but Graves was under intense local pressure to resist him.

At this point the case was complicated by an incident on January 25, 1936, in which Ozie Powell, baited by the police, attacked a deputy, Edgar Blalock, in a car, slashing his throat, and was himself shot and seriously wounded in the head. He survived but with permanent brain damage. The prosecution now decided to concentrate on his crime of assault and overlooked the original allegation of rape. He was sentenced to twenty years' imprisonment.

By July 1937 the prosecution was ready to compromise, insisting on death for Clarence Norris and prison for four others (Charlie Weems, Ozie Powell, Andrew Wright, and Haywood Patterson) and withdrawing the case against the remaining four (Olen Montgomery, Leroy Wright, Willie Roberson, and Eugene Williams). Thus four defendants were released on evidence that had convicted four others. The *Times-Dispatch* of July 27, 1937, suggested that the dropping of charges against four "serves as a virtual clincher to the argument that all nine of the Negroes are innocent." The governor then commuted Norris's sentence to life imprisonment. State authorities began to release all the remaining defendants under various terms of parole between 1943 and 1950.

Another case that provided the Communists with an opportunity to entice African-Americans was that of Angelo Herndon, arrested for leading a demonstration in Atlanta in 1932 and charged with incitement to insurrection on the basis of an old slave law. He was sentenced to eighteen years' hard labor on a chain gang. The Supreme Court overturned the verdict in 1937 after a well-orchestrated campaign for Herndon's release.

By the mid-thirties organized labor was shifting its position with regard to African-Americans. In the early decade the AFL had refused to discuss discrimination. There were few African-American unions, apart from A. Philip Randolph's Brotherhood of Sleeping Car Porters (BSCP), founded on August 5, 1925. However, the upheaval in organized labor caused by the new demands of industrial workers, leading to the creation of the CIO and its subsequent secession from the AFL, and the determination of certain Communist organizers to inject the race issue into union affairs helped promote the black case. The Communist-led National Textile Workers emphasized the need for racial equality, in contrast to the all-white exclusiveness of the United Textile Workers. Similarly, the Sharecropper Union in Alabama, the United Citrus Workers in Florida, and the Southern Tenant Farmers Union all practiced open membership. White institutions in general were showing themselves increasingly receptive to open discussion of race relations. Thus the Carnegie Foundation sponsored Swedish sociologist Gunnar Myrdal to undertake the research and writing of his mammoth study of race, *An American Dilemma* (1937).

Music and Musicians

African-American stars of entertainment, whether music, theater, or sports, made a profound contribution to the slowly burgeoning flower of civil rights in the second quarter of the century. This was despite the fact that they were not—with a few exceptions such as the multitalented Paul Robeson—political activists. It was simply that their entry into music and sports in northern society at a time when popular entertainment was becoming ever more commercialized introduced African-American artists to a wider spectrum of white society. Their art informed white society about black America. It also educated whites about the inalienable dignity of African-Americans.

The end of the 1920s and the early 1930s was a peak period of creative achievement for jazzman Duke Ellington. One of the most influential of African-American composers and musicians, Edward Kennedy ("Duke") Ellington (1899–1974) was a prolific writer of songs and of jazz pieces. Born and raised in Washington, D.C., he had little formal musical training apart from a few piano lessons as a child. He wrote his first piece, "Soda Fountain Rag," while working as a soda jerk after school. He formed his first band, the Duke's Serenaders, in 1917. In 1922 he visited New York and in Harlem heard the new improvised piano playing style of Willie ("The Lion") Smith, James P. Johnson, and Fats Waller and found their different, more flexible approach most congenial. He returned to New York in 1923 with his new band, the Washingtonians, performing first at the Kentucky Club (1923–1927) and then at the Cotton Club (1927–1932). Between 1928 and 1931 they cut 160 disks and Ellington also made radio broadcasts, introducing a signature theme, "East St. Louis Toodle Oo." His music in this period has highly original use of growling and muted brass.

His career had been synonymous with the Harlem Renaissance but his reputation survived it when he took a larger orchestra, appeared in films such as *Check and Double Check* (1930), and then reached a zenith of popularity with audiences in World War II. By this time he was composing extended concert pieces such as *Black, Brown, and Beige*, first performed in Carnegie Hall in 1953. His band was far less popular in the late 1940s and in the 1950s when "bop" and then "rock 'n' roll" were in vogue. They required far less sonority and a smaller tone palette than that of a big band like Duke Ellington's. Nevertheless, it was in this period that jazz was being taken more seriously as a high art form. Duke

Ellington tailored his compositions and arrangements to the talents and sounds of his instrumentalists, such as Johnny Hodges (alto sax), Sam Nanton (trombone), and Bubber Miley, Cootie Williams, and Ray Nance (trumpets). Their appearance at the Newport Jazz Festival of 1956, where they performed a range of sophisticated jazz pieces, was accounted a triumph and established their international reputation. For fifteen years they appeared in concert across the world in tours partly sponsored by the State Department, ever anxious to demonstrate the vitality of American art as the flowering of a free, democratic, and capitalistic society. Duke Ellington's famous songs included "Solitude," "Sophisticated Lady," "I Got It Bad," and "I Let a Song Go out of My Heart," and his shorter instrumental pieces included "Mood Indigo" and "Creole Love Call." His longer compositions included *Night Creatures* (1955), *Sweet Thursday* (1960), *My People* (1963), the musical *Beggar's Holiday* (1947), with lyrics by John La Touche, the ballet *The River* (1970), and the film score for *Assault on a Queen*. His range extended to religious music and he gave notable concerts of his own and others' sacred music in Grace Cathedral, San Francisco (1965), the Cathedral of St. John the Divine, New York (1968), and Westminster Abbey, London (1973).

Swing music was the specialty of Louis ("Satchmo") Armstrong (1900–1971), a Dixieland-style trumpeter, vocalist, and jazz-band leader whose catholic tastes were such as to allow him to move more easily into the world of standard popular music. Not only did he enjoy singular success in tours of the Mediterranean, the Middle East, and Western Europe in 1956 and of Africa in 1960 but he could also capture public acclaim equal to white artists in conventional material on disk and film with Bing Crosby in *High Society* (1956) and Barbra Streisand in *Hello, Dolly!* (1969).

However, although in the 1930s white society prized African-American singers and musicians for their range of emotional expression, it denied them full recognition as citizens. When Benny Goodman, "King of Swing," employed African-American artist Teddy Wilson in his band, various hotel managers refused to allow Wilson to play with the band on dance floors. Duke Ellington and his band were allowed to perform at Loew's State Theater on Broadway but not at the Paramount or Strand. Singer Billie Holiday had to enter hotels by the back door. In Detroit a manager thought she looked too light and she was told to put on darker makeup. She remarked of a southern tour with Artie Shaw's

Perhaps more than any other single individual, it was jazz leader Duke Ellington who raised the status and aspirations of American jazz music to the level of sophistication that put it on a par with the best of twentieth-century classical music. In this photograph by Gordon Parks the buoyant Duke Ellington is captured in conversation with members of his own orchestra at the Hurricane Cabaret in New York City in May 1943. (U.S. Office of War Information; Library of Congress.)

band, "It got to the point where I hardly ever ate, slept, or went to the bathroom without having a major NAACP-type production."

On one celebrated occasion white racism misfired and aided black pride. In 1939 classical contralto Marian Anderson planned to give a concert at Constitution Hall on Easter Day. "A voice like yours," said conductor Arturo Toscanini to her, "comes but once in a century." Nevertheless, Marian Anderson encountered serious resistance. Her proposed auditorium was managed by the Daughters of the American Revolution (DAR). Journalist Mary Johnson, sensing a story, provoked DAR president Mrs. Henry M. Robert, Jr., into announcing that neither Marian Anderson nor any other African-American artist would ever be heard in Constitution Hall. Liberals were scandalized.

However, at the suggestion of Walter White, Secretary of the Interior

Harold Ickes gave permission to hold the concert on the steps of the Lincoln Memorial, a far more prestigious and symbolic site. Eleanor Roosevelt resigned from the DAR and she and Ickes made sure that the front rows of the audience were comprised of cabinet members, senators, congressmen, and Supreme Court justices. Widespread publicity ensured an audience of seventy-five thousand, who were engrossed by the contralto's power, range, and expression in a variety of songs, from "America" to "Nobody Knows the Trouble I've Seen." Among the ensuing crush of people around Marian Anderson was a young African-American girl in her Easter best whose hands were already toughened by manual work. Walter White noticed her expression, which seemed to say, "If Marian Anderson can do it, then I can, too."

Books and Bookmen

Whereas the Great Depression and World War II inhibited certain cultural activities, they saw no lessening of artistic achievement by African-Americans in literature. The new poets included Melvin B. Tolson of Wiley College, who published a collection, *Rendezvous with America* (1944), which included his most famous piece, "Dark Symphony"; and Robert Hayden of the University of Michigan, whose first volume was *Heart-Shape in the Dust* (1940). Commentator Arna Bontemps produced *God Sends Sunday* (1931) and two historical novels, *Black Thunder* (1936) and *Drums at Dusk* (1939), before collaborating with Jack Conroy on *They Seek a City* (1945), an enthralling account of the urbanization of African-Americans. George W. Lee described Memphis life in *Beale Street* (1934) and then brought out *River George* (1936), while Waters Turpin concentrated on the upper south of Maryland in *These Low Grounds* (1937) and *O Canaan* (1939). Sculptor Augusta Savage's *Lift Every Voice and Sing* was exhibited at the New York World's Fair of 1939.

Chester Himes (b. 1909) described racial tension and friction in a wartime industrial community in *If He Hollers, Let Him Go* (1945), which vividly evokes the confusion and bitterness felt by African-Americans who had recently moved to industrial towns. In *Let Me Breathe Thunder* (1939) and *Blood on the Forge* William Attaway showed he could treat white as well as African-Americans characters and themes.

The most celebrated new talent of the second period was Richard Wright (1908–1960), who rapidly produced a collection of short stories,

A radiant photograph of the beautiful contralto Marian Anderson about to sing "The Star-Spangled Banner" at the dedication of a mural commemorating her historic free public concert on the steps of the Lincoln Memorial on Easter Sunday 1939. Refused permission to perform in Constitution Hall, Marian Anderson gained the support of Eleanor Roosevelt and Secretary of the Interior Harold Ickes to use the Lincoln Memorial and thereby brought the contribution of African-American performing artists to the fore of the burgeoning struggle for civil rights. The dedication of the mural was held in the Department of the Interior auditorium on January 6, 1943. (Photograph taken for the Office of War Information by Roger Smith; Library of Congress.)

Uncle Tom's Children (1938); a folk history, *Twelve Million Black Voices* (1941); and his account of his Mississippi childhood, *Black Boy* (1945), as well as his most celebrated novel, *Native Son* (1940).

Native Son is about the social, psychological, and physical incarceration of the marginal man. Bigger Thomas, an unemployed African-American youth, is taken on as a chauffeur by a supposedly liberal family, the Daltons, who are, in fact, the exploitive landlords of his slum home. He is compromised by their daughter, Mary, whose gestures of friendship and equality confuse and terrify him so much that he smothers her by accident and, frightened out of his wits, disposes of the body in a furnace. In the course of his getaway he brutally murders his girlfriend, Bessie.

The story is told with a series of effective dramatic metaphors, beginning with the cornered rat Bigger kills in his home and continuing with Bigger's attempted escape across Chicago, where, as with Eliza crossing the ice floes in *Uncle Tom's Cabin,* his very blackness is emphasized by the falling snow, which renders the entire city a prison of whiteness, until it is Bigger himself who is trapped like a cornered rat. The language, images, and elaborate, surreal court scenes in which the political utterances of conservatives, liberals, and Communists are shown as stereotypes of sophistry—all are effectively treated as the literary equivalent of the dramatic and stark Soviet cinema posters of the period, such as Grigory Rychkov's *The Tractor Drivers* (1939).

The genius of Wright's work is indicated not only in the way he exposes the superficiality of white understanding but also, like William Faulkner with the racially ambiguous Joe Christmas, in the way he makes articulate the hidden, confused emotions of his inarticulate hero by playing white rhetoric against black restraint and sullenness. The very title, *Native Son,* makes its own ironic comment, suggesting natives of Africa and children of the United States who have an indigenous right to equal citizenship in the country of their ancestors and of their birth.

While owing a considerable debt to the American realistic tradition of authors such as Theodore Dreiser and its European counterpart, Wright was also under the influence of such different writers as Dostoevski and Poe, both of whom had captured the inner anguish of men alienated from their surroundings. Analyst A. Robert Lee comments how "in the black American especially he saw an instance of the human psyche not only denied community with the rest of American society but frequently forced into division within and against itself."

Artist Jacob Lawrence (b. 1917) grew up in Harlem during the depression and was acutely aware of the cultural heritage and the hardships of African-Americans during the decade. His career began in a settlement-house art class that was supported by the Federal Arts Project (FAP) and his very first paintings dealt with historical figures who had played important roles in the liberation of slaves: for example, the

Haitian Toussaint L'Ouverture and the southerners Frederick Douglass and Harriet Tubman. Between 1940 and 1941 he drew directly on his experience of the depression and created the series of sixty paintings entitled *The Migration of the Negro*. These paintings provide a telling description of the plight of dispossessed blacks in the 1930s. Lawrence has pointed out that this migration was an integral part of his life: "My parents were part of the migration—on their way North when I was born in Atlantic City in 1917." His use of stark compositions, bright poster colors, and angular, often contorted figures, serve to increase the already considerable emotional impact of his subject matter.

The world of sports also attested to the continuing strength and vibrancy of African-American stars. German dictator Adolf Hitler's claims about Nordic superiority were challenged by the great African-American sprinter Jesse Owens of Ohio. At the 1936 Olympics in Berlin, German track officials deliberately handicapped Jesse Owens, who nevertheless scored signal victories. Hitler made his embarrassment obvious by refusing to make the awards of the gold medals himself. Several other American athletes protested against the insult by refusing to accept their own hard-won medals from Hitler. Two years later heavyweight boxing champion Joe Louis, the "Brown Bomber," hammered home the point by pounding German boxer Max Schmeling (who had previously defeated him) to defeat at Madison Square Garden. By the time America went to war in 1941 Joe Louis had successfully defended his heavyweight title nine times. He was well aware of his social responsibilities. "I want to fight honest," he said, "so that the next colored boy can get the same break I got. If I act the fool, I'll let them down."

Despite such prowess and sense of responsibility and achievement by Joe Louis and other African-American stars, the greater portion of African-Americans still faced considerable political, social, and economic handicaps on the eve of World War II. Yet, ironically, various factors in the tragedy of war were to play into the hands of the first civil rights leaders and to spur on the burgeoning civil rights movement.

The Incipient Movement for Civil Rights during World War II

In 1940 there were 12,866,000 African-Americans (compared with a total population of 131,699,275), and most of them worked at unskilled and menial jobs with low pay. Only one in twenty African-American males worked in a white collar profession (compared with one in three

white males). Of every ten African-American women who worked, six worked as maids (compared with one in ten white women). Although twice as many African-Americans as whites worked on farms, a much smaller proportion farmed their own land.

Four times as many African-Americans as whites lived in houses with more than two people per room and only half as many African-Americans as whites lived in houses with two rooms per person. The mortality rate among African-Americans was almost twice that of whites. Thus in Washington, D.C., for example, the infant mortality rate among whites was thirty-seven per one thousand whereas for African-Americans it was seventy-one per one thousand. If they survived infancy, African-Americans could expect to live, on average, twelve years less than whites. Of African-Americans over twenty-five, one in ten had not completed a single year of school; only one in a hundred had graduated from college. Racism was still widespread and institutionalized. Thirty states proscribed marriage between African-Americans and whites. In the South African-Americans had to use separate waiting rooms at bus and railroad stations, separate railroad cars, separate seating sections in movie theaters, separate churches and schools, separate restaurants and drinking fountains. Moreover, they had also to endure all manner of white refusals to allow them even a modicum of social respect. It was difficult, and most rare, for African-Americans to serve as police officers or become practicing lawyers. In the deep South African-Americans were almost never employed as policemen. In 1940 the states of Mississippi, South Carolina, Louisiana, Georgia, and Alabama (states in which African-Americans made up over a third of the population) had not one African-American policeman between them. Nor did Arkansas and Virginia (where African-Americans accounted for a third of the population). There were only four African-American lawyers in Alabama, compared with sixteen hundred whites, and six in Mississippi, compared with

A Christmas shopping day in Florence, Alabama, in 1941, as photographed for the Farm Security Administration, draws together various icons of American popular culture, including movie theater, bank, and sleek automobiles at a street intersection. The cityscape suggests the calm insulation of the New South from the exigency of war—a lull that would be destroyed by the dramatic domestic upheaval of American intervention (1941–1945) and would lead to an acceleration of the Great Migration of African-Americans from the South to the North; the dispersal of various ethnic communities; and arousal of a potent civil rights movement from slumber into propaganda about a war against fascism whose parallels were not lost on a vibrant generation of African-American servicemen. (Library of Congress.)

twelve thousand whites. Judges and court officials were invariably white. African-Americans seldom served on juries. In consequence, African-Americans received odd, ill-balanced forms of justice. Thus courts tended to be lenient to African-Americans accused of committing crimes against other African-Americans but were especially harsh to African-Americans accused of crimes against whites.

World War II clarified attitudes toward race as government propaganda fashioned political ideology in an attempt to cover the contradictions of fighting a war against racism abroad while maintaining segregation at home. Now the shortcomings of the American democratic system were tested to the limit. It became all too easy for liberals and radicals alike to equate poll taxes and grandfather clauses, lynching, and the segregation of African-Americans in the United States with Hitler's persecution of the Jews in the Third Reich. The *Crisis* published a photograph of a defense industry factory with a "whites only" notice outside and commented bitterly about aircrafts made by whites, flown by whites, but paid for by African-Americans. "It sounds pretty foolish to be *against* park benches marked 'Jude' in Berlin, but to be *for* park benches marked 'colored' in Tallahassee, Florida."

The New Deal and Roosevelt's foreign policy rhetoric had roused expectations of change among African-Americans but left them unsatisfied. With consummate, new-found political skills, their leaders were quick to exploit the situation. In January 1941, at a meeting that included Walter White, Mary McLeod Bethune, and Lester Grange (of the Urban League), A. Philip Randolph announced plans for a mass march on Washington to protest against discrimination in defense industries. Some commentators were skeptical of success. The Chicago *Defender* commented on February 8, 1941, "To get 10,000 Negroes assembled in one spot, under one banner, with justice, democracy, and work as their slogan would be the miracle of the century." However, Randolph was firmly convinced of solidarity among African-Americans and believed he knew how to channel their indignation into constructive political action while preventing the Communists from exploiting the situation. Indeed, Randolph's appeal transcended his immediate aims and touched a sensitive nerve in the African-American community at large. Across the country African-Americans formed committees to coordinate support and began organizing transportation to Washington. Thus encouraged, Randolph chose July 1 for the event.

Randolph's command and activities produced feelings of consterna-

Perhaps the least known of all major civil rights leaders, A. Philip Randolph (1889–1979) had the longest career and, in the opinion of history, may have exerted the greatest influence on the whole of the civil rights movement. His work was hardly invisible: it was his successful threat to organize a mass march in Washington in 1941 that forced Franklin D. Roosevelt's hand over fair employment practices during World War II. It became a model for the great March on Washington for Jobs and Freedom of August 1963, in which Randolph, then an old man of seventy-three, also played a pivotal part. In this photograph he is captured speaking to the National Press Club by *U.S. News and World Report* on August 26, 1963, around the time of the great march. (Library of Congress.)

tion bordering on panic in Roosevelt's administration. It sought national unity and FDR did not want his plans for the war to be jeopardized by ethnic divisions at home. On June 18, 1941, Roosevelt met with Randolph and White and tried to separate bluff and realism in their tactics. "Walter, how many people will really march?" he asked. "Not less than one hundred thousand," replied White. Thus cornered, on June 25 Roosevelt issued Executive Order 8802, requiring that all employers, unions, and government agencies "concerned with vocational training programs" must "provide for the full and equitable participation of all workers in defense industries without discrimination because of race, creed, color, or national origin." The march was called off. To enforce the order, FDR created a Fair Employment Practices Committee (FEPC).

The FEPC had no punitive powers and was even loath to penalize white violaters. However, because it held hearings in public, many employers preferred to change their policies rather than risk unfavorable publicity. Nevertheless, the African-American press was jubilant and greeted Executive Order 8802 as a second emancipation proclamation. Unfortunately, the FEPC was scuttled by racists at the end of the war.

During World War II (1939–1945), 1.15 million African-Americans entered the armed services and many fought overseas. However, the armed forces were totally segregated and the African-American press continued to emphasize similarities between fascist persecution of the Jews in Europe and racial segregation in the United States. Throughout the war, the Red Cross kept "white blood" and "black blood" in separate containers.

Although chiefs of staff would have preferred to think the armed services were immune from racial conflict, they came under increasing pressure to abandon their ironclad segregation code of 1941. By the terms of this code, African-Americans could not enlist in the Marine or Air Corps. In the navy they could serve only in menial tasks. The army did admit African-Americans but maintained segregated training facilities and units and retained African-American troops primarily in a supportive capacity rather than in combat. African-American officers were assigned to so-called Negro units and had to serve under white superiors. No African-American officer could ever become superior to a white in the same unit. The army rationalized this policy, partly on the sophistry that African-Americans were poor fighters, partly on the grounds that the army was not a suitable laboratory for social experiments, and partly in the belief that integration would destroy the morale of white soldiers. The War Department insisted that it could not "ignore the social relationships between negroes and whites which have been established by the American people through custom and habit." However, as the numbers of African-American soldiers increased sevenfold, from one hundred thousand in 1941 to seven hundred thousand in 1944, so did their dissatisfaction with military segregation.

African-American recruits came primarily from the North because those from the South were usually neither sufficiently healthy nor well enough educated to pass induction tests. African-Americans from the North were less likely to accept Jim Crow. One African-American leader, Edgar Brown, advised Roosevelt in a letter of May 20, 1942, how "many of these young people have lived all their lives in New York, Detroit, Philadelphia, Chicago and other metropolitan areas where their

African-American worker using a portable electric drill on a YP-38 subassembly unit in a western aircraft plant, one of the millions of artisans trained for skilled, precision work in record time. (Photograph taken for the OWI, June 1942, by Bransby; Library of Congress.)

civil rights have never before been abridged." Thus gradually (and reluctantly) chiefs of staff came to accept that military segregation was wasteful of manpower; that it was exposing the armed services to liberal criticisms; and that it was depressing the morale of an ever larger section of the army. Somewhat shamefaced, the army began to use African-Americans in combat and the navy introduced a program of cautious integration. Nevertheless, the army remained totally segregated. The agitation for integration led Army Chief of Staff George C. Marshall to declare, "My God! My God! . . . I don't know what to do about this race question in the army. I tell you frankly, it is the worst thing that we have to deal with. . . . We are getting a situation on our hands that may explode right in our faces."

The Great Migration, partially stilled by the Depression, resumed as African-Americans from the South sought new opportunities in the North.

During the 1940s, 1.24 million African-Americans left the South. The number of African-Americans working in industry, public utilities, and transportation increased from seven hundred thousand in 1940 to 1.45 million in 1944. In the same period the number working for the federal government rose from sixty thousand to over two hundred thousand. Despite continuing resistance to giving African-Americans highly skilled jobs or supervisory roles, those who worked as skilled workers or foremen doubled during the war. At the same time almost 550,000 joined the labor unions, usually those affiliated with the Congress of Industrial Organizations (CIO).

Whereas white migration was at its peak in 1943, migration by African-Americans peaked in 1945. Moreover, once African-Americans began to move, they did so in greater proportions than whites and tended to settle permanently in their new homes. The prime centers of migration were usually such centers of war production as Chicago and Detroit in the North; Norfolk, Charleston, and Mobile in the South; and Los Angeles, San Francisco, and San Diego in the West. In the period 1940–1944 the total population of the ten largest centers of wartime production increased by 19 percent but the population of African-Americans in those areas rose by 49 percent. The increase would have a profound impact on race relations in these centers.

Discrimination against African-Americans in defense industries was somewhat curbed by the persistent need for extra manpower. Unions that excluded African-Americans found it difficult to sustain open racism when the federal government announced it would refuse to certify them as accredited agents for collective bargaining unless they accepted minorities. Also, in 1943 the War Labor Board outlawed wage differences based exclusively on race.

In the North African-Americans could vote and there was not the same blatant segregation as existed in the South. In fact, in Chicago a larger proportion of African-Americans than whites went to the polls. Nevertheless, the war and renewed migration upset the delicate balance of institutional racism in the South and the North. As a result, race relations became most tense in the crucial areas of housing, transportation, employment, and military service.

For example, in Chicago African-Americans were excluded from some eleven square miles of residential districts either through restrictive covenants (under which householders agreed neither to sell nor to lease property to them) or by informal agreements by landlords and real estate

A clear indication of the social supremacy of white over black in the segregation of African-Americans from whites in the deep South. This photograph by Marian Post Wolcott of an African-American citizen entering a movie theater by the "colored" entrance in Belzoni in the Delta area of Mississippi in October 1932 is an ironic indication of injustice. (Farm Security Administration; Library of Congress.)

operators. As to employment, they were restricted to the dirtiest and least desirable jobs, partly because of color prejudice, partly because of inadequate training, and partly because of opposition from trade unions. Thus in Chicago African-Americans accounted for 8 percent of the labor force and 22 percent of the city's unemployed.

White workers looked on askance as African-Americans joined them on the factory floor, dreading that they might lose their cherished illusion of superiority. They protested the upgradings of African-Americans by walking out, by beating up African-American workers (as shipyard workers did in Mobile), or by going on strike (as trolley car workers did in Philadelphia). White workers in a munitions plant in Baltimore stopped work rather than share washrooms and cafeterias with African-Americans. Railroad unions tried to protect their white members by insisting on a union contract that restricted both the jobs open to African-Americans and their chances of promotion.

What did the federal government do? In Philadelphia the government dispatched federal troops to run the trolley cars, thereby persuading the strikers to give up the dispute and go back to work. However, in other cases, it responded timidly, settling differences by compromise rather than with justice. In Mobile the Fair Employment Practices Committee agreed to segregation of shipways, on which African-Americans could work in certain categories as welders, riggers, and riveters, but not in others as electricians, machine operators, or pipe fitters. In Baltimore the FEPC allowed the munitions company to construct a larger cafeteria and washroom and assign whites and African-Americans separate space at opposite ends of the room. As Louis Rucheson shows in *Race, Jobs, and Politics* (1948), where the government thought that intervention to promote equal opportunity might threaten war production, it took no action. Thus the railroad unions deliberately ignored the FEPC order against discrimination and retained their restrictive contract until the Supreme Court declared it unconstitutional in December 1944.

The movement of so many people to only a few centers led to especially heightened tension over housing. In certain northern cities ghettos were filled well beyond capacity and began to burst, thus upsetting traditional lines of demarcation. White householders, disturbed at the prospect of being engulfed in a black tide, took matters into their own hands. However, when they tried to stop African-Americans from moving into federal housing projects, they received deserved adverse publicity. In Buffalo threats of violence induced the government to cancel plans for a housing project. In February 1942 a mob of whites armed with rocks and clubs menaced fourteen families of African-Americans and deterred them from moving into the Sojourner Truth Homes in Detroit until April, when they were protected by a police escort.

The worst riots since 1919 occurred in 1943 as whites, enraged by African-Americans' penetration of formerly white occupations, took the law into their own hands. Troops were called in to restore order in Mobile, Alabama, after a riot broke out when African-American workers were promoted in a shipyard. Two people died after a disturbance in Beaumont, Texas, and a small-scale riot in Harlem was sparked off by rumors that an African-American soldier had been shot by a white policeman. By far the worst incident took place in Detroit, where thirty-four people died in a riot that spread after a fist fight between an African-American and a white. Moreover, police brutality towards African-Americans in the Detroit riot stunned the nation. Seventeen African-

Americans had died at the hands of the police and there was a preponderance of African-American arrests over those of whites.

After the Detroit riot Attorney General Francis Biddle proposed a government ban on further migration by African-Americans to certain cities. "No more Negroes should move to Detroit," he urged. He soon realized such an attitude was no help. Yet he had, inadvertently, touched upon the recent cause of riots—continued black migration. The forces that had led to better opportunities and rewards for African-Americans had also led to renewed and increased racial tension.

Thus the war exacerbated racial difference. As Richard Polenberg says in *One Nation Divisible* (1980), "From the black perspective, the lowering of some barriers made those remaining seem more intolerable. To many whites, however, the remaining barriers seemed even more desirable than before." A student quoted by Mary F. Berry and John W. Blassingame in *Long Memory: The Black Experience in America* (1982) expressed smoldering resentment among African-Americans: "The Army Jim Crows us. The Navy lets us serve only as mess men. The Red Cross refuses our blood. We are disenfranchised, Jim Crowed, spat upon. What more could Hitler do than that?" However, in contrast to their position in World War I, groups of African-Americans and their political leaders were now a political force to be reckoned with.

Nazi emphasis on racism helped discredit racial doctrines in the United States. For several decades progressive anthropologists such as Franz Boas and Otto Kleinberg had challenged the idea that some races were superior to others. During the war their successors argued these points for a mass audience. Ruth Benedict in *Race: Science and Politics* (1940), Gunnar Dahlberg in *Race, Reason and Rubbish* (1942), and Ashley Montagu in *Man's Most Dangerous Myth: The Fallacy of Race* (1942), all emphasized how much all human beings have in common; that individual differences are more important than racial averages; that so-called racial traits are really determined by culture and environment; and that the notion of racial purity was, at best, obsolete, especially given increasing migration and intermarriage. In short, such authors argued for the plasticity rather than the permanence of human nature. Thus Ashley Montagu in *Man's Most Dangerous Myth* declared how the rise of fascism "shows us today where we end up if we think the shape of the nose or the color of the skin has anything to do with human values and culture."

The African-American press called for a "Double V" campaign, a victory against racism at home as well as over fascism abroad. Without the domestic victory, they reasoned, the military victory would be pointless. Moreover, they implied that whites must pay for African-American support of the war effort. Blues artist Lonnie Johnson explained how in a candid lyric of 1942: "And you can tell the world that I'm fightin' / For what really belongs to me." The *Amsterdam News* of June 19, 1943, referred to "race discrimination and segregation, mob brutality—the entire Nazi pattern of U.S. racial conditions."

Nonviolent Resistance as a Model for Civil Rights

African-American leaders continued to find new strength, and their faith in progress was stimulated by radical religious groups. Quaker groups had played a part in the abolitionist movement during the nineteenth century. In the 1930s such organizations as the Fellowship of Reconciliation (FOR) of 1915, mixing Quaker and radical ideas, took a lead by placing racial equality at the heart of the Social Gospel. Initially the FOR had conceived of its work in race relations as educational but in 1941 a committee headed by J. Holmes Smith, a former missionary to India, suggested the use of nonviolent techniques against racial prejudice, as they had first been applied by Mohandas Karamchand Gandhi to unite Indians against British rule.

Strategies to achieve civil rights for African-Americans had long been nourished by the strategies and teachings of Gandhi (1869–1948). Born into a Hindu Bania, or merchant, caste in Porbandar, India, he was educated in both India and Britain and qualified as a barrister in London. His orthodox Hindu upbringing nurtured within him devotion to all forms of life, vegetarianism, and the practice of fasting as a means of self-purification. He emigrated to South Africa (1893–1914), where he had a successful legal practice. It was there that his sense of outrage at the racial humiliations meted out to Indians in South Africa cultivated within him a determination never to accept injustice. It was in South Africa that he campaigned for equal rights for Indians and developed techniques of nonviolent resistance, or *satyagraha* (truthforce).

On his return to India he began working for workers' and peasants' rights (1916–1918). In this way he also formed strong political connections that would provide the basis for his leadership of Indian nationalists, first in a series of confrontations and then by dominating the Indian

Among the many injustices of war was the enforced evacuation of Japanese-American citizens from west coast areas under an emergency order promulgated by the United States Army. The persecution of the Nisei and their being concentrated in camps were clearly violations of their due civil rights, although they were permitted as a result of wartime hysteria. Here a group of Japanese-Americans await with their baggage the trains that will take them from Los Angeles, California, in April 1942 to a relocation center in Owens Valley. (Photograph taken for the Farm Security Administration by Russell Lee; Library of Congress.)

National Congress. The Indian National Congress, founded in 1885, was the major Indian political party that began to conduct major political campaigns for India's self-rule and won most of the elections held under the terms of the Government of India Act of 1935 but withdrew from government in 1939. Many leaders were imprisoned during the "Quit India" campaign of 1941–1942.

Gandhi's main strategy until 1934 was civil disobedience through symbolic acts of noncooperation, passive acts of defiance intended to bring shame upon the British. Among these acts was the Salt March of two hundred miles from Sabarmati to Dandi of March 12–April 6, 1930. The private manufacture of salt was against the British salt tax system. The system discriminated against the poorest sections of the community. Gandhi, wanting an open, illegal, but entirely peaceful defiance of the British, led masses of protesters to make salt from the sea at

Dandi. As an immediate result Gandhi was arrested on May 5 and so, subsequently, were sixty thousand of his followers. However, the public outcry was such that the salt tax was repealed in the spring of 1931. In 1934 Gandhi resigned from the Congress party because he believed that the other leaders were using nonviolent resistance as a political expedient rather than as a manifestation of a religious search for truth. However, he remained at the center of the mass movement for Indian independence until it had been achieved by British withdrawal from India in 1947.

In 1941 Gandhi's strategies were first put to the test in America. Seven former students of Antioch College of Ohio had established a cooperative farm, Ahimsa Farm, near Cleveland. One of them, Lee Stern, persuaded the others to help his African-American friends from the city get into a segregated swimming pool at Garfield Park by going there as a mixed group and entering and leaving peaceably. Their attempt was so successful that James Farmer, secretary of the FOR for the mid-Atlantic area, and his friends George Houser and Bayard Rustin, organized a Men's Interracial Fellowship House in January 1942. It lasted only six months but led to a National Federation of Committees of Racial Equality, supported by the FOR, which met in June 1943. The following year at Detroit this organization became the Congress of Racial Equality (CORE).

Although nominally independent, CORE was led by FOR members and until 1957 the CORE office was at FOR headquarters and its leadership were on the Fellowship payroll. James Farmer was both national chairman of CORE and race-relations secretary of the FOR (1941–1945); George Houser was both executive secretary of CORE and race-relations secretary of the FOR (1945–1957) and race- relations projects secretary of the FOR (1944–1955); Bayard Rustin was a Fellowship youth and college secretary (1941–1952) who was active in the civil rights movement and, eventually, coordinated the March on Washington for Jobs and Freedom of August 28, 1963.

In short, the model of civil disobedience established by Gandhi in India against the British would prove most successful for American civil rights organizers when it was applied to abuses of segregation in the South in the 1950s and 1960s. By dramatizing the sobriety of African-Americans and the justice of their cause in mass demonstrations, these organizers would provide the news media with effective copy that would bring shame to their racist oppressors and lend dignity and hope to the oppressed.

The doyen of the civil rights movement across the world was Mohandas Gandhi, symbolic leader of India's long fight for independence from the British Raj. Gandhi's strategy and philosophy were based upon civil disobedience as expressed in nonviolent actions that were technically illegal but spiritually profound and intended to bring shame upon his adversaries. This photograph of April 6, 1925, was taken shortly after one of Gandhi's periodic incarcerations by the British. He is seen spinning cotton, being a determined advocate of home spinning by Indians, whom he tried to persuade to discard conventional cottons made by western machines.

Gandhi's ideals of spiritual resistance were translated most powerfully after World War II into effective strategies on behalf of civil rights for African-Americans by such powerful church orators as Martin Luther King. They recognized how well suited were Gandhi's techniques to a world being recorded by the mass media of film and television. Civil rights demonstrations, dramatic imprisonments, and oratory had much in common with the resolve of colored and third world peoples everywhere determined to wrest dramatic control of their own lives and institutions from colonial powers. (Library of Congress.)

PART TWO

The Second
American Revolution

Martin Luther King, Jr. (1929–1968), the young Baptist minister whose name was to become synonymous with the American civil rights movement, captured in earnest dialogue at a press conference of March 10, 1960, explaining the relationship between the strategy of nonviolent resistance and the goals of civil rights. (U.S. News and World Report; Library of Congress.)

3

Made Visible

Ralph Ellison's novel *Invisible Man* (1952) captured the imagination
of a generation in part because it prophesied something of the
metamorphosis of African-Americans who were themselves at various
crossroads on their journey to full citizenship. It was W. E. B. Du Bois
who had first discerned "the sense of looking at one's self through the
eyes of others." *Invisible Man* not only captured this sensation but also
fielded a hero who could transcend sociological, visual, and psychological imprisonment.

Invisible Man is a confessional, picaresque novel in the tradition of
slave narratives in which an unnamed protagonist takes a journey through
life from the deep South to a Harlem ghetto and discovers various types
of African-Americans and the forms they have, willingly or not, assumed. Thus its central subjects of white over black and of blackness
within the human spirit, as expressed in black words printed on white
pages, are used to unfold an emblematic human story. The journey ever
onward represents a search for understanding in place of oppression, for
consciousness instead of apathy and ignorance, and for identity made
visible. The implication of the novel's prologue and epilogue is that each
successive identity assumed by the unnamed hero has been provisional:
African-American scholarship candidate, member of the Brotherhood
(Ellison's imaginative, literary reconstruction of the American Communist party), factory worker for Liberty Paints, hipster and stud, confi-

dence trickster B. P. Rinehart, and the underground, invisible author who sets fire to all preconceived labels and, with them, the categories all African-Americans have had foisted upon them.

The other characters he has met on his journey are representative figures recalled from the past history of African-Americans. Bledsoe, the southern college president, plays accommodation as a lyre to his white benefactors in the sagacious manner of Booker T. Washington. Homer Barbee speaks the commencement address in Emersonian riddles in a manner intended to cloud insight with blindness. Mr. Norton, the college's principal and northern benefactor, seeks subliminal release from his own intimations of incest, partly by his largess, partly in his fantasies of black incest. Ras is a black nationalist in the tradition of Marcus Garvey. Brother Jack is a token black in the predominantly white Communist brotherhood. Lucius Brockway is a factory artisan for Liberty Paints whose principal product of white paint can only be achieved by application of select drops of black paint—a cruel, penetrating metaphor for white society seeking its preferred racial balance by select, token integration—until the protagonist causes mayhem. Tod Clifton, the determined imp of fun who is as doomed as his first name, starts as a Fabian on the make and ends as a rejected Feste. His picaresque journey accomplished, the protagonist makes it crystal clear that his progress from callow youth to seasoned maturity, from darkness to light, has made him an astute observer who will no longer remain locked in by the definitions of others.

I'm shaking off the old skin, and I'll leave it here in the hole. I'm coming out, no less invisible without it, but coming out nevertheless. And I suppose it's damn well time. Even hibernations can be overdone, come to think of it. Perhaps that's my greatest social crime, I've overstayed my hibernation, since there's a possibility that even an invisible man has a socially responsible role to play.

That Ralph Ellison could explain something of the future metamorphosis of African-Americans was in part due to his remarkable perception about the role any emerging individual must play in a society itself undergoing immense transformation—social, economic, and political. Various changes that occurred in America's white and African-American communities in the 1950s helped promote an emerging civil rights movement that would burst forth in the 1960s. The combination of factors stimulating and publicizing the cause of civil rights were complex. However, it was the interaction of political forces alongside demographic, economic, and cultural changes that underpinned the conflicts of the fifties and sixties, although the characterization of a coherent postwar civil rights movement with new goals, organization, and direction has been exaggerated.

The Emergence of Civil Rights

Race relations began to occupy a commanding position upon the political stage of postwar America for a variety of reasons. Among the most notable were the impact of the continuous migration of African-Americans from the rural South to the industrial urban North while whites in the North were moving from cities to suburbs; the advent of television; and the resurgence of black Africa.

The historical shift of southern African-Americans to the North, which had begun after the Civil War, reached a peak in the period 1940–1960, when three million migrated. The accompanying table illustrates trends of migration in the period 1950–1980. The percentage of African-Americans in the southern population as a whole declined while African-Americans were still moving northward. Thus between 1950 and 1980 it fell in Arkansas from 22 percent to 16 percent, in Florida from 22 percent to 14 percent, and in Mississippi from 45 percent to 35 percent. The percentages of white migrants to the South from other regions rose in Arkansas from 9 percent to 18 percent, in Florida from 30 percent to 51 percent, and in Texas from 9 percent to 20 percent.

In the single decade from 1950 as many as 1,473,000 African-Americans moved north. Hence, in this period the African-American population of New York City doubled, that of Philadelphia, Chicago, and Detroit tripled, while that of Los Angeles increased by five times. The migration was of vital political importance to both the Republican and Democratic parties. As whites moved to the suburbs, African-Americans moved into the inner cities, making the future political complexion of formerly Democratic wards uncertain. Politicians now had to take the African-American vote and, more significantly, African-American grievances, into consideration at the local as well as the national level.

Furthermore, the migration of African-Americans north and west was leading them into urban areas where the apparatus of southern Jim Crow laws did not exist. In the South, too, urbanization was beginning to place a strain on the system of segregation. Since segregation was

TABLE 1

Whites born outside the South and African-Americans in the South (as a percentage of the population)

	1950	1960	1970	1980
Alabama	3%	5%	6%	8%
	32	30	26	26
Arkansas	9	10	12	18
	22	22	18	16
Florida	30	30	42	51
	22	18	15	14
Georgia	4	6	8	12
	31	28	26	27
Louisiana	5	5	6	9
	33	32	30	29
Mississippi	3	5	6	8
	45	42	37	35
North Carolina	3	5	7	11
	27	24	22	22
South Carolina	3	6	8	12
	39	35	30	30
Tennessee	4	5	7	11
	16	16	16	16
Texas	9	10	14	20
	13	12	12	12
Virginia	11	14	18	21
	22	21	19	19

(as percentage of population)

The source of these statistics is the Bureau of the Census, "Guide to U. S. Elections," *Congressional Quarterly, Inc.* (1985).

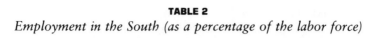

TABLE 2

Employment in the South (as a percentage of the labor force)

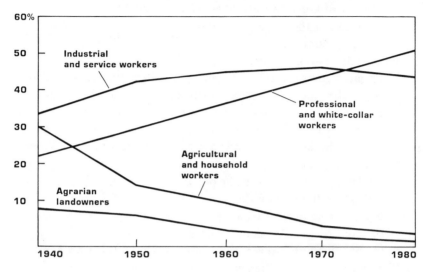

more overt in towns, the contrast between the treatment of the races was more striking than in the countryside. In urban areas, also, individuals tended to become involved in particular social, political, or religious communities and to find them mutually supportive. Between 1940 and 1950 the proportion of African-Americans in southern urban areas increased from 49 percent to 62 percent, continuing to rise to 73 percent by 1960 and then to 81 percent by 1970.

Another significant factor in the increasing urbanization of African-Americans was the mechanization of southern agriculture and its diversification away from cotton into other produce. Southern agriculture had deep problems. Right across the black belt of rich soil, former agricultural workers were being displaced by machines. The accompanying table of employment in the South as a percentage of the labor force (Table 2) shows the decline in agrarian landowners and of agricultural and domestic workers in the period 1940–1980 while the percentages of industrial, service, and professional workers were generally rising. By the end of the sixties the African-American population in the southern cities of Atlanta, New Orleans, Birmingham, and Richmond was over 40 percent of the total population. By 1970, 70 percent of the population of Washington, D.C., was African-American. Such major cities in the South, like those in the North, were developing a significant under-class of dispossessed, unemployed African-Americans.

The upshot of these various demographic changes was momentous. As the historian of the South, C. Vann Woodward, asserts, "What the South has long claimed as its peculiar problem was no longer a regional monopoly but a national problem."

Civil rights leaders succeeded in gaining presidential ears and congres-sional votes when they established a firm constituency by organizing the African-American community in the churches; by gaining the attention of the mass media through demonstrations; and by scoring victories in the courts. In the late 1940s and in the 1950s direct- action protests against racial injustice did not gain the publicity that would be forth-coming in later years. However, the persistence of certain idealists in the face of initial indifference on the part of the mass media and politicians indicates something of their tenacity. Among political parties all but the southern wing of the Democratic party committed themselves to the cause of civil rights. However, the so-called white backlash of resent-ment at African-Americans' newfound political strength eventually helped certain conservative politicians such as Barry Goldwater of Arizona, George C. Wallace of Alabama, and, much later, Ronald Reagan of California.

The 1950s also saw the advent of television across America. On January 1, 1950, three million families owned television sets. Another seven million sets were installed that year alone. For the next five years sales of television sets averaged five million a year until 88 percent of American families had at least one television. In a jibe Louis Kronenber-ger asserted that America had become a nation of peeping Toms. It was coincidence but good luck that the civil rights movement emerged just as television news was developing from its earlier rudimentary state and becoming the prime source of news for most Americans. In the fall of 1963 both CBS and NBC expanded their evening news programs from fifteen minutes to thirty minutes. Moreover, on September 2, 1963, NBC broadcast a three-hour documentary on civil rights entitled *American Revolution 1963*, a skillful montage of news footage and reporting.

The significance of television in the dramatic power play of civil rights can hardly be overemphasized. Perhaps more important than any gen-eral, sympathetic coverage television gave to the civil rights movement by way of news broadcasts was the way it educated leaders and activists about the complex and shifting nature of political power. Political power,

Lyricist Oscar Hammerstein II translated and transported Georges Bizet's most famous opera into an African-American musical as *Carmen Jones,* set around military camps, supply factories, and boxing gyms in the 1940s. In the classic film (1954) the beautiful Dorothy Danridge brought deep commitment to what might have become, in less sensitive playing, a conventional good-time part, although her singing was dubbed by the white mezzo Marilyn Horne. Having left her humble G.I. Joe for the allure of the King of Clubs, boxer Husky Miller, and his easy crowd, including Pearl Bailey (*third from right*) and Diahann Carroll (*second from left*), her smiles will soon turn to foreboding when this Queen of Hearts discovers that her next date is with the Ace of Spades. (Museum of Modern Art Film Stills Archive.)

they discovered, was not simply a static commodity like the authority invested in a medieval king or the brute force of a self-perpetuating oligarchy. It was, rather, a matter of currency carried and molded by the media of electronic communications, whether the form was press reports, speeches, live or printed, or demonstrations, with their visible show of massed energy fixed on a particular objective and colored by multiple, exciting incidents.

In the 1950s and 1960s civil rights demonstrations provided ideal media copy with their dramatic contrasts between nonviolent tactics and gestures of brotherhood on one side and profane displays of malice, discrimination, and violence by racist mobs on the other. Thus an NBC correspondent could claim with some exaggeration but essential truth, "Before television the American public had no idea of the abuses blacks suffered in the South. We showed them what was happening; the brutality, the police dogs, the miserable conditions. . . . We made it impossible for Congress not to act." Thus by its coverage of civil rights demonstrations, television suggested that a political dialogue was taking place between civil rights activists and diehard segregationists—a dialogue in which television was giving the demonstrators the winning hand.

In addition, the 1950s witnessed the emergence of a new black nationalism in the continent of Africa. World War II had disrupted the imperial systems of Europe and had irretrievably damaged the colonial empires of Britain, France, and Germany. The success of the Japanese against the combined might of the French and British Empires in the Far East in 1942 shattered forever the myth of white racial superiority and any lingering assumptions about white duty by way of paternal protection to nonwhites, the so-called white man's burden, upon which these empires rested. By the fifties African nationalism was emerging as a force in opposition to the colonial system. Between 1945 and 1960 nearly thirty black African states gained independence from white colonial rule. Since 1960 another seventeen have become autonomous nations. Moreover, descendants of Africa who were neighbors of the United States in the Caribbean were also achieving independence from colonial status in this period, notably Jamaica, which celebrated independence from British rule on August 6, 1963. This event was significant in itself and close to home.

Black people, and third world people generally, seemed to be asserting themselves for the first time. Only the former British dominion of South Africa was adamant in its policy of apartheid—the disfranchisement of black Africans, restricting their movements, and barring them from places of public accommodation. For these notorious policies South Africa earned opprobrium across the world and was forced out of the British Commonwealth of Nations in 1961. Rhodesia was equally obdurate, broke its legal ties with Britain in 1965 and only returned formally and fully to the commonwealth as an independent black state, Zimbabwe, in 1980. For its part, to maintain its credibility as the leader of the free world, America had to show emerging black nations that it cared for its own black citizens in a period of fierce propaganda rivalry between capitalist and communist nations. For the Cold War also had a part to play in the drama.

Whereas the elimination of Nazism, fascism, and other right-wing forms of government in Germany, Italy, Japan, and the countries they had oppressed should have ended World War II in 1945 on a note of jubilation for the great democracies, a darker shadow loomed. This was the Cold War of 1945–1990—a period of hostile competition of varying intensity between, first Britain, then the United States, and the Soviet Union. It arose in large measure because the United States and the Soviet Union were nations with considerable resources in a decimated world— clearly the major super powers. It also arose from ideological conflict between democratic capitalism as practiced by the U.S. and state socialism as practiced by the U.S.S.R. The hostility was at its greatest in the late forties and early fifties. One sign of this hostility was the successful attempt on the part of the Soviet Union, part defensive, part aggressive, to create a ring of satellite countries with Communist governments surrounding the western flank of Russia. In the period 1945–1948 Communist governments were installed in Poland, Romania, Bulgaria, Czechoslovakia, Yugoslavia, Hungary, and East Germany (now divided from West Germany), supported and protected by a sizable presence of the Red Army. Later on, unsuccessful revolutions against communism, notably in Hungary in 1956 and Czechoslovakia in 1968, were crushed. Another sign of Cold War tension was in scientific and technological rivalry between the United States and the Soviet Union. The Cold War was an essential fact of life for all peoples in the countries directly and indirectly involved and provided a somber backdrop to the drama of civil rights.

The propaganda of America and its allies had deliberately associated democratic ideals of freedom with racial equality and emphasized the link between fascism and racism. Cold War rhetoric continued an ideological conflict between West and East and cast the Soviet Union in the role of villain formerly taken by Hitler's Germany. But, while Cold War rhetoric had made America vulnerable to criticism on the race question, despite its role as "leader of the free world," it had also produced a virulent anticommunism that confused any calls for racial integration with radical subversion.

The immediate political shocks of 1949–1950 easily outweighed any burgeoning interest in civil rights for the time being. By January 1949 the Chinese capital, Beijing, was in the hands of the Chinese Communists under Mao Zedong. By the end of the year their opponents, the Nationalists, had withdrawn to Taiwan (Formosa) and the whole of China was controlled by the Communists. The fall of China was a tragedy for the newfound foreign policy of containment, and worse was to follow. On September 22, 1949, the federal government announced, "We have evidence that within recent weeks an atomic explosion occurred in the USSR." On February 9, 1950, in a speech to the Women's Republican Club in Wheeling, West Virginia, Senator Joseph McCarthy of Wisconsin stole the thunder of anticommunist hysteria with untrue and exaggerated accusations about Communists working in the State Department. Then, on June 25, 1950, North Korea attacked South Korea across the thirty-eighth parallel. Almost immediately, President Harry Truman (1945–1953) decided to commit American combat troops to support South Korea. The Korean War, in which the United States fought within a United Nations contingent, continued, with various vicissitudes, until an armistice was signed on July 27, 1953.

Throughout the Cold War the United States courted nations newly independent from colonial status—many of them in Africa. Hitherto, the negative image of Africa as a continent of barbarism and savagery had served to reinforce political and cultural prejudice against African-Americans generally. In the twenties Marcus Garvey had turned this spiritual link between Africa and African-Americans into a rallying point for an oppressed African-American minority in the United States. In addition, W. E. B. Du Bois had attempted to engender black political consciousness in a series of Pan-African conferences of 1900, 1919, 1921, 1923, 1927, and 1945. Many of the future leaders of the anticolonialist movements in Africa attended these events. Now, for the first time, the movement toward black independence in Africa was transforming the original home of black political, social, and cultural history into a positive political asset for African-Americans. African-American newspapers quite regularly covered the struggle of African nations against colonialism during the 1950s. Novelist Richard Wright reported his experience of African activism in his book *Black Power*. Black intellectuals, including Congressman Adam Clayton Powell, attended the conference of third world and nonaligned nations in Bandung, Indonesia, in 1955. No African-American intellectual or activist could fail to be influenced by the political transformation of Africa. Martin Luther King wrote of Egyptian President Gamal Nasser's defiance of Britain and France over the Suez Canal in 1956, "They have broken loose from the

Egypt of colonialism and imperialism, and they are now moving through the wilderness of adjustment toward the promised land of cultural integration."

The contradiction between a move toward freedom for contemporary Africans while the descendants of Africans remained second-class citizens in the United States was emphasized by civil rights activists in the 1950s and 1960s. Thus, at a time when African-Americans continued to suffer racial discrimination and oppression, they were becoming aware both of their legitimate rights as American citizens and of their heritage in a continent in the process of emerging as a major force in world affairs. The influence of African political writings, and of West Indian social philosopher Frantz Fanon, who first defined the concepts of first, second, and third world countries, would have a critical effect on the whole spectrum of black politics during the 1950s and 1960s.

Hence, the culmination of the Great Migration northward, the advent of television, and the creation of postcolonial African states created a new understanding that the winds of change would directly bear upon and enhance the burgeoning civil rights movement in the United States.

The loose coalition that came to be known as the civil rights movement in the 1950s and 1960s rested on four main organizations: the National Association for the Advancement of Colored People (NAACP); the Congress of Racial Equality (CORE); the Southern Christian Leadership Conference (SCLC); and the Student Nonviolent Coordinating Committee (SNCC, or Snick). Each of these organizations played a role in articulating, representing, and fostering the civil rights revolution. Each also represented significant, distinct, and sometimes contradictory factions within that coalition. The NAACP was by far the oldest and most conservative of the organizations. It still represented a legalistic and learned form of African-American protest and was to achieve its most famous victory in the Supreme Court's *Brown* decision of 1954. CORE would gain substantial publicity in the early sixties with the success of its Freedom Ride protests and would undergo significant changes in the mid-sixties as the character of the movement altered. It had begun as an organization committed to Christian nonviolence as a tactic in direct-action protests by small groups of dedicated individuals. This tradition would be transformed in the sixties. The SCLC brought the latent power of the African-American church into play for organized demonstrations by masses of ordinary folk, African-American and white, in the South. SNCC represented the emergence of nonviolent African-

American youth protest in the wave of student sit-ins in 1960. It, too, would change as the whole character of African-American protest shifted in tactics and location during the decade.

For thirty years after the end of World War II the great civil rights movement unfolded as an exciting drama in five acts that accomplished profound political achievements despite harrowing tragedies. First came the exposition act in the period 1945–1954, in which the problems of segregation and disfranchisement were displayed to an ever wider and more incredulous audience nationwide and in which a principal solution was proposed—desegregation in education, realized in principle by the Supreme Court's landmark decision in the *Brown* case. Second came the developmental act of 1955–1960 in which aspirant leader Martin Luther King revealed the latent political power of the African-American church and deployed an effective strategy of nonviolent demonstrations to achieve some desegregation.

In the third, dramatic act of 1961–1965 the civil rights movement surmounted searing tragedies and scored notable successes: the great march on Washington, expressing consensus between masses of African-American and white people, and the civil rights legislation of the Great Society. Two major leaders had emerged. They were both virtuoso, charismatic speakers. Their towering performances in this drama seemed, initially, at opposite ends of the political spectrum, since the Reverend Martin Luther King, Jr. (1929–1968) and Malcolm X (1925–1965) spoke, respectively, for integration and separatism. Their dazzling careers were nurtured by very different forms of organized religion. Tragically, both were assassinated. Moreover, there were deepening fissures underlying displays of ecstatic unity across the movement as the field of battle was shifting from the South to the North. Leading activists began to differ as to which was the optimum strategy to achieve their ends. Deep divisions about those ends—integration or separatism—were opened and left unresolved. This led to a fourth act of confrontations in 1965–1968, including the Selma march of 1965 and ending in the shift in emphasis from civil rights to black power. These central acts, nevertheless, represented the civil rights movement at its zenith, touching and transforming the entire spectrum of domestic politics, winning the conscience of the liberal world, and inspiring protests of their own by students, women, and other ethnic groups.

The great movement entered the final act of 1969–1974 without either of its major leaders. The potential for disintegration had always been present, both in the civil rights movement and in specific political contexts. By the time it had switched emphasis from black nationalism to Pan-Africanism in the 1970s, the civil rights movement was a variety of movements rather than one single, integral movement. In *Race, Reform, and Rebellion* (1984), Manning Marable correctly analyzes the dangers of incipient disintegration as a recurrent phenomenon in American politics to the left:

At the beginning, political themes advanced by a progressive minority are adopted at a mass level and push the boundaries of political consciousness and practice to the left. Some of the dissidents' demands are accommodated, while the militant leadership is isolated. The movement collapses as its reformist wing is co-opted and its more radical wing marginalized. The remnants of the movement begin to subdivide while losing touch with their mass base.

The final scattering of the civil rights movement on behalf of African-Americans should not obscure its profound achievements: in legislation, these were the Civil Rights Acts of 1957, 1960, 1964, and 1968, and the Voting Rights Act of 1965. Moreover, the United States entered the last quarter of the twentieth century with the environment of, and its attitude toward, its African-American citizens irrevocably altered—all in the brief course of twenty-five or thirty years. Throughout the peak years of achievement it was the Supreme Court far more than Congress and the presidents that sustained the civil rights movement by virtue of its constancy to the movement's ideals.

Civil Rights in the Truman Years

Despite the imminent potential for an effective movement on behalf of civil rights, not all the circumstances were propitious in the late 1940s. The Fair Employment Practices Committee was abolished. Nevertheless, the fight to establish a permanent FEPC resulted in cooperation between A. Philip Randolph, the AFL and CIO, and the NAACP in a National Council for a Permanent FEPC. President Harry Truman (1945–1953) was on record as favoring formation of a permanent FEPC. However, a bill to do so in the Senate was smothered by a southern filibuster lasting from January 18 to February 7, 1946. Although the FEPC foundered, Truman and his political advisers were aware of the growing role of African-American politics in national affairs. Moreover, Truman was deeply shocked by evidence of violence against returning African-American servicemen. It seemed that the tragic events of the Red Summer of

1919 were repeating themselves in 1946. Riots occurred in Columbia, Tennessee, and Athens, Alabama, and there were also disturbances in Chicago and Philadelphia. A series of murders took place in Georgia, where veteran Maceo Snipes was shot dead for voting in the local elections. In South Carolina, a much-publicized incident took place in which Isaac Woodward, a teetotaler and veteran, was accused of drunkenness by a white bus driver and arrested by police, who beat him so badly they blinded him.

Truman promised to institute a committee to investigate these violations and created it by executive order in December 1946. The widespread midterm election victories of the Republicans that year left Truman politically isolated. Nevertheless, his advisers urged on him a liberal program including civil rights. In 1947 he called for specific action on African-American disfranchisement and addressed a NAACP meeting at the Lincoln Memorial, the first president ever to do so. Truman asserted that the country's "immediate task is to remove the last remnants of the barriers which stand between millions of our citizens and their birthrights." America's imperfect record on human rights for its own citizens was highlighted somewhat ironically by the attempt of delegates from the Soviet Union to discuss a petition delivered by the NAACP to the United Nations Commission on Human Rights. Further controversy followed the publication of the Presidential Committee's Report on Civil Rights in October 1947.

The report, *To Secure These Rights,* surveyed the plight of African-Americans and set forth four essential rights due to all citizens: the right to safety and security of person; the right to citizenship and its privileges, including armed service and voting; the right to freedom of conscience and expression; and the right to equality of opportunity. The report called for the abolition of all forms of discrimination and segregation along with the establishment of fair employment and health benefits, and equality in housing and education. Truman included many of these points in his civil rights message to Congress on February 2, 1948. He asserted, "The world position of the United States in the world today makes it especially urgent that we adopt these measures to secure for all our people their essential rights." On July 26, 1948, Truman, prompted in part by demands from A. Philip Randolph, issued Executive Orders 9980 and 9981 creating a Fair Employment Board to eliminate discrimination in the civil service and establishing a President's Committee on Equality and Opportunity in the Armed Services.

While Randolph agreed with the dominant American interpretation of the Cold War—that hostility between the U.S. and the USSR was caused by Soviet imperialism and intransigence—he pointed out that the existence of widespread segregation was placing "the greatest single propaganda and political weapon in the hands of Russia and international communism today." Nevertheless, the army (unlike the navy and the air force) jibbed at the very notion of integration. It only accepted a plan of integration in January 1950 because it thought it could postpone implementation—a miscalculation brought to an abrupt end by the cruel circumstances of the Korean War of 1950–1953.

Executive Order 9981 stated that "there shall be equality of treatment and opportunity for all persons in the armed services without regard to race, color, religion, or national origin." By 1950 reports to the president asserted that, in the navy, "Negroes in general service are completely integrated with whites in basic training, technical schools, on the job, in messes and sleeping quarters, ashore and afloat." In the air force three-quarters of African-Americans were now integrated. However, it was during the Korean War, with a surplus of African-American troops behind the lines and with whites taking heavy casualties, that necessity forced integration in the army. After the test of combat, integration was applied right across the board, even extending to arrangements for eating and sleeping. As the historian of the South C. Vann Woodward comments:

The long range significance of the new military policy extended far beyond the limits of the armed services. Hundreds of thousands of men discharged from the services entered civilian life with an experience that very few, whether Northerners or Southerners, would have ever duplicated elsewhere.

But these gains were not paralleled by similar developments in American society outside the services. As Harvard Sitkoff notes, "The fear of McCarthyism [that is, of anticommunist hysteria] so inhibited blacks that they failed to use the Korean War as a lever for racial reform, as they had World War II. At mid century direct action had ceased being a tactic in the quest for racial justice."

Truman's sympathy towards civil rights was probably genuine enough but his sense of political realism was stronger. He knew he could not jeopardize his foreign policy, predicated on the containment of communism, by prodding a reluctant Congress to enact civil rights legislation and thereby risk a showdown. Thus all civil rights proposals outside those for the armed services were aborted. Eventually, Truman provided a sop to the civil rights movement in the form of the minuscule Committee on Government Contract Compliance. It had such limited powers that it was unable to cancel a single contract during the Korean War of any firm practicing discrimination, despite an abundance of evidence about discriminatory practices.

The 1948 presidential campaign clearly demonstrated ways in which African-American influence was suddenly gaining new significance. The Democrats were now divided. Henry A. Wallace, former secretary of agriculture and vice president under FDR and former secretary of commerce under Truman, who was critical of Truman's foreign policy, led a newly formed Progressive party to the left of the Democrats. Meanwhile, on the right, southern racists, outraged by the Democrats' adoption of a civil rights platform, formed a States Rights' Democratic party, the Dixiecrats, and nominated Governor J. Strom Thurmond of South Carolina for president. They justified their racism as a bastion against communism. Thus Thurmond claimed that the Democrats' commitment to civil rights had "its origin in communist ideology" and was intended to "excite race and class hatred" and "create the chaos and confusion which leads to communism." The Dixiecrats did not seriously think they could capture the presidency. However, they knew they would divide the Democratic vote and thereby might prevent Truman from winning a victory in the electoral college. Thus they might have the election decided in the House of Representatives. The consequence of the division of the Democrats was that Truman was left walking a political tightrope against the Republican candidate Governor Thomas E. Dewey of New York. Not daunted, he maintained his stand on civil rights and he became the first president to speak in Harlem. In response, the NAACP and Walter White urged African-Americans to vote for Truman. In November he carried two-thirds of the African-American vote in his remarkable surprise victory. In California, Ohio, and Illinois, African-American voters played a decisive part in giving Truman the election.

The duet: "A Good Man Is Hard to Find." Artist Ben Shahn satirized the duopoly of the Democratic and Republican parties' alternating control of the White House in this lithographic poster on behalf of the third party of Progressives in the election campaign of 1948. President Harry Truman plays a selection of old favorites, allowing himself and his Republican rival, Governor Thomas E. Dewey of New York, to carol away in unison without regard to the electorate. (Library of Congress.)

In 1949 Truman's legislation on FEPC, lynching, the poll tax, and civil rights ran into conflict with a coalition of southern Democrats and Republicans. This was partly because the position of southern Democrats was much strengthened after the 1950 election. They held a majority of the Democratic seats in the House and had only one short of a majority of Democratic seats in the Senate. Not until 1957 would any of Truman's proposals become legislation, and then only in the vaguely worded Civil Rights Bill of that year. Interpretations of this election victory are mixed. Welsh scholar Neil A. Wynn asserts that Truman had made real achievements in civil rights and that this presaged a new role for African-American interest groups in national politics. On the other hand, Manning Marable takes a very different view:

Truman's victory silenced and isolated black progressives for many years and committed the NAACP and most middle class black leaders to an alliance with Democratic presidents who did not usually share black workers' interests, except in ways which would promote their own needs at a given moment. Accommodation, anti-communism, and tacit allegiance to white liberals became the principle tenets for black middle class politics for the next decade.

Economic expansion also affected African-Americans. Despite Truman's defeat on the issue of the FEPC, the inclusion of nondiscrimination clauses in defense contracts during the Korean War helped reduce unemployment among African-Americans after 1950. In 1950 the annual average of unemployment for African-American and nonwhite races was 9.0 percent, compared to 4.9 percent for whites. In 1951 these figures had fallen to 5.3 percent and 3.1 percent, respectively. Median income levels for nonwhites rose from $1,614 a year per family in 1947 to $2,338 per year in 1950, though prices had also risen accordingly. Trade union membership among African-Americans also grew from 1.5 million in 1949 to 2.4 million in 1953. The proportion of African-Americans enrolled in school rose to 74.8 percent in 1950. More significantly, by 1950, 113,000 African-Americans were enrolled in college. The number of African-Americans registered to vote in the South rose from 750,000 in 1948 to at least 1.2 million and, perhaps, 1.3 million in 1952. Nevertheless, in the lower South little change could be detected. Senator Theodore Bilbo of Mississippi said that only fifteen hundred out of five hundred thousand eligible African-American voters were registered in his state. He asserted with ecstatic racist candor that "the best way to keep a nigger away from a white primary is to see him the night before."

There was little organized opposition from established groups. For one thing, the NAACP had never been a mass movement and had only reluctantly assisted direct-action protests. With the continuing rise in African-American prosperity, the organization concentrated upon litigation rather than protest. Thus chapters in the South concentrated on voter registration while those in the North lobbied for fair housing and employment. They counted on time to widen their base of support as the number of educated African-Americans rose. Unaffected by competition from more radical African-American groups, the NAACP preferred to follow strategies of litigation, reliance upon the Truman administration, and avoidance of direct protest.

The treatment of Paul Robeson and W. E. B. Du Bois provides an example of the frenzied interest American politics and African-American organizations showed in proving their allegiance to traditional, even conservative, ideals. This was the period when cold war hostility between the U.S. and the USSR was at its most intense. Singer and actor Paul Robeson had been known for his radical ideas and membership in the Communist party since the thirties. In the 1940s his career foundered on general intolerance of radicalism. In 1948 a police-aided riot prevented Robeson from singing in a concert in Peekskill, New York. While he was in Paris in 1949 he defended the USSR for having "raised our people to full human dignity," in comparison with the United States, whose policy to African-Americans "is similar to that of Hitler and Goebbels." Thus, opined Robeson, it was inconceivable "that American Negroes would go to war" against the Soviet Union on "behalf of those who have oppressed us for generations." The torrent of abuse Paul Robeson received, following close upon the Hollywood blacklist of suspected radicals, made it difficult for him to perform, whether as actor or singer. He was followed by FBI men and the House Un-American Activities Committee (HUAC) produced witnesses to denounce him. One of them said he aspired to be "the black Stalin among Negroes."

Among those courted by the establishment as a role model in opposition to Robeson was African-American Jackie Robinson, the second baseman of the Brooklyn Dodgers, who had broken one color barrier by gaining a position in a major league while breaking down a stereotype of African-American sports stars by providing—unlike certain African-American boxers—that he could withstand racial slurs and remain a man of high principles in his personal life. Robinson also appeared before HUAC in 1949, read out a statement that, while segregation was wrong, "we can win the fight without the Communists and we don't want their help."

After a ten-year absence W. E. B. Du Bois returned to the NAACP as research director in 1944. But Walter White pressed for his removal in 1947 because of Du Bois's involvement in various Pan-African movements and his work for international peace. White had the NAACP pursue a policy of anticommunism most aggressively and he assured its unqualified support for the Truman administration, even to the exclusion of other protest activities. In 1950 Du Bois ran in New York for the U.S. Senate as the candidate for the Progressive American Labor party and garnered 206,000 votes. However, on February 8, 1951, he was indicted for serving as "an agent of a foreign principal" because of his work with the Peace Information Center in New York. In November a federal judge acquitted him for lack of evidence. However, neither the NAACP nor any other prominent African-American spokesman came to his defense. None of the NAACP legal defense lawyers would take his case. The federal government withheld his passport for another seven years. W. E. B. Du Bois's various and prolific writings on sociology, history, and politics were eliminated from library shelves as subversive. The Chicago *Defender* asserted how "it is a supreme tragedy that he should have become embroiled in activities that have been exposed as subversive in the twilight of his years." This shift in visible African-American opinion illustrated a division that Du Bois remarked upon in his autobiography:

The reaction of Negroes [to his trial] revealed a distinct cleavage not hitherto clear in American Negro opinion. The intelligentsia, the successful business and professional men were . . . either silent or actually antagonistic. [These blacks] had become American in their acceptance of exploitation as defensible, and in their imitation of American "conspicuous expenditure." They proposed to make money and spent it as pleased them. They had beautiful homes, large and expensive cars and fur coats. They hated "communism" and "socialism" as much as any white American.

Convinced that African-Americans could not achieve justice in the United States, Du Bois emigrated to Africa. In 1962 he became a citizen of Ghana, where he died in 1963 while engaged as director of a government-sponsored *Encyclopedia Africana*.

The only other black organization engaged in active protest activity in the 1940s was the Congress of Racial Equality. By 1947 there were thirteen CORE chapters, mostly in the midwestern states of Illinois,

Ohio, Minnesota, Missouri, Kansas, and Oklahoma. Some activists staged boycotts against segregated lunch counters and schools in a number of northern cities. But the most spectacular event organized by CORE was the 1947 Journey of Reconciliation. Following various recent legal decisions outlawing segregation in interstate travel, George Houser and Bayard Rustin developed a plan for an interracial bus journey into the South. CORE members, both African-American and white, would ignore the segregation laws and by traveling peacefully together resist any attempts to divide the races. On April 9, 1947, sixteen members, eight African-American and eight white, set out from Washington, D.C., in two groups for a planned trip through the states of the upper South. Houser's original plan for a journey to New Orleans was abandoned as too dangerous.

The protesters, repeatedly arrested and intimidated by southern police, reported ambivalent reactions from many ordinary southerners. Bayard Rustin and three others were arrested in Cargill near Chapel Hill, North Carolina, and sentenced to serve thirty days on a chain gang. Although several arrests had been made and some local interest aroused, the African-American and white press virtually ignored the whole incident. The NAACP leadership flatly refused to help. Thurgood Marshall declared, "A disobedience movement on the part of Negroes and their white allies, if employed in the South, would result in wholesale slaughter with no good achieved." Even CORE was affected by the prevalent anticommunist hysteria. The San Francisco chapter's affiliation was terminated by the central office because it included Trotskyite members. A CORE convention in 1948 composed a statement on communism that condemned any connections with Communists or their organization. However, as August Meier and Elliott Rudwick note, "CORE suffered considerably from the McCarthyite hysteria of the period. The Red Scare, by labeling radical reform groups subversive, seriously impeded CORE's growth."

In 1949–1950 payments from chapters to the national CORE organization amounted to $437,000, with individual donations reaching $1,528. After a brief expansion to around twenty chapters in 1950, the number declined to only eleven in the following years. About one-third of these chapters were made up of college students, most of them white, and each chapter had between fifteen and thirty members.

When civil rights reformers tried to see what, if any, use they could make of the Cold War and the Korean War in pursuit of racial equality, they discovered that anticommunist hysteria served those who supported the existing social system far better than those who wanted to reform it. African-American activism among workers coalesced in June 1950 in Chicago at the National Labor Conference for Negro Rights. Paul Robeson addressed the conference of nearly a thousand delegates, condemning the Cold War. A committee was established to coordinate future action and in October 1951 the National Negro Labor Council was formed in Cincinnati, Ohio. Unions expelled from the CIO for retaining Communist members were represented along with unions still within the umbrella of the AFL-CIO. White union leaders denounced the council as a tool of the Soviet Union, and Lester Granger of the National Urban League called it subversive. Working against segregation in unions and industry, the council was accused of having a procommunist ideology by the House Un-American Activities Committee in 1954. Under such intense pressure, the council folded in 1956.

Affluent Society?

Progress toward civil rights in the 1950s must be considered in its socioeconomic setting. The fifties ushered in a decade of apparently unparalleled prosperity for the United States. Despite small recessions in 1953 and 1957, the economy grew at an astonishing, not to say alarming, rate. According to historian William Manchester, nearly 60 percent of all American families were reporting wages in the middle-class bracket. Since the late 1940s the median family income had risen from $3,083 to $5,657, an increase of 48 percent after allowing for inflation. With the growth of affluence went an increase in consumer spending and consumer demand. New gadgets and inventions flooded the marketplaces of the fifties. Buying on credit became commonplace, with installment credit growing by 63 percent between 1952 and 1956. BBC radio producer and commentator on America Daniel Snowman remarks on the wider social significance of the affluent society:

Material poverty was . . . relegated for the first time in history to minority status and wealthier people liked to point out that the poor in America were usually better off than even the relatively affluent in some less favorably endowed societies. . . . People were spending a smaller fraction of their incomes than ever before on the basic necessities of life, such as food and clothes, and more than they had ever done on luxuries . . . that both extended and were partly promoted by the conformist tastes of the day.

The pressures placed upon people by the whole panoply of consumer advertising to change fashions, cars, and lifestyles was considerable, and, to a certain extent, similar to those of urban society in the 1920s when a prefigurative culture also developed in which the younger generation led the older. Not surprisingly, many people dreaded change because they feared it would undermine the familiar values associated with a mythic traditional America. Thus the decade of technological change in the 1950s with the advent of television and the ever wider mass appeal of air transportation as well as the continuing revolution in automobile transportation was also a decade of ideological conformity to the belief that success was forged by virtue and hard work.

The advent of the affluent society and the election of Dwight D. Eisenhower as president in 1952 seemed to set the atmosphere of an entire decade. The political witchhunts of Senator Joe McCarthy of Wisconsin decimated critics of American society. Conflicts over fundamental issues of society and ideology were, apparently, now obsolete. Social progress could apparently be achieved through economic expansion, with the conflicts associated with inequality absorbed by ever greater levels of abundance.

But the performance of the economy as a whole and the brutal repression of dissent in the political sphere masked a series of shortcomings of American society in the 1950s. Gabriel Kolko's findings in his *Wealth and Power in America* disclosed that, although the lower half of the population lived substantially better than the poor in the past, their actual proportional share of national personal income had dropped from 27 percent in 1910 to 23 percent in 1959. The affluent society had not redistributed wealth, and the inequalities of American life were as glaring, in the case of African-Americans, as before World War II. The census data for this period is unambiguous, although the figures do not show the performance of African-Americans exclusively. In 1950, the median family income for nonwhite families was $3,828. The white family figure was $7,057. The ratio of nonwhite to white income was 0.54. By 1958 the nonwhite median family income had risen to $4,624, but white median family income had risen to $9,039, with the ratio of nonwhite to white falling to 0.51. This ratio recovered slightly to 0.55 in 1960.

In fact, poverty was a chronic problem for about thirty-nine million people, 21 percent of the population, as late as 1960. Not only was income badly distributed but the mass media's emphasis on conspicuous consumption in advertising also served to inform the dispossessed about exactly what it was that they lacked. Moreover, the formidable expansion of the federal government during and after World War II led to a much-expanded welfare bureaucracy and entailed greater revenue, both of which served to raise the expectations of groups who wanted to increase and liberalize federal social policies. Prosperity, too, had its own educational power. Politicians and social scientists preferred to imagine that the combination of an affluent society and political democracy worked together to break down class barriers and eliminate the last vestiges of want and suffering. Welfare might wither away, as would the need for it.

Such an illusion was rudely shattered by one book—*The Other America* (1962) by Michael Harrington. Michael Harrington conceded that general economic prosperity had benefitted millions since the Great Depression. However, the elimination of poverty suffered by the masses in the 1930s made the poverty endured by certain classes in the 1950s morally indefensible. The new classes of poor were old people and minorities, single-parent families—especially those headed by women—and farm workers eased off their land. These people, he claimed, lived in an "other America" that comprised a new "ghetto, a modern poor farm for the rejects of society and of the economy."

The profusion of new suburbs across the United States had a profound impact upon the assimilation of ethnic groups, class mobility, and race relations. At the very point when the federal government was making tentative steps toward better racial integration, the white exodus to the suburbs interrupted it. Although the African-American suburban population rose during the 1950s from one million to 1.7 million, African-Americans counted for less than 5 percent of all suburban residents. Moreover, given the particular definitions of *suburbs* and *suburban* applied by the Bureau of the Census, measured in terms of geographical proximity to cities rather than in the occupation of the residents, *suburban* not only signified commuter dormitories but also farming communities adjacent to cities.

In general the process of increasing suburbanization was aiding the actual basis for segregation while the legal basis was being weakened by judicial decisions, civil rights protests, and action in Washington by Congress and three presidents. In the 1950s suburban communities wanted to maintain and protect a high standard of housing by adopting zoning

President Harry Truman's insistence on the injection of a civil rights plank into the Democratic platform of 1948 still rankled among more conservative Democrats in 1952. In this cartoon by Ross A. Lewis for the *Milwaukee Journal* of August 22, 1952, the caption shows the Democratic donkey removing splinters after his experiences in 1948. The caption was first entitled "Still remembering the slivers from 1948." (Library of Congress.)

regulations requiring that houses be built on large lots, be capacious inside, and be built of high-quality materials. This meant that such houses were costly to build. Thus price alone excluded unwanted minorities. They were often refused permission to build apartment blocks and other forms of housing with multiple units and purposes.

About sixty thousand people lived in Levittown, Pennsylvania, and all of them were white. Pioneer builder William Levitt had persistently refused to sell his houses to African-American citizens. However, a furor followed the sale of a house by its white owner, William Myers, to African-Americans. Myers and his wife were harassed by anonymous phone calls, a rock thrown through their front window, and cars racing by and flying Confederate flags. In the end, the state of Pennsylvania took steps to forestall continued harassment through court orders and a statement from the governor just as the acts of intimidation were dying down. In 1958 two African-Americans who wanted to buy houses from

Levitt in New Jersey and were refused sued him on the grounds that discrimination in the sale of homes acquired with mortgages insured by the FHA was unconstitutional because it represented an attempt to misuse government funds for the purposes of unlawful discrimination. When an appellate court decided in late 1959 to hold public hearings, Levitt decided to change policy rather than risk further adverse publicity. In March 1960 he announced he would allow sale of his houses to African-Americans. The atmosphere was so tense in certain communities that Levitt undertook the most careful preparations in anticipation of public disorder. His company prevailed upon clergymen to give support to his new policy of desegregation, upon the local press to minimize coverage of the story, and upon the police to be ready for any disorder.

In addition, Levitt had prospective African-American purchasers screened in order to ensure that they really were from the middle class. Moreover, he introduced them to his suburbs on a token basis, ensuring that no two African-American families ever acquired adjacent properties and that the African-Americans only acquired the last available house on a street, thereby restricting the advent of African-American minorities.

Those few African-Americans who could afford to live in affluent suburbs often found it difficult to move because of prevalent racial discrimination by real estate agents and vendors. John H. Denton observed in "Phase 1 Report" to the National Committee against Discrimination in Housing, as cited by Michael N. Danielson in *The Politics of Exclusion* (1976), that "every routine act, every bit of ritual in the sale or rental of a dwelling unit can be performed in a way calculated to make it either difficult or impossible to consummate a deal." Banks also practiced discrimination in loans. The National Conference and Report of the State Advisory Committees to the U.S. Commission on Civil Rights, 1959, might well have been making a general point as well as commenting on the situation in the suburbs of Columbus, Ohio, when it reported that "Negro buyers, regardless of affluence, education, or credit rating, would be refused and discouraged if they should attempt to purchase a home in the new developments which cater to the white market."

When African-Americans did live in suburbs these were essentially dormitories for commuters to the city. They were usually almost entirely all-African-American communities such as Kinloch (a suburb of St. Louis), Robbins (a suburb of Chicago), Lincoln Heights (Cincinnati), and Richmond Heights (Miami). None of these and, indeed, very few genuine African-American suburbs represented anything like the typical suburban development of the 1940s and 1950s.

Court Progress to Brown

With an embarrassment of choice as far as African-American grievances to redress were concerned, including education, housing, voter registration, social segregation, and poverty, the NAACP decided to focus on education. It did so because it believed that education was the sphere in which it could most easily achieve a legal victory since education was indissolubly associated with equality. It would be far easier for NAACP leaders to argue about education to people of all classes and shades of political opinion than, for instance, to concentrate their attention upon employment or housing.

The legal process that ended in the landmark decision in the case of *Brown* v. *Board of Education of Topeka, Kansas,* by the Supreme Court in 1954 lasted about two decades. It was not sudden, nor was it achieved without a context. It was the inevitable culmination of a process that had begun over twenty years earlier.

By the time the NAACP was being formed in 1910, it was clear to those committed to raising the issue of civil rights for African-Americans that a major battle in the campaign would have to be waged in the courts. This was largely because it was the Supreme Court itself, by its notorious decision in *Plessy* v. *Ferguson* of 1896, that had sanctified racism and segregation and, indeed, confirmed that African-American citizens were at the nadir of their political and social rights. The Court had decided in *Plessy* that the Fourteenth Amendment could be satisfied by facilities that were "separate but equal." If segregation were ever to be overturned by peaceful means, then a battle must be fought in the courts where segregation had been legally identified, authorized, and protected.

Moreover, NAACP lawyers and other civil rights workers believed that the most damaging form of segregation, both in itself and for what it gave rise to, was separate educational systems. The consequences could often be seen more easily at the higher professional level than in elementary or high schools. Often someone's career in medicine or law, for example, depended on that person having a state license. It was often essential to be educated in the state where you intended to practice law or medicine in order to be able to pass the appropriate licensing exam. Moreover, African-Americans would certainly need a considerable number of fully trained lawyers in all states. In addition, judges, who were themselves lawyers, were bound to take a special interest in cases involving law schools and this fact alone would ensure keen legal interest. Consequently, pressure against segregation had been developed by civil rights activists in a whole series of court cases in the 1930s and 1940s concerning the admission of African-American students to the law schools of state universities.

It was in 1938 that the Court first ordered the state of Missouri to provide equal educational facilities for its law students. This was the first time that the separate but equal doctrine of *Plessy* v. *Ferguson* of 1896 was applied literally by the Supreme Court in ways that would have astonished and angered its original proponents. The NAACP's tactic in this case was to apply the principle of *Plessy* so thoroughly that states would find it too expensive to provide duplicate educational facilities for the two races and thus would opt to desegregate their schools. By the early fifties, white southerners had recognized the complexities of the financial situation. In fact, between 1939 and 1952 expenditures on education in the South soared 800 percent. In a series of decisions after World War II, the NAACP won victories over segregation on interstate transport in the case of *Morgan* v. *Virginia* in 1946 and against discrimination in law school facilities in *Sipuel* v. *University of Oklahoma* in 1948 and in *Sweatt* v. *Painter* in 1949. Moreover, in 1950 in *McLaurin* v. *Oklahoma* the Court stated that segregated law schools "impair and inhibit [the African-American student's] ability to study, engage in discussions and exchange views with other students and, in general, to learn his profession."

Therefore, even before *Brown,* the Supreme Court had begun a shift toward desegregation in education. Thurgood Marshall, chief attorney to the NAACP's Legal and Defense Fund, coordinated the attack on desegregation. In the early fifties he decided to shift from a policy of attacking inequalities in education generally to directly attacking the principle of school segregation itself. Accordingly, in 1951, the NAACP filed lawsuits in the names of several African-American high school and elementary school students in Clarendon County, South Carolina; in Prince Edward County, Virginia; in New Castle County, Delaware; in Washington, D.C.; and in Topeka, Kansas. Oliver Brown, from Topeka,

Chief Justice Earl Warren shattered his impeccable conservative credentials by bringing the Supreme Court around to a unanimous ruling in the *Brown* case of 1954 that separate was not equal, thereby conferring judicial support upon the growing tide of African-American protest. (*U.S. News and World Report,* 1965; Library of Congress.)

Kansas, wanted to prevent the enforcement of a state segregation law that obliged his eight-year-old daughter, Linda, to travel a mile by bus to reach an all-black school. The corresponding all-white school was only three blocks away from their home. On December 9, 1952, the Supreme Court heard oral arguments on all five cases, combined under the name of the plaintiff from Topeka, Kansas. In an unexpected move, the outgoing Truman administration filed as a friend of the Court arguing against segregation.

At first the Court was deadlocked on the issue of overturning *Plessy* v. *Ferguson*. However, after several months, two justices changed their opinions in favor of the NAACP, creating a slim majority. In the event, the Court voted for a reargument and asked the litigants to prepare briefs on the intentions of the framers of the Fourteenth Amendment and the ways in which the Supreme Court could enforce desegregation and effective compliance on the part of the states. In the summer of 1953, Chief Justice Fred Vinson died and Dwight D. Eisenhower, the new president (1953–1961), appointed Earl Warren, governor of California, to replace him. Vinson had sought to delay ruling on the *Brown* case and would have voted against a decision favorable to the NAACP. However, after the rearguments that began on December 7, 1953, and lasted three days, the Court remained silent while the nation awaited what was widely predicted to be a landmark decision. Earl Warren delayed the Court ruling until he could persuade two justices to concur in a unanimous decision on such an explosive issue. On May 17, 1954, the Court ruled that "in the field of public education the doctrine of 'separate but equal' has no place. Separate educational facilities are inherently unequal."

Citing several psychological studies of children's education, the Court held that segregation was damaging to the educational chances of African-Americans. In so doing, they were responding to the way that NAACP lawyer Thurgood Marshall and his associates had used the findings of social scientists to buttress their argument that segregation in education was absolutely unequal. They referred to the research of psychologists Kenneth and Mamie Clark, whose experiments with children and black and white dolls revealed that segregation caused psychological damage to African-Americans by inducing feelings of worthlessness and self-abnegation. Hence, in his ruling Chief Justice Earl Warren declared that to separate gradeschool children "from others of similar age and qualifications solely because of their race generates a feeling of inferiority as to their status in the community that may affect their hearts and minds in a way unlikely ever to be undone."

Nevertheless, Kenneth Clark's findings ignored certain salient data: that African-American children attending integrated schools in the North had an even lower sense of self-esteem than children in segregated schools in the South; that tests on children not yet in school revealed the same results in tests with dolls and crayons as did tests conducted upon children in school, whose psychological adjustment should, according to Clark, have been worse. In addition to taking psychological evidence, the Court also invited the two sides to argue their positions on the grounds of the original intentions of those who framed the Fourteenth Amendment of 1866–1868. The lawyers for the South argued that the same Congress that had passed the amendment had also segregated public schools in the District of Columbia. Moreover, many northern states had had segregated schools in the 1860s. In contrast, the argument for integration was that the various Reconstruction amendments were drafted so as to "revolutionize the legal relationship between Negroes and whites, to destroy the inferior status of the Negro and to place him upon a plane of complete equality with the white man." For their part, the justices averred that education was so central to modern society that it was simply wrong to try and "turn the clock back to 1868 when the Amendment was adopted, or even to 1896 when *Plessy* v. *Ferguson* was written."

Although the Supreme Court was drawing upon psychology and sociology to reach its decision, its case was far from conclusive in the simpler terms of historical precedent. All previous cases about separateness, or equality, or the lack thereof in education had concerned higher education. In fact, the justices' decision to overturn *Plessy* was rooted in morality—what one might call common decency. In this respect the intervention of Earl Warren was pivotal. It was he who had brought everyone round on the simple grounds that segregation was based on an unwarranted assumption of racial superiority and that it was essential that the eventual decision be unanimous if the Court ever hoped to persuade the United States as a whole that segregation must be abandoned.

The impact of the *Brown* decision supposedly went a great deal further than the field of education. Harvard Sitkoff comments,

Euphoric blacks declared that just as the first Emancipation Proclamation abolished slavery, so this second proclamation of emancipation would end all Jim Crow. . . . More, it offered the real beginning of a multi-racial democratic society. Brown heightened the aspirations and expectations of Afro-Americans as nothing ever had before. Nearly a century after their professed freedom had been stalled, compromised, and stolen, blacks confidently anticipated being free and equal at last.

According to Sitkoff, few white liberals foresaw any difficulties in enforcing desegregation the following year. A survey of school officials reported in the *New York Times* showed that none expected any kind of violence or crisis to develop. Indeed, many school districts in Delaware, Kentucky, Maryland, Missouri, Oklahoma, and West Virginia were quickly and quietly desegregated along with those in the District of Columbia after President Eisenhower issued an appropriate order. Nevertheless, on May 31, 1955, the Supreme Court rejected the NAACP's call for immediate desegregation everywhere. Instead, it ruled on a policy of desegregation "with all deliberate speed." Local officials and local judges were assigned to responsibility for desegregation plans. As Sitkoff notes, "For the first time the Supreme Court had vindicated a constitutional right and then deferred its exercise." The price that Earl Warren had paid for a unanimous decision on *Brown* was gradual rather than immediate school desegregation.

As to public reception of the news, opinion polls in the South showed that 80 percent of whites were against *Brown*. Moreover, the administration would not be providing federal assistance to facilitate desegregation. Eisenhower later described his appointment of Warren to the Supreme Court as "the biggest damnfool mistake I ever made." In Congress, a coalition of conservative Republicans and southern Democrats in both houses ensured the absence of any legislative initiatives on desegregation. Moreover, on March 12, 1956, 101 members of Congress signed a "Declaration of Constitutional Principles," defending the right of states to refuse to desegregate. This was the so-called Southern Manifesto. By the 1956–1957 school year, 723 southern school districts had already been desegregated and three hundred thousand African-American school children were attending "desegregated" schools. But there were still 2.4 million African-American children enrolled in separate schools and numerous white school boards expressing their determined defiance of the Supreme Court.

The "Southern Manifesto" marked a return to the rhetoric and resistance of the old Confederacy. Thus was the language of interposition, nullification, and states' rights resurrected in order to resist desegregation. Southern press and politicians competed with one another in denouncing the actions of the Supreme Court and devising ways to limit the effects of the *Brown* decision. Delaying tactics were the first method of obstruction, forcing NAACP groups to take out individual court actions. Postponement of court actions and economic intimidation followed. The result was, usually, token desegregation. Physical intimidation of African-American schoolchildren became commonplace, with white parents and teachers encouraging such activities. Just as white legislatures had enacted legal devices to prevent African-Americans from voting since the Civil War, more than 450 laws and resolutions were now being enacted to prevent or limit school desegregation. Some required schools to cease operation rather than integrate classes, or persecuted those teachers who taught mixed classes. Of these devices the most successful was the pupil placement law. It purported to guarantee the child freedom of choice in the selection of a school and gave local authorities the power either to accept or to reject pupils requesting admission to particular schools. Thus in practice African-American children remained in African-American schools and white children remained in white ones. The Supreme Court upheld the constitutionality of this rule in 1958.

Many southern states also enacted measures to hound and harass the NAACP, the only truly nationwide civil rights organization in the fifties, and the prime mover of the *Brown* case. A number of laws required the organization to make public its membership lists, made membership illegal for teachers or state employees, and made it an offense to attack local segregation laws. For several years the association was preoccupied with fighting for its very existence in the South. From 1955 to 1958, the NAACP lost 246 branches in the southern states. As well as arousing the legislative wrath of the old Confederacy, the school desegregation issue also revived the terrorism of the revived Ku Klux Klan. In December 1951 in Miami, Florida, state NAACP leader Harry T. Moore was murdered by a bomb at his home. Many leaders were arrested, threatened, and harassed. The president of the NAACP chapter in Belconi, Mississippi, was shot to death on the courthouse lawn in 1955. The idea that race relations were steadily improving seemed ridiculous with the lynching of Emmett Till in August 1955. On vacation in Mississippi from Chicago, he was beaten, mutilated, and shot by white men in a small town for allegedly saying "'bye" to a white woman. He was only fourteen years old. His relative, Mose Wright, showed great courage in identifying the murderers, knowing full well that an all-white jury would acquit them.

White Citizens Councils flourished and sharpened the conflict over race relations. In politics, southern politicians adopted the race issue to further their electoral prospects. In 1956 the white supremacist States' Rights party received 7.2 percent of the vote in Louisiana, 17.3 percent in Mississippi, and 29.5 percent in South Carolina. Those politicians who counseled caution received short shrift at the polls. Circuit Judge George C. Wallace, who ran for governor of Alabama in 1958 on a platform of racial moderation, was easily beaten by John Patterson, who advocated diehard segregation. Later Wallace swore ominously, "They outniggered me that time, but they'll never do it again." C. Vann Woodward described the period as a time when "all over the South the lights of reason and tolerance and moderation began to go out."

4

"Black and White Together, We Shall Overcome": Martin Luther King and the Emergence of the Civil Rights Movement

The Latent Power of the African-American Church

In *An American Dilemma* (1944) Gunnar Myrdal wrote, "Potentially the Negro church is undoubtedly a power institution. It has the Negro masses organized and, if the church bodies decided to do so, they could line the Negroes behind a program." The African-American church had held considerable authority in the African-American community since the Civil War. Both Booker T. Washington and W. E. B. Du Bois had commented on its importance. Writing in 1903, Du Bois called it "the social center of Negro life in the United States, and the most characteristic expression of African character." The African-American church also provided a clear distinction of the separation between white and African-American communities. During the 1950s Martin Luther King became the most significant representative of the link between protest and religion. In *Stride toward Freedom* (1958) he asserted,

Any religion that professes to be concerned with the souls of men and is not concerned with the slums that damn them, the economic conditions that strangle them and the social conditions that cripple them is a dry-as-dust religion. . . . Such a religion is the kind Marxists like to see—an opiate of the people.

Such a link had been formed before King achieved fame in Montgomery in 1956 and found expression in direct-action movements across the country. The Social Gospel, developed before and after the turn of the century by such Christian pacifist groups as the Fellowship of Reconciliation, provided fertile soil for the growth of African-American protest.

The mobilization of the resources of the African-American church in the South represented a significant shift in the orientation and character of the African-American protest movement. For the first time, large masses of African-Americans directly confronted and disrupted groups and institutions responsible for their oppression. Moreover, it was also the beginning of nonviolent protest as a mass technique in the African-American community. At various points in their history, African-American groups and individuals had confronted discrimination and oppression toward African-American people. The use of mass action was also a feature of many protests in the nineteenth and twentieth centuries. What many commentators fail to realize, as historian Charles Silberman perceives in *Crisis in Black and White* (1964), was that "Negro anger is not new; it has always been there. What is new is simply the Negro's willingness to express it and his ability to command attention when he does."

Almost all modern examples of strategy, tactics, and action in protest against racial discrimination are replicated in one form or another throughout American history. Historians Elliott Rudwick and August Meier have researched and documented some such events. For instance, mass boycotts were widely used by African-Americans at the close of the nineteenth century. As whites extended Jim Crow legislation, African-Americans conducted streetcar boycotts in twenty-five southern cities. Sustained and led by ministers or businessmen, the protests lasted from a few months in Savannah, New Orleans, and Nashville to several years in Houston, Augusta, and Montgomery. Some of these actions enjoyed initial success in preventing segregation in transportation, but within a few years, Jim Crow laws were established beyond challenge. Nevertheless, Marcus Garvey succeeded in mobilizing large numbers of African-Americans in a protest movement just after World War I. However, it was A. Philip Randolph's March on Washington Movement of 1941

Unrecognized for a century as a potent political force, the African-American or Negro church of the deep South remained an untapped source of African-American activism until after World War II. This photograph of a church at Moncks Corner, South Carolina, of March 1941, by Jack Delano, attests to the simple dignity of modest churches across the South and suggests why they were potent and inspirational sanctuaries, despite widespread oppression. (U.S. Department of Agriculture, Farm Security Administration; Library of Congress.)

that provided the first modern example of a direct-action organization with a mass membership. In short, the apparently spontaneous development of mass action in the late 1950s was a new manifestation of a long tradition of protest against discrimination.

Aldon G. Morris examines a case in Baton Rouge, Louisiana, as the beginning of what he calls the modern civil rights movement. In March 1953 African-American leaders in Baton Rouge successfully petitioned the City Council to allow African-Americans to be seated on the city buses on a first-come-first-served basis. As in the more famous Montgomery incident, African-Americans merely wanted to be seated from the rear to the front and have whites seated from the front to the rear. Accordingly, the city issued Ordinance Number 222 on March 11, 1953.

However, white bus drivers refused to accept the ordinance and went on strike. The city attorney general then ruled that the ordinance was in conflict with state segregation laws and the buses went back into operation with Jim Crow regulations. In response, the African-American community began a bus boycott in June 1953, led by Reverend T. J. Jewison, pastor of Mt. Zion Baptist Church. The protest was characterized by a series of large public meetings and a system of car transportation. It was said that the bus company was losing sixteen hundred dollars a day. After six days the white establishment in Baton Rouge offered a compromise. The agreement was to reserve two seats at the front for whites and the back seat for African-Americans, with the rest to be filled on a first-come-first-served basis. This limited victory brought the Baton Rouge boycott to an end on June 25, 1953. The boycott and its outcome represent a significant development in the postwar civil rights movement. It was organized through the local churches and directed by the United Defense League, an organization specifically created to manage the protest. Finance was directly provided by the African-American churches, with collections at services and at the mass meetings held in church buildings.

In short, the Baton Rouge boycott was a church-based direct-action movement involving large numbers of people that not only predated the Montgomery bus boycott of 1955–1956 but also the famed *Brown* decision by the Supreme Court in 1954. Although the local NAACP was involved, its leaders decided that it was incapable of directing the whole boycott. Hence, the creation of the United Defense League. The impact of the Baton Rouge boycott was discussed across the country in the national churches. T. J. Jewison was national secretary of the National Baptist Congress. In 1956, he made details of the movement's organization available to the National Baptist Convention. Among his disciples were Ralph Abernathy and Martin Luther King, who consulted Jewison over the launching of the Montgomery boycott in 1955. Reverend C. K. Steele, who led a boycott in Tallahassee, Florida, in 1956, and Reverend A. L. Davies from New Orleans, which experienced a bus protest in 1956, were also both aware of the dynamics of the Baton Rouge boycott.

The Montgomery Bus Boycott

Rosa Parks was arrested for refusing to give up her seat to a white person on a Montgomery municipal bus on December 1, 1955. Eldridge

Cleaver later wrote of the incident, "Somewhere in the universe a gear in the machinery had shifted." Martin Luther King enlarged in characteristic style on this theme when he remarked how "she was anchored to that seat by the accumulated indignities of days gone by and the boundless aspirations of generations yet unborn." In fact, the refusal of Rosa Parks to leave her seat was anything but spontaneous, just as the swift organization of a boycott was not conjured up on the spur of the moment.

The persecution of the NAACP in the South after the *Brown* decision united all classes in the African-American hierarchy and represented a severe attack on the middle-class aspirations of African-American lawyers, doctors, and, significantly, ministers. The church had the organization, the meeting places, and, crucially, the fund-raising capacity to replace and, in the event, to out-perform the NAACP. Thus out of necessity the church, and church leaders, became the focus of resistance by African-Americans to a wave of white oppression. Consistent with the charged situation was the notion that the boycott emerged spontaneously. In fact, intimidation and violence had made organizers wary of publicizing their plans, methods, and influence for galvanizing the African-American community in Montgomery and other communities throughout the South.

The most prominent activist in Montgomery in the 1950s was Edgar D. Nixon, a railway porter who had a long history of struggle on behalf of African-Americans in Alabama. Nixon's credentials as an active participant in movements to help the African-American community reveal the deep roots of protest in Montgomery and the South. Nixon had been head of the local branch of A. Philip Randolph's March on Washington Movement during World War II and president of the Montgomery local of the International Brotherhood of Sleeping Car Porters, the union Randolph had established in the 1920s. In the late forties and fifties he became more active outside the union and was the dominant figure in the Montgomery NAACP, serving as president of Alabama's NAACP in 1948–1949. He was also president of the Montgomery chapter of the Alabama Progressive Democratic Organization, an African-American alternative to the white-dominated Democratic party. In 1954 he gained renown as the first African-American within living memory to run for public office in Montgomery, as a candidate for the County Democratic Executive Committee. Other prominent figures included Rufus A. Lewis, chairman of the Citizens' Steering Committee, and Mrs. Jo Ann Robinson, a leader of the Women's Political Council, which had been formed in 1949 to encourage African-American women to register to vote. These groups sought redress for African-American grievances from the city government.

Three main complaints dominated the African-American political agenda before 1955: the lack of African-American policemen; the inadequacy of city parks in African-American areas; and the treatment of African-American people on Montgomery's buses. The Women's Political Council had already met the City Commission to complain that African-Americans had to stand on buses even though there were unoccupied seats in the white section; that they had to pay at the front of the bus, then alight and reboard at the back door; and that buses stopped only at every other corner in African-American sections of the city instead of at every corner as in white areas. The truculent attitude of drivers to African-Americans also caused offense.

African-American leaders considered that the city elections of 1955 provided them with a firm opportunity to exercise their new influence. Before the city elections on March 21, 1955, Clyde Sellers, a racist candidate for mayor, campaigned on a ferociously racist platform, and was aided by an incident on the buses arising from the segregation rules. On March 2, Claudette Colvin, a fifteen-year-old girl, was arrested for refusing to leave her seat and became the first person so arrested to enter a plea of not guilty to the charge in Montgomery. Clyde Sellers won the election on March 21 and was subsequently declared duly elected. The supposed influence of the African-American vote in favor of another candidate had succumbed to a virulently racist campaign that had heightened tensions. The refusal of white politicians and the bus company to standardize rules over seating was made clear at a series of stormy meetings at which the bus company's attorney, Jack Gershaw, maintained that the proposal to seat African-Americans from the back forward, on a first-come-first-served basis, would be in breach of the state statute, even though such a system existed in Mobile.

By the end of 1955, tension over race relations in Montgomery had reached a critical level. E. D. Nixon explains that African-American community leaders had talked about a bus boycott all year. Then, on December 1, 1955, Rosa Parks was arrested for refusing to leave her seat on a Montgomery bus. She had been secretary of the local NAACP chapter for nearly a decade. She was adviser to the NAACP's youth auxiliary and had been concerned with the Claudette Colvin case. Mrs.

New Deal photographer Jack Delano captured the sobriety and intense concentration of this African-American congregation during a church service in Woodville, Greene County, Georgia, in October 1941. Contentment and stoicism are captured during rapt attention on the service in progress. (U.S. Department of Agriculture, Farm Security Administration; Library of Congress.)

Parks was also a friend of E. D. Nixon and she and her husband were prominent figures in the African-American community. J. Mills Thornton described them as civic leaders and, at least socially, members of the middle class. Often characterized as a simple seamstress, on the basis of her much-quoted reason for refusing to move on that December day because "her feet hurt," Rosa Parks had a history of resistance against segregation on the buses.

Immediately after Rosa Parks was arrested, E. D. Nixon began phoning prominent members of the African-American community to suggest a bus strike in response. They included Reverends Ralph S. Abernathy, H. H. Hubbard, and Martin Luther King. As word spread, the protest began to take on its own momentum. Attorney Fred Gray phoned Jo Ann Robinson of the Women's Political Council. It was this call that

THE SECOND AMERICAN REVOLUTION

ensured definite action. Without waiting to consult Nixon and the meeting he had arranged in Dexter Avenue Baptist Church for the evening of December 2, 1955, Jo Ann Robinson prepared a handbill protesting the Parks arrest and calling for a bus boycott on December 5.

The one-day boycott was overwhelmingly successful. Over 90 percent of African-Americans refused to use the city buses. Meanwhile, Mrs. Parks had been convicted and fined ten dollars. Those attending a mass meeting decided to create a formal organization called, at the suggestion of Ralph Abernathy, the Montgomery Improvement Association (MIA) and chose Martin Luther King as president. Nixon was in favor of King partly because of his superb oratory and partly because he was new to Montgomery and not influenced by community rivalries. King was also very well and widely educated. Born in Atlanta, Georgia, on January 15, 1929, he had received his bachelor's degree from Morehouse College in 1948, his B.D. from Crozer Theological Seminary in 1951, and his Ph.D. from Boston University in 1955. King's election confirmed the younger Baptist's leadership in the MIA over older, more conservative individuals.

On December 8 a meeting was scheduled between the MIA, the City Commission, and the bus company. King put forward three demands: greater courtesy from bus drivers; the hiring of African-American drivers; and seating on a first-come-first-served basis from the back to the front for African-Americans and vice versa for whites. However, Jack Gershaw, the bus company's attorney, was intransigent. He flatly declared that the new seating proposal was illegal. In fact, the proposal simply required separate but equal accommodations with no specific rules governing seating arrangements. Ironically, although the African-American representatives were integrationists, they only sought to make segregation acceptable whereas Gershaw, a firm segregationist, was forcing the African-American community to seek the full abolition of segregation through the courts. He urged African-Americans who were dissatisfied to try and change the law, not to boycott the bus company.

The general approbation with which his attitude was greeted in the white community set the conflict in deadlock and confirmed the African-American community in the rightness of its cause. As the two positions widened, actions became more extreme. King's home was bombed on January 30, 1956. On February 1, African-American attorney Fred Gray filed suit challenging the constitutionality of bus segregation. On the

128

same day E. D. Nixon's home was bombed. Although negotiations between business leaders and the MIA continued in February, the refusal of whites to compromise fueled the determination of African-Americans. It was white retaliation that aroused the interest of the media. African-American protesters had many supporters within the white community, including white women who employed African-American women as maids and gladly gave them rides to work and back in order to keep their households running smoothly. By the end of February the search for a compromise had ended, and the court battle had begun. As it turned out, the courts were instrumental in ending the boycott and proved to be the prime weapon against bus segregation. In addition to its immediate achievement the boycott accomplished the education of the entire African-American community in the South. This is the opinion of J. Mills Thornton, who remarks in the *Alabama Review* of July 1980:

What the boycott taught the city's black leaders as it dragged on was that their quarrel was—had to be—with the law. Compromise with segregation was impossible because segregation so forged and underlay social relationships that even the most modest reform of its requirements threatened—just as the white politicians claimed—the entire social fabric. In such a situation reform was impossible; only "revolution" would do. The white response to the boycott revealed this truth forcefully to the blacks; that revelation is the boycott's supreme achievement, and it is something which no court suit could ever have accomplished.

On February 21, 1956, city officials took out injunctions against King and another 114 participants in the boycott for breaking a 1921 law prohibiting hindrance to a business without just cause. As the nation awaited an outcome, the boycott, fueled by violence and white intransigence, began to be transformed into a religious crusade against all forms of racial oppression. At a meeting the following evening King asserted, "We are not struggling merely for the rights of Negroes but for all the people of Montgomery, black and white. We are determined to make America a better place for all people." King went on trial in March 1956 with the world's media watching intently. He was found guilty and fined one thousand dollars.

On June 4, a federal district court declared bus segregation unconstitutional but stayed the decision until it could be appealed to the Supreme Court. Meanwhile, the state of Alabama outlawed the NAACP and Montgomery charged the MIA with operating the car pool scheme as a business without a license. This charge was brought before a court in

November. However, on November 13, the Supreme Court itself ruled against bus desegregation.

Thus, no matter how wide the base of support for the boycott—and its support was wide, uniting all African-Americans and dividing whites, of whom a liberal minority were well disposed toward the African-American cause—the final victory was, once again, the result of a decision by the Supreme Court. That decision rested on a highly moral but rather narrow legal argument.

The boycott had lasted 381 days. On December 21, 1956, King and his supporters boarded a bus, watched by the international media. The *New York Times* reported, "For the first time in the 'cradle of the Confederacy' all the Negroes entered the buses through the front door." On an early bus journey a white passenger was supposed to have said, "I see this isn't going to be a white Christmas," to which an African-American passenger responded: "That's right."

By the end of the boycott, Martin Luther King had not only emerged as a new national figure but had also forged a new ideology based on nonviolence with the struggle of African-Americans. King's powers of oratory and his education in religious philosophy helped to foster this new direction. Significantly, Bayard Rustin of the Congress of Racial Equality and the Reverend Glenn Smiley of the Fellowship of Reconciliation had arrived in Montgomery in February 1956. They had greatly influenced King, who took their advice and presented the boycott as a nonviolent movement. The Christian roots of the African-American community and the southern reality of whites outnumbering African-Americans made nonviolence an ideal strategy. Montgomery firmly established King as a leader of nationwide repute and demonstrated the political efficacy of nonviolence, which seemed to offer a sure chance of success for southern African-American protest. Moreover, the importance of the historical tradition of resistance in Montgomery and other communities provided the basis for the future success of Martin Luther King as a political activist.

Other incidents illustrated the endurance of protests against racial injustice throughout the South. In Tallahassee, Florida, in May 1956, two students from the local A & M College refused to give up their bus seats to whites. In response to their arrest, a boycott was initiated through church organizations. The Reverend C. K. Steele was elected president of the Inter-Civic Council that coordinated the protest and its financing. Ralph Abernathy and Glenn Smiley visited Tallahassee to

While lavatories and restroom facilities were separated simply according to gender, drinking fountains were separated by race according to the edicts of Oklahoma City, Oklahoma, in July 1939. Here a man is drinking at a separate water cooler in the streetcar terminal. (Photograph taken for the U.S. Department of Agriculture, Farm Security Administration, by Russell Lee; Library of Congress.)

explain nonviolent tactics to the protesters. In Birmingham, Alabama, the banning of the NAACP led to the creation of the Alabama Christian Movement for Human Rights. Reverend Fred Shuttlesworth, a leading figure in Birmingham in the sixties, became its president. Like King in Montgomery, his home was dynamited and his children attacked. Again all finances were raised through church collections, emphasizing what Aldon G. Morris calls "the fervent religious culture that undergirded the movement." The organization demanded the employment of African-American policemen and the desegregation of Birmingham's buses.

The SCLC

The most significant development of the period 1957–1960, along with the passage of civil rights legislation and the establishment of civil rights as a national political issue, was the formation of the Southern Christian Leadership Conference, or SCLC.

The founding of SCLC marked a significant departure from the traditions of African-American protest represented by the NAACP. In fact, the Montgomery Improvement Association signaled this change in 1956. After the success of the boycott, several figures recognized the need to continue the activism of Montgomery. According to political activist Ella Baker, the SCLC grew out of discussions among Stanley Levison, a white lawyer from New York, Bayard Rustin, and herself. Similar conversations between Martin Luther King, Fred Shuttlesworth, Ralph Abernathy, and A. Philip Randolph and Baker, Levison, and Abernathy confirmed the general desire to establish a firm organization. Steele, King, Shuttlesworth, and Levison issued a call to African-American church leaders for a conference in Atlanta on January 11 and 12, 1957. This meeting was called the Southern Negro Leaders' Conference on Transportation and Integration. All the proposers of the meeting had been, or were, instrumental in organizing protests in their native cities. King's standing and fame earned for him a reputation that attracted other figures to him.

In a profound way, SCLC represented the new political orientation and determination of the southern African-American church. In this role it was, as John White, an English analyst of the African-American leaders, notes, "uniquely equipped to communicate ideas on the grass roots level." As Adam Fairclough also asserts in "The SCLC and the Second Reconstruction, 1957–1973" in the *South Atlantic Quarterly,* "SCLC's leaders clothed political ideas in a religious phraseology that blacks readily understood, and used Christian tenets to give the civil rights movement a divine sanction." The adoption of the Social Gospel as a philosophy in the fight against southern segregation was perhaps the most significant single achievement of any civil rights organization in the whole period of the Second American Revolution.

The SCLC was formally founded on February 14, 1957, in a meeting in New Orleans, and King was elected president. From the beginning, the organization was identified with its charismatic leader and vice versa. Never an individual membership organization, SCLC merely required a twenty-five dollar fee from other groups. To a considerable extent, it superseded the middle-class NAACP and, being based on group rather than individual membership, it immediately encompassed vast numbers of individuals in numerous African-American church organizations throughout the South. This was crucial. These established organizations were able to support SCLC as soon as it appeared, without the need to canvass individual support and grow before it could act. As Joseph E. Lowery asserts about the foundation of SCLC,

It emphasized in the social struggle the moral aspects. Whereas they were there before . . . the political and legal aspects [had] overshadowed them. But with the coming of SCLC, the struggle was put in its proper perspective . . . in the moral arena, and that's what got people marching. It opened up people's eyes for the first time to how ugly and immoral segregation was.

Notwithstanding its advantages in the early days in 1957, the actual focus of the organization was not yet established. Although most members of SCLC were also members of the NAACP, there was considerable rivalry between them for church funds. King's ideas on protest had not fully emerged and, as several commentators have pointed out, King *was* the SCLC. Kenneth B. Clark wrote in his article "The Civil Rights Movement, Momentum and Organization" for *Daedalus* of winter 1966, "To understand this movement one has to understand King because SCLC is Martin Luther King, Jr." In May 1957 King addressed the Prayer Pilgrimage in Washington, D.C., and repeatedly asserted the African-American community's desire to be able to vote in all elections. However, as Ella Baker, temporary executive director of SCLC, later realized, the organization at this time simply reflected King's own confused ideas on protest. Thus, for the first three years, in the wake of the 1957 Civil Rights Act, SCLC initiated a Crusade for Citizenship to register African-American voters in the South. However, a lack of resources and an absence of strategy produced indifferent results. John White comments: "Certainly before 1960, SCLC was without a clearly defined purpose and strategy, undecided whether to instigate its own protests or simply to assist in local actions."

Nevertheless, the emergence of SCLC represented a profound development in African-American protest. As Harvard Sitkoff points out, "Until the founding of the SCLC, the struggle for racial equality had been largely the domain of a Northern elite oriented primarily towards legal action." The Montgomery bus boycott marked and encouraged the transformation of the southern African-American church into a significant agent of southern African-American protest. Hence, in its early years, the strategy of the SCLC was to mobilize the African-American church community for massive demonstrations to impress public opinion both locally and nationally. Thus it planned to wring concessions from local authorities and, also, to persuade the federal government to commit itself unequivocally to the cause of civil rights. Its tactics were rooted in nonviolence. As Martin Luther King observed in his open letter from the Birmingham jail of 1963, reprinted in *Why We Can't Wait* (1964), "One who breaks an unjust law must do so openly, lovingly, and with a willingness to accept the penalty." King always warned of the dangers of extremism, should nonviolence fail to achieve civil rights. For, "Millions of Negroes will, out of frustration and despair, seek solace and security in black nationalist ideologies—a development that would inevitably lead to a frightening racial nightmare."

Martin Luther King himself was becoming a national symbol of the new importance of civil rights. The Democratic National Committee invited him to appear at the platform meeting of the 1956 Democratic National Convention and he met Vice President Richard Nixon in 1957 and President Dwight D. Eisenhower in 1958. In 1957 he went to Ghana to attend the independence ceremonies along with Dr. Ralph Bunche of the United Nations and Congressman Adam Clayton Powell. This did not mean he was accepted by white racists. In 1958 he almost died after being stabbed in a New York bookstore by a deranged black woman while signing copies of *Stride toward Freedom*. Later that year he visited India and went to Gandhi's shrine. Gandhi remained the principal inspiration for nonviolent strategies. In November 1959 King resigned as pastor of the Dexter church in Montgomery and moved to Atlanta to concentrate on his duties as president of SCLC.

The Civil Rights Act of 1957

The presidential and congressional elections of 1956 could have resulted in a most damaging split in the Democratic party. The fragile coalition between northern liberal Democrats, dependent on a proportion of African-American votes, and southern states' rights Democrats, determined to exploit the race issue for white support, was under severe strain. The racial issue had not been such a potent national issue since Reconstruction, what with the Supreme Court's ruling on school desegregation and national attention focused on the Montgomery bus boycott. Concerned about social stability, in early 1956 Attorney General Herbert Brownell urged President Dwight D. Eisenhower to submit a civil rights bill to Congress. Brownell was scandalized by the South's wanton disregard of democratic procedures. He believed it was essential to have a civil rights bill passed. He also had three blatant political motives: to help the

Soldiers in the schoolyard. The drama of the Little Rock crisis of 1957 led to the first intervention of federal troops against southern states since 1877 and made news headlines across the world. America's allies reacted with profound disbelief that the admission of nine black students to Central High could unleash virulent confrontations by jeering whites and necessitate military control. (*U.S. News and World Report*; Library of Congress.)

Republicans build upon a constituency of new voters; to divide the Democrats by exposing their racism in the South as an impediment to reform; and to embarrass Lyndon Baines Johnson, the Senate majority leader who was already presenting himself as a candidate for the Democratic presidential nomination in 1960. Moreover, Brownell calculated that the Republicans would gain these advantages whether or not Congress passed the bill.

The effect of such an issue upon the Democratic party in an election year could be critical. In 1956 African-Americans represented a balance of power in seven states, with an aggregate of 197 electoral ballots. They formed 5 percent of the electorate in another fourteen states, with an aggregate of 261 electoral votes. With some Democrats espousing massive resistance to desegregation and with the signing of the "Southern Manifesto" by 101 members of Congress on March 12, 1956, the Democratic party looked extremely frail as a unit. However, Eisenhower refused to contemplate stirring up an already controversial issue. He asserted that any action by Congress would be counterproductive in the same way as he had perceived the *Brown* decision to be. He asserted, "I personally believe if you try to go too far too fast in laws in this delicate field that has involved the emotions of so many millions of Americans, you are making a mistake." Eisenhower also wanted to make the Republican party the haven for southern conservatives and thus decided not to introduce any civil rights legislation. The silence on racial matters within the Democratic party in the 1956 elections matched the relief of party managers at not having to address these issues.

Nevertheless, the election itself significantly altered political assessments of civil rights matters. Just as new international obligations were beginning to affect the standing of civil rights as an issue, electoral considerations in a nation increasingly served by national electronic media began to favor new initiatives. Harlem Congressman Adam Clayton Powell endorsed Eisenhower during the election, providing him with many thousands of African-American voters. Eisenhower increased his earlier proportion of the African-American vote, winning majorities in several cities. It seemed that the party of Lincoln had, once again, begun to remember its roots. Recognizing this significant shift in political loyalties among African-Americans, Vice President Richard Nixon pressed Eisenhower to promote a civil rights bill and northern Democrats were eager to win back African-American support. Consequently, Democratic liberals refused to respond to the howls of protest from the South when a civil rights bill was proposed.

The Civil Rights Act of 1957, the first civil rights legislation since Reconstruction, established a Civil Rights Commission of six members and a Civil Rights Division in the Department of Justice. Although the Civil Rights Act of 1866 that awarded the president the power to use troops to enforce civil rights laws was repealed, the new act prohibited attempts to intimidate or otherwise prevent people from voting and it authorized the attorney general to seek injunctions in district courts if people were deprived of their right to vote.

The passage of the bill through the Senate encountered the longest personal senatorial filibuster on record when Senator J. Strom Thurmond of South Carolina spoke for twenty-four hours and eighteen minutes on August 28 and 29, 1957, but failed to stop passage of the bill. Lyndon Johnson's parliamentary skills were so formidable that, in the Senate at least, he protected the Democratic party's reputation and managed to conciliate all factions while promoting his own presidential aspirations. The Senate eliminated all provisions except those concerning voting rights and this reduced bill was acceptable—just—to the South. Moreover, LBJ secured a provision for trial by jury for any registrar charged with abridging the right to vote in disobedience of a federal court order. In 1960, despite more southern opposition, a second Civil Rights Act was passed that authorized the selection of "referees" by federal judges to register African-Americans to vote if local officials obstructed registrations.

These limited reforms represented the first federal action on behalf of African-Americans since the nineteenth century. The idea of an impending Second Reconstruction began to look increasingly possible. However, between 1957 and 1960 only two hundred thousand African-Americans registered to vote. But, although this legislation had little real impact on African-American disfranchisement, it encouraged and legitimized aspirations among African-Americans in a way not observed in twentieth century America hitherto. Paradoxically, these moves increased African-American desire for change and justified its implementation, but did very little to bring about reform. As Harvard Sitkoff notes of these reforms:

They produced among blacks both soaring expectations that Jim Crow could soon be eliminated from American life and a growing rage toward all temporizing. Cumulatively, they generated a determination that segregation and discrimination, however wrong and unconstitutional, would cease only when blacks themselves acted massively and militantly enough to guarantee that end.

Racial inequalities, and the nation's failure to address them comprehensively, were repeatedly emphasized by the news media and by the new responsiveness of politicians to civil rights issues.

The Little Rock Crisis

In Arkansas, some state schools had already been integrated when Little Rock began its integration program in the fall of 1957. It was generally recognized that Orval Faubus would have an uphill struggle in his campaign for reelection as governor of Arkansas. He had offended liberals by approving rate increases for railroads and utilities and had offended practically everyone by raising taxes. Moreover, the state had a strong tradition against third-term governors. He decided to build a new base of support in eastern Arkansas, a section that was notoriously provincial—what was usually referred to as redneck. Although the city of Little Rock under Mayor Woodrow W. Mann had planned a careful strategy of integration to be phased in over seven years, beginning with nine African-American children at Central High School, Faubus decided upon his own strategy of racial politics and sent ominous warnings to William Rogers, the deputy attorney general in Washington, that he expected trouble.

When on August 29, 1957, Faubus obtained an injunction from a state court to prevent integration because it would lead to violence, it was overruled by U.S. District Judge Ronald Davies. Determined not to be outmaneuvered, Faubus decided to call out the National Guard and prevent the nine African-American children from registering.

On the evening of September 2 the National Guard encircled the school and their commanding officer established himself in the principal's office. Faubus himself appeared on local television and justified his actions, claiming that the city was about to explode into riot: "The evidence of discord, anger, and resentment has come to me from so many sources as to become a deluge." The mayor disagreed: "We had no reason to believe there would be violence." After all, three other Arkansas communities—Ozark, Fort Smith, and Van Buren—were being integrated peacefully that very same month. Moreover, an FBI report indicated that there was no evidence at all to suggest impending violence. The case was now dominating news headlines at home and abroad. This forced Eisenhower to act. When he met with Eisenhower on September 14, Faubus was obdurate.

On September 29, 1957, Eisenhower mobilized the National Guard and ordered in federal troops to disperse mobs of racist whites. For the first time since Reconstruction, federal soldiers were used to intervene in a southern state. To carry out the president's tardy commitment to law, order, and integration, Secretary of Defense Wilson and General Maxwell Taylor, army chief of staff, assigned a crack unit, the 327th Battle Group of the 101st Airborne Division, to control the situation, if necessary by riot-control methods. Four platoons shielded the children from station wagon to schoolhouse door and, either by their presence or physical force, kept troublemakers at bay. By November the crisis was waning and the army removed all but a token force to protect the children. That one academic year from September to May cost the government $4.05 million to keep the soldiers in Little Rock. Faubus

The Supreme Court's decisions against the State of Arkansas in its attempt to delay full implementation of integrated education compelled a shamefaced President Eisenhower to meet with civil rights leaders in a symbolic gesture of solidarity. It was also intended to convince colored nations of the third world that the United States was a democratic country. (*U.S. News and World Report.*)

was reelected governor by 255,086 votes and won successive victories until his retirement in 1967.

Yet the presence of northern troops in the South fueled southern antagonism toward the federal government. Senator Olin Johnson of South Carolina declared, "If I were Governor Faubus, I'd proclaim an insurrection down there, and I'd call out the National Guard, and I'd then find out who's going to run things in my state." Senator Herman Talmadge of Georgia, referring to the contemporaneous, abortive uprising by Hungarian students and workers in Budapest against Russian control of their government that had ended with Soviet tanks and soldiers repressing the revolt and leaving the streets of the capital carpeted with bodies, remarked, "We still mourn the destruction of Hungary. Now the South is threatened by the President of the United States using tanks [sic] and troops in the streets of Little Rock. I wish I could cast one vote for impeachment now." Public opinion polls disclosed that

"Mr. Chief Justice, why don't you trust us?" Governor Orval Faubus of Arkansas, seeking reelection, explains his decision to bar entry of the nine black children to Central High in Little Rock to a press conference in a virtuoso performance that cruelly exposed his narrow mind and monotonous vocal range. (*U.S. News and World Report;* Library of Congress.)

only a third of southerners agreed with Eisenhower's decision to send troops to Central High whereas only a tenth of northerners disagreed with him. Disagreeable though the situation was within the United States, it was most damaging abroad. After a waitress in a Howard Johnson restaurant near Dover, Delaware, told two Africans, "Colored people are not allowed to eat here," it was discovered that the two men were the finance minister of Ghana and his secretary. The minister had previously received Vice President Richard Nixon in his home. As news of the crisis spread around the world, Little Rock disgraced the United

States and made it next to impossible for the federal government to continue a pose of providing racial freedom in a democratic society—most damaging to America's reputation across the world during the height of the Cold War, when the U.S. was competing with the Soviet Union for the allegiance of third world nations, most of whose citizens were not white. During the tense period of the Little Rock crisis six thugs in Alabama kidnapped an African-American, Judge Aaron, on a deserted country road, castrated him with a razor blade, and poured turpentine into the wound. "We just wanted some nigger at random," one said later.

In spite of the federal government, Governor Faubus closed down the high school that fall. And by 1964 only 123 African-American children out of several thousand attended desegregated schools in Little Rock.

The most notable epilogue to the Little Rock crisis was provided by actor Paul Robeson, who commented, in an epigrammatic phrase that would resound through the 1960s, that society and the government's failure to react significantly in Arkansas clearly showed that what African-American citizens in America needed was "black power."

The White Negro

The *Brown* case, the Montgomery bus boycott, Little Rock, and the emerging civil rights movement in general had a profound impact on American artistic sensibility. Indeed, it was a major novelist who appreciated the significance of these events far more than any leading politician at this time.

In 1957 novelist Norman Mailer published his prescient article "The White Negro" in the *Independent*. In it he noted the appearance of a new existentialist, the hipster, among American whites. The model for this new rebel was provided by African-Americans. Mailer described the white Negro as a "philosophical psychopath," someone who lived for the moment, used a new argot or street language attractive to adolescents, pursued orgasm rather than love, and smoked marijuana. For Mailer, the white Negro was, in fact, a new breed of adventurer who had absorbed the existential values of African-Americans, values that Mailer believed were rooted in the notion of action as expression of emotional need. This was a form of religion—certainly a form of religious need. Hipsters derived their political succor from a need to rebel against orthodox behavior and conventional wisdom.

Mailer's starting point was the impact that the Nazi gas chambers and the destruction of European Jewry and the nuclear devastation at the close of World War II had had upon the generation who lived through the Holocaust and Hiroshima and then the generation who grew up in their wake. People's understanding of mass extermination had resulted in an appreciation of the fragility of civilized society and even of human existence.

For Mailer, African-Americans were the true archetypes of white hipsters. Their experience of racism and the diverse ways individuals had chosen to react to it had led many to forge a special existential approach to society.

Any Negro who wishes to live must live with danger from his first day, and no experience can ever be casual to him, no Negro can saunter down a street with any real certainty that violence will not visit him on his walk. The cameos of security for the average white: mother and the home, job and the family, are not even a mockery to millions of Negroes; they are impossible. The Negro has the simplest of alternatives; live a life of constant humility or ever-threatening danger. In such a pass where paranoia is as vital to survival as blood, the Negro had stayed alive and begun to grow by following the need of his body where he could.

Mailer's article was one part of a tapestry provided by various writers and artists, including beat poets such as Allen Ginsberg, Gregory Corso, and Jack Kerouac and abstract expressionists such as Jackson Pollock and Mark Rothko. In general, their work amounted to a plea for individuals to be allowed freedom to express themselves spontaneously against bourgeois conformism as represented by McCarthyism, white racism, and materialistic obsession with sheer size, whether of corporations or of motor cars. The lament for lost individualism was also taken up by social analysts David Riesman in *The Lonely Crowd* (1950), William H. Whyte in *The Organization Man* (1957), and Vance Packard in *The Status Seekers* (1960). The anthem was provided by Allen Ginsberg in his most famous poem, *Howl,* first read by Ginsberg in fall 1955 in San Francisco's Six Gallery and published in 1956. It was a provocative rejection of American materialist values that, according to Ginsberg, had perverted the highest expectations of American youth.

Mailer described the language or street argot of hip as artful, shaped by experience, "pictorial like non-objective art," and meaningless to those outside its subculture. The emphasis of the language was on movement and energy since stasis was inertia and death to the hipster. The

It was novelist Norman Mailer, enfant terrible of postwar American literature, who analyzed the psychological, spiritual, and cultural contribution of African-Americans to the unfolding patterns of contemporary culture. He foresaw the social problems for individuals in the coming African-American revolution in a remarkably prescient article on hipsters, "The White Negro," in 1957. This photograph was taken by Carl Van Vechten in 1948, shortly after Norman Mailer had hit mature form in *The Naked and the Dead,* a searing emotional novel of young servicemen in the Pacific war that established him as a young lion of letters. (Library of Congress.)

vocabulary included "man," "go," "put down," "make," "beat," "cool," "swing," "with it," "crazy," "dig," "trip," "creep," "hip," "square." However, these words carried diverse resonances depending on context and nuance. Hence "go" carried the sense that, after long stretches of monotony, boredom, and depression, "one has finally had one's chance, one has aroused enough energy to meet an exciting opportunity with all one's present talents for the trip (up or down) and so one is ready to go, ready to gamble." The contemporary popular music phenomenon of rock and roll that first surfaced with the disks of Bill Haley and the Comets and reached its greatest craze with the overwhelming popularity of Elvis Presley in 1956 was a laundered version of the same adolescent yearning.

Mailer's article not only described something of a counterculture that was emerging but also the directions it would take much later:

The organic growth of Hip depends on whether the Negro emerges as a domi-nating force in American life. Since the Negro knows more about the ugliness and danger of life than the white, it is probable that if the Negro can win his equality, he will possess a potential superiority, a superiority so feared that the fear itself has become the underground drama of domestic politics. Like all conservative political fear it is the fear of unforeseeable consequences, for the Negro's equality would tear a profound shift into the psychology, the sexuality, and the moral imagination of every white alive.

Demographic Currents and the Greensboro Sit-In

Various changes in the African-American community were influencing the general climate of opinion within it. In 1960 there were 18,871,831 African-Americans in the United States out of a total population of 179,323,000. In 1960, 55 percent of all nonwhites were living below the poverty level and 24.4 percent of all nonwhite youths were unemployed. With the continuing migration of African-Americans from the South to the North, the expectations of these migrants who moved north were often severely disappointed. Despite a general increase in income, be-tween 1952 and 1959 the gap between white and African-American income widened. In 1952 median income among African-Americans was 57 percent of the white median income. By 1959 this figure had fallen to 52 percent. One-third of African-American families, compared to 7.5 percent of whites, earned less than three thousand dollars a year. Many unions contributed to unemployment among African-Americans in the North by barring them from apprentice positions, preserving all-white locals, and securing blatantly segregationist contracts with employers. The AFL-CIO did little to attack these practices among its affiliated unions. A. Philip Randolph struggled to amend some of these abuses, but with little success. Southern unions actively participated in the massive resistance movement and only a few locals, along with Randolph's Brotherhood of Sleeping Car Porters, supported the Montgomery boycott. Most AFL-CIO unions ignored the 1957 Prayer Pilgrimage in Washington, D.C. The avenues that might have provided expression for the economic and political aspirations of African-Americans were continuously blocked by massive and systematic discrimination in the North and the South.

By the early 1960s the various civil rights groups were searching for a more effective and possibly revolutionary way of achieving true civil rights in two areas, free access to places of public accommodation and equality in education. They set aside equality of economic opportunity and housing until later. The impetus and strength of the civil rights movement at the beginning of the 1960s arose from the hopes and only fitfully satisfied expectations of African-Americans in the 1950s. This was not a time of despair. As political analyst Alexis de Tocqueville observed on the last days of the ancien regime at the onset of the French Revolution, the worst time for a bad government is when it begins to undertake reforms. This is partly because it further educates people about the shortcomings of the existing system, partly because it illustrates what, when, and how reforms are possible, and partly because it releases a dam of pent-up hopes and aspirations that it can satisfy only partially.

Various changes had prepared a new generation of African-American students for this dramatic moment. They were part of a southern generation who could expect to live beyond segregation, even if they were presently in segregated colleges. Even here, the politics of race infused student debate. On February 1, 1960, four students from the African-American North Carolina Agricultural and Technical College (Ezell Blair, Jr., Joseph McNeill, Franklin McClain, and David Richmond) asked to be served at a Woolworth's luncheon counter in Greensboro and were refused. They remained quietly in their seats until the restaurant closed. At first they were ignored but later whites gathered to jeer and insult the protesters. This protest, widely reported, led to a wave of nonviolent "sit-ins" by about fifty thousand people in seventy-eight cities across America, some of which were supported by CORE.

Woolworth's in Greensboro would probably never have given in to the ever-increasing number of young African-Americans patiently awaiting service. However, F. W. Woolworth was a nationwide chain with nationwide responsibilities and thus the company's omnipresent status played into the activists' hands. In Boston alone four hundred students from the universities nearby—Harvard, Boston, MIT, and Brandeis—picketed twelve Woolworth stores. Demonstrators also targeted Walgreen, Liggett, Kress, and Grant lunch counters. On June 5 the Southern Regional Council reported that nine different cities on the border between north and south had desegregated lunch counters. On July 25 Woolworth and Kress capitulated to the activists in Greensboro. However, certain sections of the South were adamant. On October 15, 1960, Martin Luther King and fifty-one demonstrators were arrested in Atlanta. When they refused to give bail, they were jailed.

The civil rights movement was rekindled by the Greensboro sit-ins and over the next five years it reshaped race relations across the country while shifting various balances in American politics. Protest within the civil rights movement amounted to an effective and sustained use of civil disobedience. When they challenged practices and laws of segregation, African-Americans and their white allies sustained a new, rigorous discipline. However, not only did they direct their protest at practices that were blatantly unjust but they also had to accept legal punishment and extralegal reprisals by racial interests.

SNCC

The Greensboro sit-in led directly to the establishment of the Student Nonviolent Coordinating Committee (SNCC or Snick). Ella Baker, executive director of the SCLC, saw the need for young activists to work independently of their elders. First she organized a conference of two hundred young African-American and white leaders at Shaw College in Raleigh, North Carolina, over Easter 1960. Subsequently, she provided Robert Moses and Julian Bond with a corner of SCLC offices from which they could run SNCC.

At first, SNCC had a theological basis. It was an elite group rather than a group with a large, widely based organization. It never had more than 150 field workers at any one time and about four-fifths of them were African-Americans. It comprised two groups, the Nashville group from Fisk and Vanderbilt universities and the Atlanta group from Atlanta University. The Nashville group from Fisk, Vanderbilt, and the local seminary included Rev. James Lawson, Rev. C. T. Vivian, Rev. James Bevel, Diane Nash, Marion S. Barry, a student at Fisk University and later at the University of Kansas, and John Lewis. The Atlanta group from Atlanta University and its colleges was initially dominated by Julian Bond. Later, these two groups lost their initial leadership. This was especially true after the arrival of more irreverent African-American students from northern colleges, notably the Nonviolent Action Group from Howard University in Washington, D.C., led by Courtland Cox and Stokely Carmichael. With the shift from clerical to secular leadership SNCC lost some of its earlier allegiance to the strategy of nonviolent resistance. Nevertheless, the newcomers increased the influence of SNCC over the course of civil rights.

Although certain critics charged SNCC with being a Communist cadre, this was nonsense. Instead, it attracted young activists who were effective in public relations and whose improvised, often abrasive activities influenced the lifestyle and, indeed, the ethics of a whole generation, both African-American and white. Here was the model of African-American rebellion affected by Norman Mailer's hipsters. Initially convinced of the relevance of Christian teaching and the traditions of American democracy, SNCC activists found their political attitude changed by successive disappointments when their strategies were ignored or buried by the system. Changed by pain and fear, they came to reject the American political system outright. Thus SNCC proved a pivotal group in the shift of African-American protest from civil rights to black power in the course of the 1960s as its own elite moved from policies of integration to those of separatism. By the mid-1960s SNCC was motivating and organizing African-Americans to seize power for themselves.

During the years when SCLC was gaining strength and SNCC was being organized, an earlier organization, the Congress of Racial Equality (CORE), was being guided by a series of progressively radical national directors—James Farmer, appointed in 1961, Floyd B. McKissick, appointed in 1965, and Roy Innes, appointed in 1968. Certain activists appreciated the need for coordination among the various civil rights organizations lest the grand strategy fail through confused tactics. Thus in 1962 Robert Moses created the Council for Federated Organizations (COFO) to provide a working coalition among local branches of the NAACP, CORE, the SCLC, and SNCC.

The symbolic presence of Eleanor Roosevelt in support of Democratic presidential and vice-presidential candidates John F. Kennedy and Lyndon Baines Johnson during the final mighty rally of their campaign at the New York Coliseum on November 5, 1960, was intended to provide evidence of their supposed continuation of the welfare policies of the New Deal. The photograph was taken from below its subjects in order to emphasize their monumental status as giant caryatids in support of democracy. (UPI; Library of Congress.)

5

A Dream beyond
the New Frontier

In his campaign for the presidency in 1960, Democratic candidate John Kennedy spoke out against the lack of equality for African-Americans whose votes he then garnered by a symbolic act of assistance.

In October 1960 Martin Luther King and fifty-one other people were arrested for taking part in a mass sit-in, asking for service in the restaurant of Rich's department store in Atlanta, Georgia. However, after all the others had been released, King was held in jail on the purely technical offense of not having a current Georgia driving license. He was then given a four months' prison sentence. This was a conventional enough instance of police harassment of civil rights leaders in the South. In Washington officers of the Federal Department of Justice composed a special draft requesting King's release. However, neither President Eisenhower nor Vice President Richard Nixon, the Republican presidential candidate, would act.

The Kennedys saw how to turn a situation in which they had no ostensible connection to considerable political advantage. First, John Kennedy telephoned Coretta Scott King to express his concern over the injustice of her husband's imprisonment. Meanwhile, his brother and campaign manager, Robert, pleaded with the judge in Georgia who had sentenced King. The very next day King was released on bail. This prompted his father, who had earlier expressed his opposition to Kennedy's candidacy on the grounds of his Catholicism, to change his mind. Martin Luther King, Sr., said he had a "suitcase of votes" he was going to "dump in the lap" of John Kennedy. Indeed, in a somewhat controversial election that Kennedy won by a comparatively diminutive margin, any one of a series of marginal factors could have accounted for Kennedy's hairsbreadth victory over Republican candidate Richard Nixon. The African-American vote certainly gave Kennedy his crucial slender majority in South Carolina, Michigan, and Illinois—one of the two states in this election where returns stirred the greatest controversy.

Civil Rights and the New Frontier

Despite this auspicious prelude, the first two years of the Kennedy administration of 1961–1963 disclosed exactly how circumscribed was the New Frontier (Kennedy's general title for his political program) when it came to civil rights. John Kennedy was not a notable champion of civil rights. When he did emerge as an advocate it was on account of effective external political pressures. Comparing him with his successor as president, Lyndon Baines Johnson, we might say that, in the field of race relations, Kennedy's policy was accommodation and his strategy was law observance whereas LBJ's policy was integration and his strategy was law reform. Nevertheless, both John Kennedy and his brother Robert, the attorney general, were acutely aware that widespread publicity about racism in America was having a deleterious impact upon the United States's relations with third world countries. They realized that they must succor American propaganda about freedom with some tangible gesture.

Kennedy's initial actions in appointing African-Americans to government positions, instituting a program of equal opportunity in the civil service, and speaking hesitantly on behalf of race relations were all intended to propitiate liberals across the country and mollify racists in the South. By selective appointments he raised the percentage of African-Americans employed in the middle grades of the civil service by 36 percent and the percentage of those in higher grades by 88 percent. Moreover, he used his executive authority to place African-Americans in various federal offices. Thus Andrew Hatcher became public relations secretary in the White House; Carl Rowan became deputy assistant secretary of state for public affairs; Robert C. Weaver became housing

Six at the summit. Bill Sauro took this picture of the collective leadership of the civil rights movement on July 3, 1963, when they met to discuss the march on Washington. *Left to right:* John Lewis, Whitney Young, A. Philip Randolph, Martin Luther King, James Farmer, and Roy Wilkins. (*U.S. News and World Report;* Library of Congress.)

administrator; and Clifton R. Wharton was appointed American ambassador to Norway.

The Second American Revolution in the South was now being advanced by freedom rides—the valiant attempt by mixed groups of whites and African-Americans to desegregate such facilities as waiting rooms, restaurants, and lavatories at interstate bus terminals, airports, and railroad stations. Although these amenities were segregated, much of the actual transportation was not. The strategy was to break customary racism by acts of integrated defiance. Three civil rights groups—CORE, SCLC, and SNCC—had all developed strategies whereby mixed groups of African-Americans and whites were dispatched to certain areas to break down racist barriers.

The Freedom Rides brought to the surface the dilemmas confronting those whom they touched. There was exasperation and outrage from the racist white South. There were special opportunities for gaining political capital for ambitious governors seeking reelection. The Kennedys were on the horns of a dilemma, torn as they were between wanting both desegregation and African-American votes and harmony in Congress and southern votes. From the point of view of John Kennedy, the timing of the first Freedom Rides could hardly have been worse. The Russians had just sent the first astronaut (Yuri Gagarin) into space and thus won another round in the war of propaganda and technical superiority. Moreover, the counterrevolutionary attack on Fidel Castro's regime in Cuba, supported covertly by the CIA and the Kennedy administration, had fallen in ignominious defeat at the Bay of Pigs. Within a month Kennedy was scheduled to meet Russian leader Nikita Khrushchev in Vienna. The very last thing Kennedy wanted was an unfortunate racial incident to compound America's newfound image of technological incompetence with racial intolerance.

Three pivotal incidents illustrate the sort of turmoil that could ensue. They took place in Montgomery, Alabama; Albany, Georgia; and Oxford, Mississippi.

In the spring of 1961 a CORE group led by James Farmer was attacked and beaten up by mobs of Alabama thugs in Anniston, Birmingham, and Montgomery. One bus was burned. At first the governor, John Patterson, refused to take appropriate action. John Kennedy sent a special ambassador, John Seigenthaler, to reason with him. However, the hapless envoy was dragged from his car while trying to rescue two African-American women. He was knocked out and an ambulance summoned to aid him was delayed for thirty minutes. The riot in Montgomery got completely out of hand and white racism degenerated into new depths of barbarism. The crowd poured flammable liquid over an African-American boy and set him alight. Robert Kennedy sent six hundred deputy marshals in order to restore order. This was only the first of various occasions in the 1960s when federal officers had to uphold law and order that neither state nor local officials were ready to maintain.

Robert Kennedy treated the controversy surrounding the freedom riders as if he were the arbitrator between two responsible sides. He issued a statement that "in order to insure that innocent people are not injured, maimed, or even killed, I would call upon all people who have a paramount interest in the future of our country to exercise restraint and judgment over their activities over the next few weeks or the next few days." Although the riders promised not to attack the Alabama rowdies, the rowdies said nothing, confident in the knowledge that actions speak louder than words. This prompted Bobby Kennedy to issue a second statement: "What is needed now is a cooling-off period." A CORE spokesman rejoined that this was the last thing that was needed since African-Americans had been cooling off for a hundred years.

When Martin Luther King announced that he would speak at a

Baptist church in Montgomery, the Ku Klux Klan reacted with redoubled hysteria. The atmosphere was now so tense that Governor Patterson was shamed into protecting him. His shift from outright opposition to truculent support was sufficient signal that, in Alabama, segregation on interstate transport and its facilities would be brought to an end. Robert Kennedy obtained a ruling from the Interstate Commerce Commission on September 22, 1961, banning segregation on all interstate facilities and providing for the institution of suits against towns and cities that still resisted desegregation.

This achievement led one community, the African-American citizens of Albany, Georgia, into rising to challenge segregation in the first sustained campaign since the Montgomery bus boycott of 1955–1956. It united SNCC workers led by Charles Sherrod and Cordell Reagan with the local NAACP chapter in the Albany Movement. However, the results were disappointing. Tom Hayden, the student activist who subsequently drafted the Port Huron Statement for the Students for a Democratic Society (SDS), was arrested in one incident in December 1961. Martin Luther King was arrested three times. He was only released on bail after a compromise between the town and its African-American citizens that conceded them very little. The *New York Herald Tribune* referred to the compromise as a "stunning defeat." Thus, when King left Albany, the movement disintegrated, having achieved little. This was a clear defeat for the civil rights movement.

A most serious situation developed around James Meredith in Oxford, Mississippi. Meredith was an African-American air force veteran who had been refused admission to the University of Mississippi in 1961, whereupon the NAACP filed a suit against the university on the grounds of racial prejudice. The following year a circuit court decided that Meredith, who was duly qualified, must be admitted. The decision was upheld in the Supreme Court. Thus on September 30, 1962, Meredith arrived at Oxford, Mississippi, to register for the fall semester. He was accompanied by federal marshals. But he was barred by no less a person than the governor himself, Ross Barnett, who was supported by a voracious student mob. Robert Kennedy produced an injunction against the governor, who continued his opposition. Ross Barnett had thrice failed to win the governorship during his days as a racial moderate, and now boasted to a crowd before a television film crew, "Friends, I'm a Mississippi segregationist and I'm proud of it." Despite the university authorities' support for Barnett's position, they dreaded that the school might have to be closed down, perhaps by a withdrawal of funds, perhaps by federal intervention.

An initial suggested compromise between Robert Kennedy and Ross Barnett involved a show of force, a charade played out before the campus, whereby thirty U.S. marshals shielding Meredith would draw their (unloaded) pistols to oblige Mississippi state troopers to step aside. Meredith would then be admitted. It went wrong when Barnett realized the crowd was so large that he could control neither it nor the outcome. He called Robert Kennedy to say so. A convoy of thirteen cars carrying Meredith and his party had to turn back. This was the fourth time Meredith had failed to register. In an attempt to appeal to public honor, John Kennedy made a television broadcast urging that Meredith be allowed to register. However, the federal marshals sent to Oxford to continue to protect Meredith were attacked by a mob who threw bottles and stones. They retaliated with tear gas until they were reinforced by federal troops from Memphis, Tennessee. Together the marshals and the troops brought the situation under control. Tragically, in the ensuing turmoil two people were killed, one of whom was a French journalist sent to report the situation. Of four hundred federal marshals protecting James Meredith from the campus mob, over a third were injured— twenty-eight by sniper fire. Nevertheless, Meredith was duly registered. Meredith received his degree on August 18, 1963.

Stokely Carmichael, elected chairman of SNCC later in May 1966, recalled that it was in the early 1960s that splits in the civil rights movement began to develop between King and the moderates on one hand, and the radicals in CORE and SNCC on the other. He characterized this split as between organizers and mobilizers. Mobilizers, like King, relied on white help to abolish the more blatant aspects of racism. However, organizers wanted to register African-Americans to vote and take power themselves. As the decade progressed they came to reject the help of liberal whites as well as liberal society. More militant African-American leaders resented King but they needed him for the publicity he could provide them with. For his part, he needed the flexible organization and mercurial strategies of the SNCC, which were more responsive to changing circumstances than those of his own SCLC.

Although Martin Luther King was the most widely known and most preeminent leader of the civil rights movement, his campaigns were sustained and nourished by his considerable team. One of King's most

U.S. federal troops leaving the airport at Oxford, Mississippi, on October 8, 1962, to protect African-American air force veteran James Meredith, who succeeded in enrolling and studying for a law degree at the law school of the University of Mississippi. The integration of "Ole Miss" was a signal victory for the civil rights movement in the unfolding and turbulent drama of desegregating education at all levels. (*U.S. News and World Report;* Library of Congress.)

able lieutenants was Wyatt Tee Walker—well-organized, officious, and indispensable. Another was his friend and sounding board, the white Stanley Levison; another was Harris Wofford of Alabama, who was the closest thing SCLC had to a civil rights "mole" in the White House during Kennedy's term in office.

The target of the civil rights movement shifted to voter registration. In August 1961 SNCC was divided by a strategic debate at a meeting in the Highlander Folk School near Nashville when Tim Jenkins of the National Student Association proposed that SNCC should begin to concentrate on voter registration. Some SNCC members wondered if Jenkins was speaking on behalf of the administration, whose interest would certainly have been served by such a shift in policy. Several radicals moved to direct political action, such as Robert Moses in Mississippi, and, later, Stokely Carmichael in Alabama. If Tim Jenkins's suggestion

Young and mature faces of Roy Wilkins, head of the NAACP. Although the NAACP was the most venerable of all civil rights organizations and for decades had led the vanguard of civil rights, by the 1960s it was losing ground to the more assertive techniques of nonviolent resistance of the SCLC and SNCC, and Roy Wilkins proved unequal to the more aggressive standards of leadership set by the young lions of the movement. (Photographs by Carl Van Vechten and *U.S. News and World Report;* Library of Congress.)

was inspired by government policy, it was, nevertheless, self-defeating. For the shift entailed competing with the Democratic party for radical, and even, liberal allegiance.

John Kennedy understood that Congress would not pass comprehensive civil rights legislation and he was unwilling to jeopardize other bills by antagonizing southern Democrats over civil rights. In 1962 a bill to create a new cabinet post, the department of urban affairs and housing, was defeated. Kennedy had intended to nominate African-American administrator Robert C. Weaver to this position. Stymied, Kennedy issued an executive order prohibiting discrimination in housing, but his authority over housing extended only to housing insured by the federal government, that is, to 15 percent of all housing.

In April 1963 the nation's conscience was further roused by dramatic events in Birmingham, Alabama, several of which were filmed and shown on television. Throughout these years Martin Luther King had continued to mount sit-in protests to draw public attention to continuing discrimination in places of public accommodation. Not only were schools segregated but also theaters and restaurants, parks and playgrounds, drinking fountains and lavatories, and churches. However, here the protesters encountered ugly resistance from Police Commissioner Eugene ("Bull") Connor, who secured an injunction banning an SCLC march scheduled for April 12, 1963—Good Friday. King and other leaders were arrested. King then drafted his famous open letter, fiercely rounding on those who wanted African-Americans to wait longer.

Letter from Birmingham Jail

Martin Luther King's open "Letter from Birmingham Jail" of April 16, 1963, soon became one of the most significant documents of the civil rights movement. It was significant for its pithy summation of the injustices experienced by African-Americans and its eloquent argument in favor of the most appropriate forms of African-American protest at that time—nonviolent resistance and civil disobedience.

Now that the legends of history have ennobled the civil rights activities of the late 1960s and their leaders, it is all too easy to forget that acts of civil disobedience were most controversial at the time—especially when performed by clergymen, who were, after all, inciting their followers to defy and break duly processed laws. This dislike of civil disobedience on the part of many conservatives and liberals was partly because many regarded civil rights defiance of race laws as wanton and as a precedent so bad that it would undermine the entire fabric of laws; partly because civil rights demonstrations were intended to lead to civic disruption and often did end in mayhem; and partly because undignified involvement of the clergy breached an unwritten rule that the church must not interfere in affairs of state. The immediate goal of civil rights agitation—of bringing shame upon the oppressors, as Mohandas Gandhi had done to the British in India years earlier—was hardly welcome to moderates who were sympathetic to the civil rights movement with regard to voting and desegregation but who did not want to see government itself changed in the process.

Martin Luther King used the opportunity to respond to a published statement critical of him by eight fellow clergymen from Alabama to write an open letter explaining his faith, his political convictions, and his strategy. The critical clergy were Bishops C. C. J. Carpenter, Joseph A. Durick, Paul Hardin, and Holan B. Harmon; Reverends George M. Murray, Edward V. Ramage, and Earl Stallings; and Rabbi Hilton L. Grafman. The eight critical clergy had condemned recent civil rights activities because, although they were peaceful in themselves, they precipitated violence. King began his letter of reply on the margins of the newspaper in which the statement appeared while he was still in jail, continued it on scraps of paper provided by an African-American trusty sympathetic to him, and concluded it on pads provided by his lawyers. In its definitive form, the "Letter from Birmingham Jail" was subsequently published in more polished prose in *Why We Can't Wait* (1964).

Martin Luther King first explained that he was active in the Birmingham demonstrations partly because the local affiliate of the Alabama Christian Movement for Civil Rights—an organization that pooled resources with the SCLC—had invited him. However, the most crucial reason was far more insistent: "I am in Birmingham because injustice is here."

He analyzed the dangers of two extreme and opposing forces in the Negro community: complacency from those who had accommodated themselves to segregation and bitterness and hatred from black nationalists, such as the Muslims. In between stood the Negro church and the doctrine of nonviolence—both of which provided the opportunity for the Negro community to release pent-up resentment in productive ways such as marches and freedom rides.

The four basic steps of any nonviolent campaign were collection of facts to ascertain whether there was injustice; negotiation; self-purification; and direct action. With regard to the first, assembling the facts: Birmingham was probably "the most thoroughly segregated city" in the United States. "Its ugly record of brutality" was widely known and included "more unsolved bombings of Negro homes and churches . . . than in any other city." Martin Luther King recounted a veritable litany of the social injustices, major and minor, on a wider canvas, experienced by African-Americans that had resulted in their crippling and degenerating sense of "nobodiness":

When you have seen vicious mobs lynch your mothers and fathers at will and drown your sisters and brothers at whim; when you have seen hate filled policemen curse, kick and even kill your black brothers and sisters; when you see the vast majority of your twenty million Negro brothers smothering in an airtight cage of poverty in the midst of an affluent society; when you suddenly find your tongue twisted and your speech stammering as you seek to explain to your six year old daughter why she can't go to the public amusement park that has just been advertised on television, and see tears welling up in her eyes when she is told that funtown is closed to colored children, and see ominous clouds of inferiority beginning to form in her little mental sky, and see her beginning to distort her personality by developing an unconscious bitterness towards white people; . . . when you are humiliated day in and day out by nagging signs reading "white" and "colored"; . . . when you are forever fighting a degenerating sense of "nobodiness"—then you will understand why we find it difficult to wait.

As to the second step, all negotiations to eliminate segregation, whether with the Birmingham city fathers or merchants, had been unfulfilled, either because promises of reform were made by whites but not kept or because African-Americans miscalculated their tactics or could not sustain economic boycotts.

The third stage of self-purification took the form of a soul-searching analysis of the situation. The crux of King's argument was the need for the civil rights movement to resort to civil disobedience to break unjust laws on the basis that "an unjust law"—one that is out of harmony with moral law and degrades human personality—is no law at all. Segregation ended up by treating persons as mere things. Another factor that made laws of segregation unjust was the fact that they were inflicted on a minority who had been denied the right to vote and therefore had had no part in enacting them. The Alabama state legislature was not even democratically elected since African-Americans were prevented from becoming registered to vote.

Since earlier strategies had failed, the civil rights movement was turning to the fourth stage of direct action in order to oblige whites to negotiate. "Nonviolent direct action seeks to create such a crisis and foster such a tension that a community which has constantly refused to negotiate is forced to confront the issue. It seeks so to dramatize the issue that it can no longer be ignored."

Thus came King's classic example that

one who breaks an unjust law must do so openly, lovingly, and with a willingness to accept the penalty. I submit that an individual who breaks a law that conscience tells him is unjust, and who willingly accepts the penalty of imprisonment in order to arouse the conscience of the community over its injustice, is in reality expressing the highest respect for law.

He praised those whites who had spoken or written eloquently on behalf of the civil rights movement and those who had marched with Negroes and languished in filthy jails on their behalf. Yet King confessed his grave disappointment with the sort of moderate who was devoted more to order than to justice and who failed to appreciate that the present tensions in the South existed because African-Americans were determined to resist the sort of law and order that was blocking social progress. Moreover, he also expressed profound disappointment with the white church, many of whose leaders had been outright opponents of civil rights and had never supported African-Americans' outrage at their treatment by Governors Ross Barnett or George Wallace. He was particularly dismayed that the clergy had commended the Birmingham police force for keeping "order" and "preventing violence":

I doubt that you would have so warmly commended the police force if you had seen its dogs sinking their teeth into unarmed, nonviolent Negroes. I doubt that you would so quickly commend the policemen if you were to observe their ugly and inhumane treatment of Negroes here in the city jail; if you were to watch them push and curse old Negro women and young Negro girls; if you were to see them slap and kick Negro men and young boys; if you were to observe them, as I did on two occasions, refuse to give us food because we wanted to sing our grace together. I cannot join you in praise of the Birmingham police department.

During his incarceration King's followers protested by marching and were, indeed, menaced by savagely grinning police dogs. There followed a bizarre series of practically continuous demonstrations. Yet there were no arrests. The most dramatic incident occurred on May 2, when a march by African-American children and students was attacked by an ugly mob throwing glass bottles and bricks. On May 5 the little children and defenseless students were dispersed by police, who unleashed fire hoses and dogs upon them. The most shocking example of this racism was the bombing of a church Sunday School in which four young African-American girls were killed. The courage of African-American activists and their adherents had a profound effect on national consciousness as a whole. Faced with outrage from the local African-American community in Birmingham, Robert Kennedy and the assistant attor-

John F. Kennedy resigned himself to the March on Washington for Jobs and Freedom of August 1963 and played a decisive part in shifting its emphasis from a march upon the administration to a march on behalf of the administration to lobby Congress for civil rights and welfare legislation. He stands with uninvolved toleration among African-American leaders Whitney Young, Martin Luther King, John Lewis, and A. Philip Randolph (*respectively fourth, fifth, sixth, and eighth from left*) and Roy Wilkins, as often, to the right. (*U.S. News and World Report;* Library of Congress.)

ney general, Burke Marshall, worked out a compromise with Birmingham's civic leaders to desegregate public facilities in the city. King hailed it as a great victory.

Moreover, as Theodore Sorenson put it, it now dawned upon John Kennedy that it was his duty as president to "lead and not be swamped" by the civil rights movement. In a television address on June 11, 1963, Kennedy declared that the issue of racial justice posed a great moral crisis: "A great change is at hand, and our task, our obligation, is to make that revolution, that change, peaceful and constructive for all." Having summoned a modicum of courage, John Kennedy used three strategies in the interests of civil rights. The first was a civil rights bill of significant proportions. The second was to convert a great civil rights march upon Washington into a rally for that bill. The third was to promote support for voluntary integration among leaders of labor, business, women, and the churches.

The civil rights bill Kennedy sent to Congress on June 19, 1963, would have banned discrimination in all places of public accommodation pertaining to interstate commerce. Further, the bill awarded new powers to the attorney general in order that he might better urge the desegregation of public education. Thus the bill was intended to redress the two immediate areas of grievance that African-Americans themselves had targeted in their various demonstrations.

The March on Washington

Some African-Americans despaired of Kennedy's proposed civil rights legislation ever reaching the statute books. However, they were determined to show their resolve. Thus, encouraged by A. Philip Randolph—now an old man of seventy-three—they organized the March on Washington for Jobs and Freedom, the apogee of the drama of civil rights in the 1960s. The prime mover was Bayard Rustin.

One of the leading proponents of civil rights, Bayard Rustin was born in West Chester, Pennsylvania, on March 17, 1912. He was educated at Wilberforce University, Cheyney State Teachers College, and the City College of New York. A committed pacifist, he was imprisoned for twenty-eight months during World War II on account of his conscientious objection to military service. He subsequently served the Fellowship of Reconciliation (1941–1953), the War Resisters League (1953–1955), and Martin Luther King, Jr. (1955–1960). The chief organizer of the march on Washington in 1963, his speeches against injustice and on behalf of humanity were delivered in places as diverse as Africa, Asia, and Europe. In 1964 he joined the A. Philip Randolph Institute, an educational, civil rights, and labor organization named after the great civil rights leader and based in New York City. Bayard Rustin moved from a position as executive director to that of cochairman and president of its educational fund, posts he held at the time of his death in New York on August 24, 1987.

The Kennedy brothers were, at first, suspicious and even hostile toward the proposed march on Washington. However, once they realized that, unlike FDR in 1941, they could not stop such a demonstration of mass purpose, they adjusted themselves to it. Indeed, they almost appropriated it. They tried to direct the leaders into some action for voter registration for which the requisite funds were to be secured from the Tacoma Foundation.

Tragedy strengthened the resolve behind the great purpose. On June 12, Medgar Evers, chapter secretary of the NAACP and the most respected civil rights leader in Mississippi, was shot and killed. A week later, Stephen Currier, head of the Tacoma Foundation, chaired a meeting of ninety-six bankers and corporation executives in the Hotel Carlyle, New York, at which $1.5 million was pledged for civil rights. This fund was later distributed by a new coordinating committee, the Council for United Civil Rights Leadership (CUCRL), chaired jointly by Currier and Whitney Young of the Urban League.

Hence the march was transformed into a march in, not upon, Washington—a march not to put pressure on the Kennedy administration but, rather, to help the administration by lobbying Congress. To that end Kennedy himself met with about thirty civil rights leaders in the White House on June 22, 1963. This meeting was held partly so that each side could coopt the other, partly for each side to demonstrate unanimity to the nation.

This show of unity was a form of accommodation most disagreeable to certain African-Americans, such as Malcolm X, prominent leader in the Nation of Islam. He declared that African-American unity was being achieved by the white man's money. Malcolm X pointedly referred not to the march on Washington, but to the "farce on Washington." Not surprisingly, the moment of ecstatic unity betrayed undercurrents of instability and division.

At the actual demonstration on August 28 the show of numerical strength quite exceeded the wildest expectations of the organizers. Perhaps 250,000 people, both African-American and white, young and old, attended what was evidently the largest public demonstration to that time, a march that moved resolutely from the Washington Monument to the Lincoln Memorial. Organizer Bayard Rustin realized that the presence of Martin Luther King was needed to help unite the civil rights movement, already beginning to divide. King's speech at the Lincoln Memorial, "I have a dream," became his most famous memorial. It was an impassioned plea for equality:

I have a dream that one day this nation will rise up, live out the true meaning of its creed: "We hold these truths to be self-evident, that all men are created equal." I have a dream that one day on the red hills of Georgia sons of former slaves and sons of former slaveowners will be able to sit down together at the table of brotherhood. I have a dream that one day even the state of Mississippi, a state sweltering with the heat of injustice . . . will be transformed into an oasis of freedom and justice. I have a dream that my four little children will one day live in a nation where they will not be judged by the color of their skin but by the content of their character.

Not only did the march display peaceful solidarity between African-American and white, but it was also the first public recognition that employment and the elimination of poverty were the only true bases for enduring racial equality. Thus the march signaled a shift from protests about equality in accommodation and education to the troubled areas of poverty, housing, and work. Already in July 1963 the NAACP had decided at its annual convention in Chicago to mount a campaign against de facto segregation in northern school districts, fully realizing that this would probably antagonize many northern whites. *Newsweek,* in its issue of July 29, 1963, noted that the reform movement of civil rights was turning revolutionary. "Vast majorities" of African-Americans wanted "complete equality, nothing less."

At the march on Washington John Lewis of SNCC used his ten-minute speech to criticize shortcomings in the administration's civil rights bill. Lewis's original draft began as follows: "In good conscience, we cannot support the administration's civil rights bill, for it is too little, and too late." He referred to "cheap political leaders who build their careers on immoral compromises." Reviewing the wide spectrum of opinion on civil rights within the Democratic party, he pointedly asked, "Which side is the administration on?" Learning of this, Archbishop (later, Cardinal) O'Boyle refused to give the invocation and benediction at the rally unless the speech were altered. James Forman, also of SNCC, then rewrote the speech under guidance from Randolph, Rustin, Walter Reuther, and Dr. Eugene Carson Blake, later head of the World Council of Churches. Blake even objected to an original reference to "masses" as "communist talk; we don't talk about the common people as masses in this country."

There were also a few incidental ironies in the jostling for position by some leaders. Taylor Branch records in *Parting the Waters* (1988) how King and his associates were concerned that any public knowledge about Bayard Rustin's affairs with men would tarnish the civil rights movement, and thus they ensured that he was not prominent in any photographs. King himself came in for censure for his affairs with women from his friend Ralph Abernathy in Abernathy's own memoirs of 1989.

Essayist Marya Mannes described the scene as the crowd flocked down Constitution Avenue toward the Lincoln Memorial on the momentous day of the March on Washington for Jobs and Freedom: "There was . . . no attempt at lines, at rhythm, at any formation whatsoever. They did not even stick together except in the loosest way by groups or states, or organizations, or bus-loads. They just walked—mostly black, partly white—like people who know where they are going but are not making a show of it. . . . A people serious but relaxed; almost festive. Among the neatly suited men, who did not even in the sun take off their coats and ties, were many handsome and stalwart young negroes, many middle-age ones of substance and gravity. Many of the young women were beautiful, many of the older ones distinguished. To one of them, by the banks of the pool, under the trees, I said, 'I think Lincoln was moved by this: he must know what is happening.' She glanced suddenly and said, 'The dead know much more than we think they do. I am so proud of my people.' "(*U.S. News and World Report;* Library of Congress.)

Abernathy's revelations caused him to suffer coals of fire of adverse criticism. It is certainly the case that the significance of the champions of civil rights lies in their public achievements and that their private lives should remain their own. The danger of too much personal historical revelation is of losing a sense of proportion by emphasis on tittle-tattle; the danger of historians eliminating the personal foibles of their subjects is in creating a false ennoblement of their characters and implying that only men and women free of personal appetites and idiosyncracies can transform and change society, thereby implying that the task of social reform is for others—and not for the rest of us.

This apogee of the civil rights movement set the presidency at the crossroads of a dilemma between national and individual sensibility. Hitherto, it had seemed that a just solution could be achieved by legislation. For a time, civil rights expectations of the president grew and the institution of the presidency was enhanced. It seemed that the president represented a national consensus of liberalism ready to take a stand against an entrenched, regressive minority in Congress. The march on Washington had served to draw the sting of embattled wasps. The subsequent assassination of John Kennedy on November 22, 1963, and the skillful way his successor, Lyndon Johnson, used circumstances and his command of Congress gave added emotional impulse to the civil rights bill that was passed with wider provisions in 1964.

The Civil Rights Act of 1964 entered congressional folklore. This was partly for its controversial debates. It was also partly because the Senate, for the first time, voted to end a filibuster over civil rights and against the opposition of hostile Judiciary Committee Chairman Senator James O. Eastland of Mississippi. It was partly on account of Republican support awarded to LBJ. Quite simply, civil rights was to the southern Johnson what parochial schools had been to the Catholic Kennedy—a test of his credentials as a leader of liberal reform. Biographer Doris Kearns quotes Johnson as saying, "If I didn't get out in front on this issue, then the liberals would get me. They'd throw up my background against me, they'd use it to prove I was incapable of bringing unity. . . . I had to produce a civil rights bill that was even stronger than the one they'd have gotten if Kennedy had lived. Without this, I'd be dead before I could ever begin."

The Civil Rights Act of 1964 banned discrimination in such places of public accommodation as theaters, hotels, restaurants, and gas stations. It authorized the attorney general to bring an end to segregation in public schools, hospitals, libraries, and playgrounds. It forbade discrimination by businesses with one hundred or more employees or in trade unions with one hundred or more members, and it extended the ban to smaller organizations within three years. Later, the Supreme Court upheld the act, especially its controversial sections about public accommodation. Some of the justices based their decisions on interpretations of the Fourteenth Amendment. Others ruled on the grounds that Congress had the power to regulate interstate commerce. The scope of the bill allowed the canceling of federal programs in areas where discrimination existed. The bill also provided for government suits to desegregate schools.

Like bees swarming around a giant honeycomb, spectators and participants alike are seen on the steps of the Lincoln Memorial on the historic occasion of the civil rights march on Washington in 1963. (Library of Congress.)

However, the act was not very effective in safeguarding the right to vote. It presumed that education up to the level of sixth grade entailed sufficient literacy and prevented people from being rejected for slight mistakes on their application forms. Nevertheless, it gave southern registrars wide discretionary powers.

The Civil Rights Act of 1964 passed the House with the support of 152 Democrats and 138 Republicans. In June it passed the Senate by the considerable margin of seventy-three votes to twenty-seven. Public support for the bill was revealed incidentally in the elections of 1964. Twelve southern Democrats who had supported the bill survived and were reelected and a third of the Republicans who had opposed the bill in the House were defeated.

Ironically, although the act could be interpreted as the culmination of everything in the civil rights movement since the *Brown* case, one consequence was a repudiation of the arguments upon which the Supreme Court had based its ruling in 1954. The act of 1964 specifically entrusted the commissioner of education to conduct a survey "concerning the lack of availability of equal educational opportunities for individuals by reason of race, color, religion or national origins." The survey was to be led by Professor James Coleman.

One of the most enduring legacies of the Kennedy period was little known at the time. This was affirmative action, a term first used by John Kennedy in Executive Order 10025 of 1961. Affirmative action came to signify positive discrimination in favor of African-Americans in the spheres of employment and education on the grounds that only by way of such race-conscious selection of African-Americans could the crippling legacy of centuries of institutional racism be overcome and African-Americans rewarded with the same opportunities of employment and education as whites. Always controversial, the strategy could be put into effect most easily in those institutions, such as universities and colleges, that received, directly or indirectly, at least a modicum of public, federal, or state funds. Controversy stemmed from the way official emphasis upon the strategy hardened progressively; from concerns that positive discrimination defied selection according to preeminent merit; and from misgivings about its efficacy and long-term effects.

The Coleman report, published in 1966, disclosed that attainment by the average African-American, American Indian, Mexican, and Puerto Rican child was below that of the average white and Oriental child at every grade. The difference was large to begin with and progressively greater in the higher grades. Moreover, the spectrum of variation could be found within each particular school, rather than by comparison between schools. It was clear that the majority of African-American and white students still attended different schools. However, the similarities between schools in terms of facilities and equipment and formal curricula were far greater than the differences. Yet there was little correlation between the quantity and quality of the facilities and curricula and the results in terms of student attainment as indicated, for example, in standard reading tests.

The only aspect of schools that showed a consistent correlation to student attainment was the major factor denied poor African-American children—an affluent home background. Thus Coleman and his team concluded that the prime source of inequality was the home. The schools' part was secondary.

The Rediscovery of Poverty

John Lewis's arguments about chronic poverty and the need for effective federal action to combat it at the time of the March on Washington struck a responsive chord among those administrators embarrassed by their realization that poverty persisted in the United States.

Previously, a congressional subcommittee led by Senator John Sparkman of Alabama had reported several times on the particular problem of low-income families, families living on less than two thousand dollars per annum and comprising between a fifth and a quarter of the population. Others who reviewed poverty in America in this period included economist John Kenneth Galbraith and social analysts Richard Cloward and Lloyd Ohlin. In the mid-1960s poverty and its victims received more attention in journals, books, and Congress than they had since the worst days of the Great Depression. Yet public opinion polls suggested that Americans persisted in believing cherished inaccurate stereotypes about poor people as work-shy or immoral. Nevertheless, there was a slowly developing realization that economic growth was slowing down. Economists generally believed that they knew how to run things better. Thus, for instance, James N. Morgan, Martin H. David, Wilber J. Cohen, and Harvey Z. Brazer, joint authors of *Income and Welfare in the United States* (1962) concluded that the "elimination of poverty is well within the means of federal, state, and local government." They thought it could be achieved by strategic use of $10 billion per annum, less than 2 percent of the GNP and less than a fifth of the cost of defense. More than the precise prescription, the prediction by Morgan, et al., displayed a beneficent assumption that a rich country could, should, and must be able to afford to eliminate poverty.

The rediscovery of poverty was restricted to the elite of high power politics—Kennedy, Johnson, and their advisers—rather than understood by the great mass of people. Yet, as the 1960s moved on there was a growing awareness both within government and without that a "culture of poverty" not only existed but was also the major factor governing certain cultural patterns and helped explain the behavior of certain social, economic, and ethnic groups. Scholars were more precise. They convinced themselves that a culture of poverty did not have to be passed inexorably from one generation to another. Poverty was essentially an economic problem, not a cultural one. As analyst James Patterson put it, it stemmed from demographic changes, notably the increase in numbers of old people and broken families and the oscillations—vagaries, almost—in a market economy. Only racism—one of the most potent adversaries of social improvement—could be described as culturally inherited. It certainly served to impede the needs, rights, and aspirations of minorities. The inevitable conclusion of the school of thought that minimized the cultural legacy of poverty was that the federal government must enhance welfare, provide additional employment, and protect civil rights.

The political reassessment of poverty had already resulted in legislation in 1962 whereby John Kennedy had been empowered to provide funds to assist depressed areas with high unemployment and, in the same year, a Manpower Development and Training Act to help people improve their skills. The Public Welfare Amendments of 1962 increased federal funds to train social workers and allowed federal support of 75 percent of the cost of the states to provide rehabilitation for the indigent poor. Such measures provided training and services but not work, which was what was most needed. Even so, the programs were inadequately funded.

This was certainly the case of the most widely publicized program, the War on Poverty, administered by the Office of Economic Opportunity (OEO) established under the administration of Lyndon Johnson (1963–1969). The War on Poverty was waged across a long frontier and included such diverse features as loans to indigent farmers and businessmen, aid for needy college students, Volunteers in Service to America (VISTA), the Job Corps (a program to develop skills among the poor), and Community Action Plans (CAPs). There were over a thousand CAPs. Their brief was to support various community-based programs, including Head Start, for young children who had not entered school, and legal services for the poor. The solutions were applied ahead of due and sufficient analysis, grossly underfunded, and inadequate to the task in hand since they failed to provide jobs and income.

Civil rights activists also engaged state and local government agencies

Street scene in Harlem, New York, the most famous African-American residential district in the Americas, photographed by Joe Cavello in May 1964 before the summer uprising that was to tear apart prospects of African-American and white unanimity. (*U.S. News and World Report;* Library of Congress.)

for due apportionment of federal funds. In so doing they alienated mayors and antagonized Congress. It responded by curtailing the way local communities could allocate the monies it awarded them.

Liberals believed at the time that right would, and must, inevitably triumph over might in the crusade for civil rights and the war on poverty. But many African-Americans were becoming impatient. The torch of freedom was being passed from moderate to radical reformers, notably advocates of separation.

Malcolm X and the Nation of Islam

The Black Muslims, or the Nation of Islam, formed the most enduring and controversial sect of African-American nationalists in the postwar period. This religious sect, created around 1931 by Wali Fard, practiced a form of Islamic worship. The leader was still Elijah Muhammad and by 1960 the Nation of Islam numbered between sixty-five thousand and one hundred thousand members.

Malcolm X (1925–1965) caught in reflective mood before a press conference in March 1962. The most charismatic of all advocates of black separatism, Malcolm moved from spellbinding oratory of hate in the Nation of Islam and contempt for civil rights strategies of integration to a doctrine of greater toleration and a strategy of realpolitik. When he broke from the Black Muslims in 1964, he established a separatist movement, the Organization of Afro-American Unity, and, as El-Hadj Malik El-Shabazz, he embraced orthodox Islam. His assassination in 1965 was a tragic loss for the civil rights movement, which could only have benefited from a leader who was beginning to reconcile the diverse strands of thought on integration and separatism. His autobiography, as recounted by Alex Haley, has become an icon of cultural protest. (*U.S. News and World Report;* Library of Congress.)

The aims of the Black Muslims were radical separation; the establishment of an all-black state; and racial economic development. Their most articulate spokesman was Malcolm X. Born in Omaha, Nebraska, on May 19, 1925, he grew up in Michigan. After a youth of crime in New York and Boston, he had become a convert to Islam in prison and, following his release, played a significant part in the expansion of the group in the 1950s. Malcolm X's spell-binding oratory was enhanced by his dramatic appearance. He had a narrow face upon which the flesh was so tightly drawn as to seem almost like a skull, crowned with steel-rimmed glasses. He damned whites to their faces. To Malcolm X, American society was feral, with the races in combat. Thus, for African-Americans, expertise in individual self-defense was more important than collective strategies of nonviolence; racial separation was more important than integration. The recurrent theme of Malcolm X's preaching was that African-Americans were in exile in the United States. "No, I'm not an American. I'm one of twenty-two million black people who are the victims of Americanism . . . and I see America through the eyes of the victim. I don't see any American dream; I see an American nightmare."

In 1959 the Nation of Islam became a focus of the mass media with the broadcasting of a television documentary by Louis Lomax for the Mike Wallace Show. It was entitled, simply and brutally, *The Hate Which Hate Produced*. Shortly afterwards, Dr. C. Eric Lincoln published his scholarly study, *The Black Muslims in America* (1961). The media's outraged response to the "messengers of hate," with its suspicions of Communist inspiration and "black racism," alarmed whites, whom it titillated, and it also disturbed middle-class African-Americans. Yet the publicity resulted in a new wave of poor African-American recruits to the Nation of Islam. More conservative African-American leaders were intimidated by such a radical repudiation of their cherished ideal of integration as the Black Muslims provided. In August 1959 Roy Wilkins of the NAACP said the Muslims had a "hate white" doctrine as dangerous as any white racism. Thurgood Marshall accused the Nation of Islam of being "run by a bunch of thugs organized from prisons and jails and financed, I am sure, by Nasser or some Arab group." Foreshadowing his emergence as one of the most significant African-American political theorists of the period, Malcolm X replied that "it is not integration that the Negroes in America want, it is human dignity."

For their part, social workers admired the success with which Muslims reclaimed heroin addicts. Muslims were not appalled by the addiction that they could blame on whites. Moreover, their religious rites and, indeed, the entire organization would become paramount in the lives of those whom they reclaimed. This was also true of their success with former convicts who had survived another form of slavery. The Nation of Islam could redeem its converts because it renewed their self-respect, loss of which was the most deadly curse of ghetto dwellers.

BBC commentator Gerald Priestland summed up his impressions of a Black Muslim ceremony:

Inside the Hall, Muslim sisters in white nun-like robes were carefully segregated from the Brothers in smart business suits. Stalls at the back of the auditorium were selling portraits of "The Messenger of Allah, the Honorable Elijah Muhammad," copies of his books, pamphlets from the United Arab Republic featuring Gamal Abdel Nasser, ideological textbooks for children and a lugubrious record entitled "A White Man's Heaven Is a Black Man's Hell." . . . The Messenger appeared at the microphone without ever having been seen in transit to it. Wild applause, all rise. As well they might, for Elijah Muhammad is a tiny man who might easily be overlooked but for his sequined cap. . . . His hold on the organization is evidently based upon his abilities as a schemer, rather than any charisma, and his speaking voice is weak and ill-modulated.

The Muslim's most charismatic leader, Malcolm X, remained loyal to Elijah Muhammad long after it was clear that his authority exceeded his patron's, notably in his ability to recruit. Perhaps this was because he appreciated that it was Elijah who had enabled him to reclaim his life. Yet there was a fundamental political difference yawning between them. Elijah Muhammad's rejection of white society was essentially passive; Malcolm wanted to move that rejection to self-assertion. Moreover, Malcolm X recognized that the emerging civil rights movement was a considerable competitor in the quest for young African-American recruits. It could offer them a new identity. The civil rights movement in the South had shown African-Americans in northern ghettos that they could challenge white racism and, after a struggle, attain some of their political ends. Nevertheless, in April 1962 the Muslims' assertion of black integrity was threatened by a serious incident in Los Angeles when seven unarmed Muslims were shot, one fatally, by police who arrested sixteen other Muslims for a "criminal assault on the police."

By 1963, Malcolm X and Elijah Muhammad were disagreeing quite openly over the role of the Nation of Islam in the civil rights movement. Elijah Muhammad then disciplined Malcolm X for his impolitic com-

This photograph of a Black Muslim rally at Uline Arena of June 25, 1961, underlines the interesting mix of influences upon Nation of Islam Meetings—part devout church service, part plangent rally, part psychological cabaret. (*U.S. News and World Report;* Library of Congress.)

ment upon John Kennedy's assassination that the "chickens were coming home to roost." Presumably, he meant that a state that licenses violence across society should not be surprised when violence is turned against its leaders. Whereas Malcolm wanted to organize a nationwide campaign for black separation, Elijah first hesitated and then, finally, forbade it. In December 1963 Malcolm disagreed openly with the messenger:

The Messenger has seen God. . . . He is willing to wait for Allah to deal with the devil. Well, sir, the rest of us Black Muslims have not seen God, we don't have this gift of divine patience with the devil. The younger Black Muslims want to see some action.

In March 1964 Malcolm X parted from the Nation of Islam. He made two trips to North Africa and the Near East. His friendly reception by Muslims there—white, Arab, and black—led him to conclude that, perhaps, some accommodation between African-Americans and whites was possible in the United States after all. He thus created a new separatist movement, the Organization of Afro-American Unity, with its headquarters in New York City. He preferred to believe that his friendly reception by the Arab world represented genuine religious recognition of his sect rather than a gesture of political opportunism. Malcolm's African pilgrimages had made him aware of the provincial nature of the teachings of Elijah Muhammad, with their constant obsession with color. Moreover, he could now consider black people in a new global context. They were not only a dispossessed ethnic minority in certain countries but also members of a majority in the world of people who were not white. Thus in a speech at Columbia University four days before his assassination, he showed how greatly he had been able to transcend racism: "It is incorrect to classify the revolt of the Negro as simply a racial conflict of black against white. Rather, we are seeing today a global rebellion of the oppressed against the oppressor."

Hence, in diverse ways, Malcolm X indicated that he was ready to participate in the civil rights movement: "Our political philosophy will be black nationalism. . . . The political philosophy of black nationalism means we must control the politics and politicians of our community. They must no longer take orders from outside forces." Tragically, on February 21, 1965, Malcolm X himself was assassinated, gunned down by Black Muslims in the Audubon ballroom, New York, in full view of his congregation. This was a calamitous loss of a major African-American leader. Malcolm was already showing such qualities of vision, political dexterity, and practical strategy that he might have reconciled the schism between civil rights and black power.

The story of Malcolm X is now best known through the work of his ghost writer, Alex Haley, in *The Autobiography of Malcolm X,* published shortly after his assassination in 1965. While this enthralling account turns the searing experiences of Malcolm X to maximum effect and unfolds the traumas of young African-Americans dispossessed of their self-respect by the institutional racism of the white establishment, it does so in a way that might very well have surprised its subject had he lived to read the completed work. The form of the novel—a more accurate description than autobiography—is very traditional, taking five acts as in classical tragedy, leading inevitably to Malcolm's murder, told first in a prologue. We begin with the exposition of Malcolm's youth as the son of a murdered preacher in act 1; progress through a developmental second act of Malcolm's career as a hustler in the demimonde of dead-end street life; come to the central crisis of act 3 and his years in prison, where he experiences a cathartic religious conversion to Islam;

move to a fourth act of denouement or unraveling, with his career as a public speaker and organizer of the Nation of Islam; and finally, in act 5, face the catastrophe of his assassination, following his break with Elijah Muhammad and his discerning reinterpretation of the more humanistic possibilities of white society. For each successive act he bears a different name: Malcolm Little, Detroit Red, Satan, Malcolm X, and finally, El-Hadj Malik El-Shabazz.

Yet, for all his artifice, Alex Haley tells us more than might appear at first glance. Although the most crucial experiences in the structural progress of the work should be Malcolm's cathartic conversion in prison and his ministry for the Nation of Islam, they are by no means the most interesting to read. It is the sequence of act 2 that clearly aroused Alex Haley's greatest interest and sharpened his powers of evocation and, possibly, of invention. Here the nether world of theft, reefer-smoking, and promiscuity carries the traditional racial stereotype of the no-good black stallion, a latter day Sportin' Life from *Porgy*, despite Malcolm's own intrusive insistence that easy street is a dead end of hopeless self-abnegation.

The central section, however, implicitly discloses why some young African-American hoodlums who fell foul of the law and went to jail were educated and radicalized there rather than earlier. For one thing, since all the smaller routines and chores of life were decided for them by prison regulations, they had time not on their hands but for their minds to reconsider what had happened and why in a larger context. Moreover, unlike life in the ghetto, they had access to a library and occasion to concentrate their minds upon what they were reading. Then, too, the very hierarchical nature of prison existence expressed in literal as well as metaphorical terms the dominance of white bars upon black society. This, in turn, deepened the understanding of such prison converts to radicalism as Eldridge Cleaver and George Jackson, as well as Malcolm X, of the need to reform society. Moreover, Alex Haley, as a consummate artist, was well aware of the dramatic ironies of Malcolm X beginning life as a slain minister's child, sowing his wild oats as a prodigal son, and then returning to a religious fold as a preacher—first of hate, then of humanity—who would also be slain in turn. Here he was conforming to a long religious tradition of reclaimed sinners, for which the precedents included St. Francis of Assisi and St. Augustine. Thus the odyssey of Malcolm X was from psychological needs to spiritual aspirations and, thence, to political solutions.

The enormous prestige of Malcolm X, which grew ever stronger after his tragic assassination, contributed to the Nation of Islam's most unstable political situation. He had, after all, left the Black Muslims in 1964 to form the Organization of Afro-American Unity. After his murder his reputation and ideas were respected and upheld by every shade of opinion within the black power and, later, Pan-Africanist movements throughout the 1960s and 1970s. Yet the Nation of Islam was criticized by the younger generation of black nationalists, partly for being too conservative in economics and politics and partly for its association with Islam, a religion that had countenanced Arab participation in the slave trade. It was, therefore, somewhat suspect. Moreover, Malcolm X had abandoned the Nation of Islam.

In 1975 Elijah Muhammad died. He had been the patriarch of the Nation of Islam for forty years. The Black Muslims were unable at first to respond constructively to the loss of their spiritual leader. Elijah's appointed successor was the fifth of his six sons, Wallace Deen Muhammad, who moved the Nation into a period of religious reformation that entailed fundamental ideological changes. The Nation adopted the tenants of Sunni Islam and changed its name to the World Community of Al-Islam in the West. *Muhammad Speaks,* the black nationalist weekly newspaper created by Malcolm X in the 1950s, changed its name to the *Bilalian News.* Members were known as Bilalians, after Bilal, an African Muslim who became Islam's first *muezzin,* or crier. Somewhat surprisingly, whites were permitted to join the World Community while such traditional nationalist goals as the demand for a separate bloc of states for African-Americans in the American South were abandoned. These religious and political shifts led various ministers to leave the revised organization.

Shifting Sensibilities

Disagreement over means and ends would become the most significant issues to face the African-American protest struggle in the 1960s. The rejection of the Black Muslims by other African-American leaders did not make the undercurrents of racial pride and violent self-assertion go away either. In Monroe, North Carolina, Robert Williams, head of the local chapter of the NAACP, asserted that African-Americans would have to meet force with force and recommended armed self-defense. In early 1959 he was suspended from the NAACP and later expelled.

Muhammad Speaks, the newspaper of the Nation of Islam, rolls off the press and its contents are perused by print workers in this publicity still of the 1970s. (*U.S. News and World Report;* Library of Congress.)

Nevertheless, his example, and that of the Muslims, proved that nonviolence, although extremely effective as a strategy, was merely that—a strategy. It was not truly the *satyagraha* taught by Mohandas Gandhi in India, in which nonviolence becomes a creed, a philosophy, and a way of life to the protestor. The undercurrents of black nationalism, unobserved and ignored since Marcus Garvey, were just as powerful within African-American communities in the North and South as the new commitment to nonviolence by some sections of the African-American community in the South. The 1960s would see the emergence of both traditions as African-Americans in the North and South gained new opportunities to express grievances. In the South their problems were legal and constitutional. In the North they were economic and social. In the South the system of institutional racism was already on the defensive. In the North the extent and depth of racism were imperfectly understood.

As David L. Kirp, a professor of public policy at Berkeley, observed in a review for the *New York Times* of April 22, 1990, "It was easy enough to secure formal legal equality for blacks ... since that left whites unthreatened, but real change meant giving blacks more than the vote and a seat at the lunch counter. It meant securing political and economic power for blacks, guaranteeing them places at schools and factories and executive suites, even—necessarily—at the expense of whites." What about "innocent" whites? asked Congressman Peter Rodino of James Farmer of CORE in a colloquy about preferential treatment during hearings on the 1964 Civil Rights Act. "You see," answered James Farmer, "none of us are really innocent." This was never a popular, never an accepted view. Indeed, some congressmen tried to eliminate affirmative action from the 1964 act.

Hitherto, civil rights had moved to the front of the political stage but had been treated by federal and state governments at face value only, as a specific, separate problem, capable of rational solution. Now it was to play a decisive role in the way other crucial issues unfolded. It was part of an unraveling tapestry of social reform and war in Indochina that dominated the later 1960s and in which the diverse threads snarled and tangled with one another. Not since the First Reconstruction of 1865–1877 had the history of African-Americans become so interwoven with the complexity of federal politics. Thus, the history of President Lyndon Johnson's administration of 1963–1969, the fate of the Great Society, the tragedy of American involvement in Vietnam, and the shift in emphasis of African-American protest from civil rights to black power were all interrelated.

The Great Society

Lyndon Johnson's reform program was known as the Great Society, a phrase adopted by Richard Goodwin from the title of a book by Graham Wallas, an English socialist at the turn of the century. It was first used by LBJ in an address he gave at the University of Michigan on May 22, 1964. His theme was that it was time for the United States to be concerned about equality of life for all American citizens and not just about the quantity of affluence for a privileged few. The very notion of providing liberty and abundance for all citizens was somewhat radical in itself because such statements made by the president to this end implied that they did not exist already. The traumatic effect upon society of John Kennedy's murder was turned to powerful effect by LBJ. Not only did he retain Kennedy's men for the initial period of his administration but he also used Kennedy's presumed commitment to reform as a justification of the need. Johnson, who had exercised considerable authority as Senate majority leader in the 1950s, had both the special knowledge of key congressional figures and superb parliamentary skills to forge a consensus of opinion as to what should be achieved. Thus were John Kennedy's ideas on poverty and Harry Truman's ideas on medical reform transformed by Lyndon Johnson.

After the Democrats' landslide victories in the presidential and congressional elections of 1964, the Eighty-ninth Congress voted the president about two-thirds of the legislation he proposed—a record exceeded only by the New Deal. Among the most significant of all Great Society legislations were the various new laws on civil rights: the Civil Rights Act of 1964; the Voting Rights Act of 1965; and the Civil Rights Protection Act of 1968. LBJ knew that, as a southerner, his commitment to civil rights would always be suspect. He knew that to overcome any residual suspicion of lack of sincerity, he had to exceed all expectations. Moreover, it was only full-hearted, unprecedented commitment to civil rights that would ensure his credibility as a social reformer.

The tragedy of Lyndon Johnson was akin to certain traditional interpretations of heroes of classical tragedies, who are led to their destruction by fissures in their characters that destroy both them and those around them. LBJ was a man of terrifying contradictions. A southerner, he came from the rural oligarchy of provincial machine politics and yet he understood the advent of the African-American revolution better than many northern politicians; a humanitarian, he was capable of cruel ridicule of his administrators, whom he sometimes believed failed him. Yet his hypersensitive nature made him resistant even to constructive criticism. He had a self-conscious aspiration to become a great president and modeled himself on the lines of FDR. Not only had Roosevelt led the United States through the tragedy of the Great Depression but also to victory in a war against tyranny. Johnson allowed this obsession to warp his sense of perspective. Moreover, his concentration and enthusiasm wandered.

One instance of drift in the Great Society legislation is provided by the Economic Opportunity Act of 1964. Of considerable interest to the African-American community, it was designed to create employment by community action (rather than simply work), a strategy advocated by the President's Commission on Juvenile Delinquency and the Council of Economic Advisors. Johnson named a Kennedy brother-in-law, Sargent

Shriver, as head of the Office of Economic Opportunity, spearhead of the declared "war on poverty." In fact, the War on Poverty was an academic strategy devised by social scientists and imposed on Congress by the administration. Furthermore, it was managed without due consideration of the niceties of electoral politics.

Sargent Shriver's strategy was to follow the path of LBJ's consensus and, particularly, to gain the goodwill and support of business. During its zenith of 1965–1970, the OEO received an average of $1.7 billion per annum, about 1.5 percent of the federal budget, or .33 percent of the GNP. In a period when the number of poor people rose from about twenty-five million to thirty-three million, had all OEO funds been distributed evenly to the poor (instead of being siphoned away for the bureaucracy), each poor person would have received between fifty and seventy dollars per annum. Analyst Joseph A. Kershaw commented in his *Government against Poverty* (1970), "The war on poverty has rarely scratched the surface. Most poor people had no contact with it, except perhaps to hear the promises of a better life to come." Yet the rhetoric of hope raised expectations—especially of rising funding—that resulted simply in frustrating those whom they were intended to help. The brakes LBJ and Congress put on the OEO undermined public confidence in the government's probity and resolve with regard to social reform and contributed to public cynicism in the 1970s and 1980s about what could and could not be achieved.

Furthermore, city governments and their bosses did not like the results of programs that turned the poor against their established political machines. In *America in Our Time* (1976) Godfrey Hodgson puts it bluntly: "The poor were being organized against the establishment and, not surprisingly, the establishment didn't like it a bit." For example, the Mississippi Child Development Group provided preschool education for disadvantaged children and used some funds to campaign against congressmen it regarded as too conservative. Another beneficiary of OEO funds was Imamu Amiri Baraka, the former LeRoi Jones's Harlem Theater, which staged plays that criticized whites in virulent terms. Political machines, whether federal or local but always duly elected, simply would not long tolerate an opposition funded, albeit covertly, from federal resources.

Despite tears in the fabric of reform, African-Americans took significant steps to achieve political or judicial power in the Johnson years. A few gained significant political influence. Thus Edward W. Brooke, the attorney general of Massachusetts, became the first African-American senator since Reconstruction, representing the Republicans. Thurgood Marshall, the noted attorney who had represented the NAACP in the celebrated *Brown* case in 1954, was appointed to the Supreme Court in 1967. Furthermore, the way the African-American urban electorate and white liberals decided to cast and concentrate their votes in favor of certain African-American candidates led to the election of African-American mayors in Cleveland, Ohio; Gary, Indiana; and Washington, D.C.

In addition, the courts insisted upon further desegregation in schools. Thus in 1965 the Supreme Court ruled against the states of Florida and Louisiana that their "delays in desegregation" were "no longer tolerable." In the case of *Harper* v. *Virginia State Board of Education* of 1966, the Supreme Court ruled that the state poll tax violated individual rights guaranteed by the Fourteenth Amendment. In 1967, in the case of *Loving* v. *Virginia,* the Supreme Court ruled unanimously that a state law of Virginia prohibiting marriage between people of different races was unconstitutional and also in violation of the Fourteenth Amendment.

However, the gains did not meet the awakened expectations of a steadily increasing African-American population. Although African-Americans were increasingly able to move into reasonably well-paid jobs in the cities, their gains were disproportionately behind those of whites. African-American unemployment was twice that of white and rising continuously. Moreover, various demographic changes affected African-Americans more adversely. As certain industries moved out of inner cities and even beyond the suburbs, they left millions of undereducated, unskilled urban African-Americans without jobs in impoverished ghettos. One index of exploitation was health. While the United States was eighth in rank among industrial nations as far as the general health of its population was concerned, African-American infant mortality was twice that of white.

6

Civil Rights and Black Power

After almost a hundred years of faltering progress in civil rights, African-American protest underwent in the space of only six short years a momentous shift in emphasis from civil rights to black power. The new form of protest was characterized by a change from nonviolent, peaceful protest to violence and riots that some commentators characterize as African-American uprisings. Various civil rights organizations reflected the change. The advocates of nonviolent resistance lost control of the leadership and those whites who were also leaders in the civil rights movement were displaced by African-Americans. The first white volunteers were often affluent children of the culture that had produced the Pax Americana of the postwar world. They had shown increasing impatience with the fumbling African-American organizations. For their part, African-Americans resented their assertions of experience and, indeed, their actual experience in organization.

The Summer of 1964

In addition to unexpected problems in social and economic reforms, confidence in the American political system and the way it was supposed to be able to monitor and absorb change democratically was much disrupted by dramatic, tragic events in the summer of 1964. These events shook African-American confidence and respect for the federal government. It seemed it could neither protect the legitimate protests by civil rights workers nor mete out justice to their murderous adversaries. In 1964 SNCC workers began to carry guns to protect themselves.

The troubles of the Mississippi Summer Project illustrate the erosion of confidence. In the summer of 1964 SNCC was organizing white and African-American students in a drive to persuade African-Americans in Mississippi to claim their legal right to register to vote. At this time more than two-fifths of the population in Mississippi were African-American citizens yet only one out of every twenty duly qualified African-American adults was actually registered to vote. Not a single African-American had held elective office since the end of Reconstruction in 1877.

The Mississippi Summer Project of the Mississippi Freedom Democratic party attempted to change this. It was led by Robert Parris Moses. He was born and raised in Manhattan and had attended Hamilton College on a scholarship before studying for a master's degree in philosophy at Harvard. After some initial successes with registration drives in Mississippi, Moses planned to draw in ever more students from such leading universities as Stanford and Berkeley, Swarthmore and Yale to help the registration drive.

Robert Moses knew his project would require lawyers to advise how best to challenge the laws of Mississippi. Sensing that funds to pay the lawyers might not be made available by Jack Greenberg, head of the Legal Defense and Education Fund, Inc. (the "Inc. Fund"), of the NAACP, Robert Moses accepted an offer of assistance from the National Lawyers Guild, which in the 1940s had been generally thought of as a front for communism. Greenberg told Moses that if SNCC or COFO worked with the Guild, he would get nothing from the Inc. Fund. Consequently, Moses and the Guild resorted to subterfuge, calling it a Lawyers Committee for Civil Rights.

Robert Moses gave classes in Oxford, Ohio, training volunteers in civil defense against police harassment. The first cadre had just left on their mission when, on June 21, Moses heard that three of that group had been arrested in Neshoba County and were now missing. Six weeks later, on August 4, 1964, their bodies were found in an earthen dam outside Philadelphia, Mississippi. They had been beaten and then shot. These civil rights martyrs were Michael Schwerner of Brooklyn, aged twenty-four; Andrew Goodman of Queens College, New York, aged twenty; and James Earl Chaney of Meridian, Mississippi, aged twenty-one. The pathologist who reported on the bodies said that the wounds inflicted by chains on Chaney, the only African-American, were so terrible that he had only seen such damage on humans as the result of aircraft crashes at high speed.

It was Lyndon Johnson himself who insisted that the atrocious crime and its perpetrators be brought to light. On December 4, 1964, the sheriff and deputy sheriff of Neshoba County and nineteen other people were arrested. However, six days later, all charges against them were dropped on the grounds that evidence gleaned by the FBI was insufficient. Quite simply, FBI efforts to ascertain the true facts and provide hard evidence had been frustrated by the Mississippi officers. In that summer, eight civil rights workers altogether were beaten up in Mississippi and about one thousand were arrested. It was not until 1967 that seven people were found guilty of the civil rights murders of 1964.

During the election campaign of 1964, the Democratic party's attempt at a show of unity was also undermined by a dramatic incident at the Democratic National Convention held in Atlantic City in August. The incident shows how profoundly disillusioned African-Americans were with the administration. Sixty-eight delegates from the Mississippi Freedom Democratic party (MFDP), of whom four were white and the others African-American, arrived at the Convention. Their purpose was clear: to assert that they were the true representatives and democratic delegates from the state as opposed to those from the state Democratic party, which had, after all, connived for numerous years at the exclusion of African-Americans. Embarrassed, Lyndon Johnson from behind the scenes proposed to seat the MFDP delegates as "honored guests" and to accept three members of the usual delegation—from the state Democratic party—as regular delegates. This compromise won the consent of Governor Paul Johnson of Mississippi but not that of the MFDP. One member, Fannie Lou Hamer, told an investigating committee how she had been beaten when she tried to register to vote in Ruleville, Mississippi. "They beat me with a long, flat blackjack. I screamed to God in

Whatever their disagreements on political aims and strategies, Martin Luther King and Malcolm X had more in common than was widely understood until it was too late, with the assassinations of Malcolm in 1965 and Martin in 1968. This candid picture of their meeting of March 24, 1964, in the presence of Ralph Abernathy (*behind*), suggests a deeper warmth that extended beyond surface professional courtesy. (*U.S. News and World Report;* Library of Congress.)

my mind. My dress worked itself up. I tried to pull it down. They beat my arms until I had no feeling in them." Fannie Lou Hamer was, like Martin Luther King, a virtuoso speaker. Although she was relatively uneducated and her career was that of a simple sharecropper, she rivaled King in her ability to mix intelligence and appeal in her powerful rhetoric.

Her evidence and the unassailable conclusion that African-Americans were unconstitutionally being deprived of their voting rights in Mississippi forced the president to retract and provide a second compromise whereby two delegates from the MFDP would be seated as delegates at large. However, LBJ would go no further. John Connally, governor of Texas, had advised him, "If you seat those black buggers, the whole South will walk out." Johnson really did fear Democratic defections not only in the rural South but also in the urban North, where he knew that ghetto riots might yet provoke what the press called a "white backlash" of resentment against African-Americans and their problems and needs. He knew that maverick Democratic aspirant Governor George C. Wallace of Alabama might be able to build on smoldering blue-collar resentment against African-Americans in the cities, especially among new immigrants and their descendants.

The weight of opinion among Democratic delegates and emotional pressure within the Democratic party as a whole was thrown in the scales against the MFDP. Even Martin Luther King and Bayard Rustin also urged them to accept LBJ's compromise solution. However, the MFDP was adamant. In a moralistic statement the delegates refused to yield and accept a token of recognition: "The compromise was not designed to deal with the issues raised by the FDP" for "the FDP delegation came to Atlantic City to raise the issue of racism, not simply to demand recognition. It could not accept a token decision which had as its goal the avoidance of the question of racism."

If we return to Norman Mailer's prophetic analysis in "The White Negro," we can understand the reasons for the MFDP's reluctance to compromise:

The unstated essence of Hip, its psychopathic brilliance, quivers with the knowledge that new kinds of victories increase one's power for new kinds of perception; and defeats, the wrong kind of defeats, attack the body and imprison one's energy until one is jailed in the prison of other people's habits, other people's defeats, boredom, quiet desperation, and muted icy self-destroying rage.

The Selma March

The fissure of unease that had developed in the confidence of the civil rights movement over such incidents as the Mississippi Freedom Democratic party's reception at the Democratic National Convention in Atlantic City and the tragedy of the civil rights martyrs in Mississippi deepened inexorably and opened wide with the Selma Crisis of 1965. As Martin Luther King once observed, "The paths of Negro-white unity that had been converging crossed at Selma and like a giant X began to diverge."

Following his award of the Nobel Prize for Peace in December 1964, in January 1965 Martin Luther King called a press conference to announce a voter registration drive in Selma, in Dallas County, Alabama, where only 335 of 15,115 potential African-American voters (about 2.1 percent) were registered. The election board was open only two days a month and it processed applications with undue sloth. However, African-Americans in Selma seemed indifferent to King's registration drive until rural whites murdered an African-American in nearby Perry County, Alabama. SNCC resented the entry of King in Selma because SNCC workers had been involved in a voter registration drive there since 1963. They dreaded that he would appropriate their work, bring it to a successful conclusion, enjoy the reclame and with it the promise of more funds from local philanthropists, and then move on to another project.

The first Selma demonstrations began in January 1965. On February 1 King and another 770 participants were arrested. On his release on February 6 he went to Washington, D.C., where the vice president, Hubert Humphrey, and the attorney general, Nicholas de B. Katzenbach, assured him that the administration would soon introduce an effective voting rights bill.

King now proposed that the demonstration should take the form of a peaceful march on March 7, 1965, from Selma to Montgomery along fifty-four miles of Route 80, also known as the Jefferson Davis Highway. Governor George Wallace banned the march on the specious grounds that it was a threat to commerce and public safety alike. He sent a hundred state troopers to the area to reinforce his man there, Sheriff Clark. However, on the appointed day—Black Sunday—about six hundred African-Americans and a few white activists started to march in defiance of the ban. They proceeded from Brown's Chapel to the

Edmund Pettus Bridge across the Alabama River, where they were met by state troopers who employed tear gas, wet bullwhips, and billy clubs against them.

On Tuesday, March 9, 1965, Martin Luther King, who had been absent from the earlier march, returned to head another march of about three hundred African-Americans and white clergy, including rabbis and nuns. Rather than become embroiled in another violent confrontation, King and Clark agreed to compromise on a select token march only across the bridge. This compromise now seemed like outright betrayal to SNCC activists, who openly ridiculed Martin Luther King as a second Uncle Tom. In the meantime, several white youths attacked a white Unitarian minister, Reverend James J. Reeb of Boston, who had come to take part in the march. They beat him to death outside a Selma cafe. This scandalous murder led to an atmosphere pregnant with such turmoil that Wallace was obliged to seek extra help from the president. He condemned the marches but said he could neither prevent them from taking place nor protect them. In reply, Johnson dispatched 1,863 national guardsmen, 250 marshals, and two army battalions, supported by helicopters and ambulances, to Selma.

Thus fortified, King and his followers embarked on a third march from Selma, beginning on March 21, 1965, that was televised across the country. It started with only thirty-two hundred people on the first day, but more and more people joined the procession until the numbers had swelled to twenty-five thousand people, who arrived at the final destination, Montgomery, four days later on March 25. If anything, television disclosed even more than the actual event the sharp contrast between the cheerful sobriety and composure of the African-American and white marchers led by Martin Luther King and Ralph Bunche, an assistant secretary general of the United Nations, and the truculence and disorder of the Alabama rowdies who had gathered to jeer and intimidate them.

The Selma crisis reached a tragic climax with yet another brutal murder. Mrs. Viola Liuzzo, a Detroit housewife and tender mother of five children, was a civil rights volunteer whose task after Selma was to drive Alabama marchers back to their homes once the march was over. On her last journey, when she was carrying a nineteen-year-old African-American barber, she was fired on by Ku Klux Klansmen and killed.

The various trials of those accused of her murder proved sensational. It transpired that one of the Klansmen in the car that had sprayed her car with bullets was an undercover FBI agent who identified the others.

Governor George Wallace of Alabama testifying before a Senate Commerce Committee on July 16, 1963. Having started and risked his political career as a moderate on race issues, Wallace became the most widely know racist politician in the United States, determined to hold a color line at whatever cost to America's reputation as a bastion of democracy across the world. His failure to turn the tide of civil rights in the Selma March of 1965 did not deter his political ambitions and he became the presidential candidate of an American Independent party in 1968 that helped break Democratic control of a solid South and assisted the emergence of Richard Nixon as a leader of a new conservative majority. A political realist, he began to court the African-American vote when it was sizable enough to be decisive. When Wallace ran for president again in 1972 he was shot by an assassin, paralyzed from the waist down, ending his natural political ambitions. (*U.S. News and World Report;* Library of Congress.)

At the first trial, defense attorney Matt M. Murphy, Jr., dared to say, "When white people join up with them [African-Americans], they become white niggers." At the trial's conclusion, the jury was divided by ten votes to two and would only find the defendants guilty of man-slaughter—not murder. At the second trial, the Klansmen were actually acquitted. However, the federal government insisted on a new trial on the grounds that the Klansmen had violated Mrs. Liuzzo's civil rights by killing her. In the end, the murderers were convicted and sentenced to the maximum penalty—ten years' imprisonment.

A third murder was of a white Episcopalian student from New Hampshire who was killed in a grocery store by a part-time deputy sheriff. The accused sheriff pleaded self-defense and was acquitted by a white jury. Meanwhile, three men charged with killing James Reeb were also acquitted.

According to the president, it was the Selma crisis that inspired the Voting Rights Act of 1965. It was passed in August and public opinion generally attributed it to the influence of Martin Luther King. After all, King was the symbolic leader of the entire civil rights movement. It was he who had conceived of the Selma march with the intention of getting African-Americans registered to vote. The Voting Rights Act of 1965 allowed direct federal action to enable African-American citizens to register to vote and to vote. It awarded the attorney general power to appoint federal registration officials in those areas where activity by voters had fallen below a specified level. These areas included the states of Alabama, Georgia, Louisiana, Mississippi, South Carolina, and Virginia; twenty-eight counties in North Carolina; and a number of miscellaneous counties in certain western states. Furthermore, the act suspended literacy tests and similar qualifying devices and provided penalties for criminal interference with voting rights.

The act had an immediate, dramatic effect. On August 14, 1965, 381 African-Americans were enrolled in Selma—more than the number registered in all preceding years of the twentieth century. Moreover, whereas in 1964 only 35 percent of African-Americans were registered to vote in the South, by 1969 almost 65 percent were registered. The most dramatic changes occurred in the deep South, where the percentage of African-Americans registered to vote rose form 19 percent to 61 percent in Alabama; from 7 percent to 67 percent in Mississippi; and from 27 percent to 60 percent in Georgia.

The Selma crisis brought a chapter in civil rights history to an end for three reasons. First, it taught strategists among white racists that open resistance in the form of organized brutality was self-defeating. This was primarily because it earned much adverse publicity on television and resulted in federal intervention. (The rank and file remained adamant in its hubris.) Second, it exorcised the collective guilt of white liberals, who believed, erroneously, that civil rights had achieved its ends through due legislation. Once laws were passed, they believed their contribution was over. Third, it showed African-Americans that they must continuously work to maintain the interest and morale of their followers at the grass-roots level. Such local leaders included Ronnie Moore of Louisiana, Charles Sherrod of Georgia, and Charles Evers of Mississippi (brother of Medgar Evers).

The diminuendo of enthusiasm for civil rights within and without the movement in the mid-1960s should not obscure its profound achievement—the uprooting of America's tragic racial traditions. Critic Ella May Norton commented in the *New York Times* of November 27, 1988, how extensive was this achievement in which

oppressed and powerless people moving together changed themselves and their country profoundly and permanently. Small steps by timid leaders had proved unavailing for a century. Finally, the people did it themselves with the brilliant combination of strategy and philosophy that became the southern nonviolent civil rights movement. What has in other countries been changed through mindless violence was transformed by the principled suffering of those who had already suffered most.

It's Gettin' Hotter in the North Every Day

Hitherto it had seemed, at least on the surface, that there was nothing in the civil rights movement that contradicted general liberal optimism and consensus. Its philosophy was equality; its strategy was integration; its tactics were nonviolent. Many assumed that integration could be achieved without changing white society in any fundamental way. Yet, despite its high moral tone, nonviolent resistance did not automatically melt the hearts of those Americans who saw it either directly or on television. Polls suggested that many people disapproved of the tactics of the civil rights movement and the speed with which civil rights hit its various targets.

Moreover, problems in the northern cities disclosed that African-Americans' psychological need for attention and respect from whites was as potent as their political and physical needs. It was, in part, a question of African-American consciousness. Certain militants also discovered white fears about the way African-Americans in ghettos might express their anger and the very fact of that anger deeply perplexed many white liberals. Urban African-Americans were not poor in absolute terms but, rather, were poor in cultural and material terms in comparison with the affluence of bourgeois whites surrounding the ghettos.

The temporary lapse of white confidence allowed the torch of political initiative to pass from white to African-American, from liberal to militant. Furthermore, the threat of violence in northern cities undermined confidence that racism could be overcome. Hence, the civil right movement moved quickly from nonviolent resistance to riots, or, as some maintain, African-American uprisings, as the accumulated frustration of urban African-Americans reached a peak in the heat and humidity of several long, hot summers. During the epidemic of riots and uprisings between 1964 and 1972, sixty thousand people were arrested for looting, arson, or resisting arrest, ten thousand were seriously injured, and around 250 were killed. Moreover, the tumult caused psychic and social turmoil over several years. The riots were always ended by displays of massed force by government, whether local, state, or federal.

During the Selma crisis of 1965 a hundred copies of Assistant Secretary of Labor Daniel Patrick Moynihan's report, *The Negro Family: The Case for National Action,* were circulated among LBJ's policy makers. Moynihan had been a prime mover of the War on Poverty. The substance of Moynihan's analysis was the continuous relationship among unemployment, deprivation, and social problems in urban ghettos, and their impact upon African-American families. Moynihan's lengthy parade of statistics was most disturbing. A third of nonwhite children were being raised in broken families. In Harlem the rate of illegitimacy was over 40 percent. Moreover, "unemployment among Negroes outside the South has persisted at catastrophic levels since the first statistics were gathered in 1930."

Not all the evidence was disturbing—at least in economic terms. A steadily expanding African-American professional and middle class was beginning to profit from the system. Yet an underclass of disadvantaged African-Americans was falling further behind. The deterioration of the African-American family stood at the eye of the political storm. This was, in part, a consequence of slavery. "It was by destroying the Negro family under slavery that white America broke the will of the Negro people." However, chronic unemployment was eroding the African-American family even further. Oscillations in the business cycle that led to another round of greater employment or unemployment were followed within a year by the decreases or increases in the number of separations and broken marriages.

The main constructive suggestion in Moynihan's argument was that if African-Americans were ever to overcome their social disadvantages, then the government would have to institute positive discrimination: "If you were ever going to have anything like an equal Negro community, you are . . . going to have to give them unequal treatment."

LBJ accepted the principle of federal policies to achieve equality as a fact rather than just a theory. Thus he discussed the subject in his speech at Howard University, in Washington, D.C., on June 4, 1965—a speech first drafted by Daniel Moynihan himself. Yet, when LBJ called a White House conference to translate rhetoric into policy and strategy, he consulted such white liberals as Erik Erikson, Robert Coles, Talcott Parsons, and Urie Bronfenbrenner, and only one African-American, Kenneth Clark. Leading participants at the conference included successful businessmen —people who could be presented as concerned about poverty without any possible suggestion that they were revolutionaries. LBJ himself was preoccupied with the war in Vietnam. Moreover, Johnson was particularly incensed at certain civil rights leaders for the way he thought they were trying to make his war strategy for him. Not surprisingly, when the conference finally began in June 1966 it had far less significance than had been originally intended. Civil rights was only a priority for the administration insofar as it wanted to reduce any embarrassment caused by activists—as had happened at the Democratic National Convention in 1964.

Since the conference extended to two thousand people, the most it could achieve was to endorse proposals recommended in advance by a committee chaired by Ben Heinemann of the Chicago and North Western Railway. Roger Wilkins, an aide with the Department of Justice, commented that "there is widespread belief among Negroes interested in civil rights that there will be no significant follow-up to or implementation of the recommendations of the conference by this administration." This was proved correct. Conference discussions were overtaken by the tide of events.

The strategies for equality in the North were far harder to find than the demolition of segregation in the South—and that had proved difficult. They would include the rapid raising and faster disbursing of billions of dollars and affirmative action in favor of African-Americans. This strategy expected a great deal both of whites and the federal government. Great nationwide institutions illustrated the ambiguity. Thus television networks in the greatest metropolitan centers might adopt liberal attitudes to civil rights on television that their local southern affiliates eschewed in favor of racist propaganda. Hence, U.S. Steel would hire African-Americans in Pittsburgh or Gary in the North while its Birmingham subsidiary, Tennessee Coal and Iron, refused to hire them.

Whereas African-American sharecroppers in the South had more than enough to do to stay alive, urban African-Americans in the North often had time on their hands, especially if they were unemployed. Yet every time they watched television, glanced at a newspaper, or listened to the radio the panoply of advertising told them that social status and fulfillment could be acquired by buying consumer goods. Nevertheless, the gulf between aspiration and achievement was so great as to be almost ludicrous—certainly bizarre.

The prelude to the terrible series of summer riots or uprisings came with the Harlem riot of July 16, 1964. It began with a minor incident in which a janitor turned a water hose on African-American youths outside 215 East 76th Street in Manhattan. One boy was pursued by a policeman until he turned on his captor, drew a knife, and was himself killed.

The Watts uprising of 1965 began on August 11 when a white police officer stopped a car in the Watts district of Los Angeles, a district that was 98 percent African-American in population. He gave the African-American driver, Marquette Fryer, a test for drunkenness and this provoked a riot lasting six days that encompassed arson, looting, general mayhem, and destruction of property. In all, thirty-four people were killed and 856 injured. As many as thirty-one hundred people were arrested in the Watts riot. The uprising was ended by fifteen thousand National Guardsmen and another one thousand law enforcement officers. Estimates of the damage varied from $45 million to $200 million. The Watts riot was the most severe since the Detroit race riot of 1943 but was really in an entirely new category. LBJ summed up the outrage felt by many liberals after Watts when he said, "Neither old wrongs nor new fears can justify arson and murder." He did not mention that the killings had been by white men and, moreover, by white men in uniform.

What people suspected were killings by organized cadres of African-American snipers were in fact, it later transpired, the fatal product of haphazard firing by police and the National Guard.

Lou Smith, formerly of CORE, called the Watts riot a "tremulous community tantrum":

What happened was that people had sat here and watched all the concern about black people "over there." And there wasn't a damn soul paying one bit of attention to what was going on in Watts. So the black people in Watts just spontaneously rose up one day and said: 'Fuck it! We're hungry, our schools stink. We are getting the shit beaten out of us. We've tried the integration route. It's obvious the integration route ain't going to work. Now we've got to go another way."

A comparable, but less extreme riot began in Chicago on August 12, 1965, and there were other riots that year in Cleveland, New York, Jacksonville, Florida, and South Bend, Indiana.

It seemed a new tier of militant African-American activists had discovered something that eluded established civil rights leaders—that potent, if destructive expressions of African-American anger, such as those of the Harlem and Watts riots, proved especially plangent copy in the mass media of newspapers and television. It sold papers, provided television with eager audiences, informed a nation about the perils of city ghettos, and made a more pressing case for reform than anything else. The more militant activists understood that liberals would attend closely to urban problems if only to anticipate and prevent renewed, perhaps legitimate, expressions of anger by violence and riot. The most tragic irony of such African-American protests in the mid-1960s was that many were directed against Lyndon Johnson, who was undoubtedly the greatest president for civil rights in American history.

The Shift from Civil Rights to Black Power

The impact of the Selma crisis, the summer uprisings, and the faltering moves of the administration was such that, from 1965 onward, the organized American civil rights movement itself presented two faces—an outward face of victory and an inner face of disillusionment. In only fifteen months, from the Selma march of Easter 1965 to the summer of 1966, both CORE and SNCC began to disintegrate. They were divided by three issues. Could the civil rights movement maintain its strategy of nonviolence? Could African-Americans and whites continue to work together harmoniously and productively? Was the civil rights movement essentially reformist or revolutionary?

The SNCC cadre transformed itself from an interracial group using nonviolent resistance in the cause of civil rights to a militant elite openly advocating African-American separatism. In October 1964 ten SNCC members returned from Guinea, Africa, where they had been guests of the Marxist president, Sekou Touré. Their advocacy of separatism led to a schism between moderates and revolutionaries from which SNCC never really recovered. At a SNCC staff meeting in Waveland, Mississippi, in November 1965, Courtland Cox wrote on the blackboard: "Get power for black people. The people want power, power to control the courthouse, power to control their own lives." James Forman then added, "Power, Education, Organization." Nevertheless, the schism in SNCC was such that in 1965 it proved impossible for SNCC to launch a significant summer program. Robert Moses simply withdrew and, to emphasize his departure, took his mother's name as Robert Parris.

"Black Power"—the phrase coined so memorably by Paul Robeson in the wake of the Little Rock crisis of 1957—became a potent rallying cry in 1966 following a second crisis around James Meredith. Meredith, having gained entrance to the University of Mississippi at Oxford in 1962, now tried to encourage African-Americans to claim their legitimate right and register to vote by demonstrating that it was safe for them to do so. He decided to walk to the state capitol but was shot and badly wounded by an assassin, Aubrey James Norrell, and was too weak to continue. Both Martin Luther King and Stokely Carmichael went immediately to Mississippi to continue the march Meredith had started. This was done in part as a gesture toward solidarity in the civil rights movement. Early on, one of Carmichael's adherents, Willie Ricks, a young member of SNCC, used the phrase "black power" in Yazoo City, Mississippi. Stokely Carmichael appropriated it and made it popular.

The march by Martin Luther King and Stokely Carmichael in place of the wounded Meredith ended at Canton, Mississippi, on June 24, 1966. The police there refused to allow African-American marchers to pitch their tents in a schoolyard playground. However, twenty-five hundred marchers were determined not to abide by the police ruling. When it seemed that Martin Luther King had agreed to accept the police decision, SNCC abandoned him. He was no longer the acknowledged leader —although, of course, SNCC had originally developed out of Martin

Luther King's own SCLC. SNCC was also abandoning the old guard. For example, SNCC leaders refused to take part in a rally organized by the NAACP in Jackson, Mississippi, and scheduled for June 1966. Under pressure from A. Philip Randolph and Bayard Rustin, Stokely Carmichael agreed to cooperate with the NAACP, but only temporarily. Then, he himself was succeeded as chairman of SNCC by a more extreme separatist, H. Rap Brown.

In CORE the contest between traditional civil rights and black power took the form of a power struggle between James Farmer and Floyd McKissick. James Farmer was married to a white woman and was fully committed to integration politics and nonviolent strategy. Floyd McKissick was a lawyer from North Carolina who held more militant views. He became CORE national director in 1965 but was succeeded in his term by the radical separatist Roy Innes in 1968. Two years earlier CORE had endorsed the philosophy of black power.

The African-American protest movement had once been a mainly southern and integrated, Christian and optimistic movement working for civil rights. Now it was a largely northern, urban, secular, and militant movement favoring black power. The movement was now far more radical in purpose and militant in tactics than anything envisioned only ten years earlier.

Stokely Carmichael and political scientist Charles V. Hamilton projected their particular concept in *Black Power: The Politics of Liberation in America* (1967):

[Black Power] is a call for black people in this country to unite, to recognize their heritage, to build a sense of community. It is a call for black people to begin to define their goals, to lead their organizations and to support those organizations. It is a call to reject the racist institutions and values of this society. The concept . . . rests on a fundamental premise: *Before a group can enter the open society, it must first close ranks.* By this we mean that group solidarity is necessary before a group can operate effectively from a bargaining position of strength in a pluralistic society.

Among newly elected congressmen sympathetic to black power were John Conyers of Detroit and Ronald V. Dellums of Oakland, California. Congressman Adam Clayton Powell of Harlem also used the phrase "black power" to emphasize the significance of his break from Lyndon Johnson and the Democrats. Labor unrest among African-Americans led to the formation of the Dodge Revolutionary Union Movement (DRUM) in Detroit and the United Black Brothers of Mahway Ford Plant in New

Jersey and culminated in the creation of the League of Revolutionary Black Workers. This new militant pose among African-Americans was rejected by orthodox unions such as the United Auto Workers as an attitude fostered by "black fascists" and compared with the subversion of Communist cadres in the 1940s. In Memphis Martin Luther King helped organize thirteen hundred black sanitation workers in Local 1773 in their 1968 strike for higher wages and better terms.

At this time, black power was more a declaration of no confidence in the political strategy of nonviolent civil rights than an assertion of black nationalism. It was perhaps the very allusive nature of the slogan of black power that accounted for its wide appeal to unfulfilled workers, radicals, and the unemployed. Moreover, it provided a rod for all African-Americans adopting orthodox ideologies, whether of the right or the left, with which to beat traditional civil rights organizations who, they might claim, had sold them short of true equality.

This was all ironic. For it was the very victories of the civil rights movement that provided a social and political basis for the renewal of black nationalism. There were various contributory factors to this phenomenon, including desire by African-Americans to control their own economic and political destiny; group solidarity in the face of white ethnocentricity; resistance toward confinement in a lower caste; rejection of cultural assimilation within a white majority; and ethnic pride.

Civil rights activists of the traditional school spared no invective to denounce the new slogan and the school of thought it represented. In its editorial for June-July 1966 the *Crisis* explained how "in a pluralist society the slogan 'black power' is as unacceptable as 'white supremacy.' Moreover, it is fantastic to believe that so disadvantaged a minority [as African-Americans] can surmount the polarized opposition of an entrenched and powerful majority." In one editorial, "On Learning What the White Boys Learn," for May 1969, the *Crisis* used especially grim invective and insisted that "the basic problem of the ghetto will not be solved by courses in 'black studies.'" The old guard of civil rights issued a public statement of their policy, "Crisis and Commitment," and it ran in almost every African-American-owned newspaper, including the *Crisis,* for November 1966, and in the *New York Times.* It was signed by Bayard Rustin, Roy Wilkins, Whitney Young, Dorothy Height (president of the National Council of Negro Women), Marion E. Bryant (president of the National Association of Negro Business and Professional Women's Clubs), and Bishop Carey A. Gibbs of the AME Church. However, most significantly, it was not signed by Martin Luther King, Jr. The statement rejected the advocates of black power as immature products of bitterness and frustration and praised the loyalty of African-American soldiers fighting in Vietnam.

The group most associated with black power were the Black Panthers. The Black Panthers, founded in Oakland, California, by Huey Newton and Bobby Seale in 1966 and later led by Ron Karenga, comprised a self-proclaimed revolutionary black nationalist movement dedicated to African-American self-defense. Originally roused by concern about police harassment of African-Americans in urban ghettos, the Panthers formed groups of vigilantes who patrolled ghettos with guns. They achieved a bizarre radical chic with claims that they controlled institutions in African-American areas, demanding African-American juries and African-American exemption from military service as belated compensation for centuries of exploitation. Espousing an unformed, vague Marxist philosophy, the Panthers, together with the largely white Peace and Freedom party, in 1968 promoted Eldridge Cleaver, Panther minister of education, as their presidential candidate on a platform of social revolution. By the early 1970s the Panthers had between one thousand and two thousand members. In 1972 Eldridge Cleaver, who favored revolution by violence if this was the only way it could be achieved, split with Huey Newton and Bobby Seale, who preferred reform by peaceful means. At one point Cleaver jumped bail in Los Angeles in 1968 and fled to Cuba. After sojourns in Algeria, North Korea, and France, he returned to the United States in 1975 to face criminal charges. By the mid-1970s, having lost many members and fallen out with various African-American leaders, Bobby Seale and Huey Newton, who also had had significant brushes with the law, preferred to concentrate on providing social services in African-American neighborhoods. J. Edgar Hoover, director of the FBI, called the Panthers "the most dangerous and violent prone of all extremist groups." Yet the irony about cries for black power was that, despite the threat to use it, in reality there was none.

Although black power accomplished only minimal changes to political institutions, it succeeded in revolutionizing the cultural and intellectual attitudes not only of African-Americans but also of whites. Whereas African-Americans and liberal whites came to think it insulting to describe Negroes as black men before 1968, it was rank insult to call them anything but black for about twenty years thereafter.

The concept of the black aesthetic was much discussed by literary critics in such journals as *Dasein Dasein* (1961–1969), *Negro Digest* (1942–1951, 1961–1970), subsequently retitled *Black World* (1970–1976), and *Black Scholar* (since 1969). Discussion became controversial on the issue of whether black art could only be truly appreciated by blacks, whose sense of self was directly related to black communitarian values. Thus, in *The Black Aesthetic* (1971), Addison Gayle, Jr., declared,

The question for the black critic today is not how beautiful is a melody, a play, a poem, or a novel, but how much more beautiful has the poem, melody, play or novel made the life of a single black man? The Black Aesthetic, then, as conceived by this writer, is a corrective—a means of helping black people out of the polluted mainstream of Americanism.

When such writers as Chester Himes, Samuel R. Delany, and Ishmael Reed were reworking the conventional genres of, respectively, detective, science, and romantic fiction, they were also finding new ways to recover black experience. As critic A. Robert Lee says, "Blackness thus serves as both theme and means, an inescapable subject yet also a departure point for attempting new reaches of voice or, in author [James Alan] McPherson's phrase, 'fresh forms.'"

Some radicals disliked the idea of responsible African-American fiction, believing that the cause of civil rights would be better and more appropriately served by direct confessions in the form of autobiographies, diaries, and letters and essays that turned such varied but contingent experiences as prison, the ghetto, the nether world of hustling and drugs, and military service into overt political declarations. The most widely read and most plangent included James Baldwin's record of survival against racial odds in three books, *Notes of a Native Son* (1955), *Nobody Knows My Name* (1961), and *The Fire Next Time* (1963); Eldridge Cleaver's prison essays, *Soul on Ice* (1968); George Jackson's prison observations, *Soledad Brother* (1970); and the autobiographies of Martin Luther King, Huey Newton and Bobby Seale, Angela Davis, and Claude Brown. Most popular of all was *The Autobiography of Malcolm X* (1965), as told by Alex Haley. In his "Myth of a Negro Literature" in *Home: Social Essays* (1972), Imamu Amiri Baraka (LeRoi Jones) by implication praised the stark, uncompromising nature of this school of writing when he declared, "A Negro literature, to be a legitimate product of the Negro experience in America, must get at that experience in exactly the terms America has proposed for it, in its most ruthless identity."

Heightened awareness of the contribution of African-Americans to the history of the United States extended to material culture, notably painting, sculpture, and other art forms. In 1964 Bowdoin College mounted "The Portrait of the Negro in American Painting," which included sixty paintings mainly by white artists, drawn from the period 1715–1960. In 1974 the National Portrait Gallery in Washington mounted "The Black Presence in the Era of Revolution, 1770–1800."

In 1970 the Menil Foundation of Houston began an extensive research project in the documentation and interpretation of African-Americans in western art that led to its publication of four volumes on the subject, notably *The Image of the Black in Western Art: From the American Revolution to World War I,* by an English historian, Hugh Honour.

Vietnam—The Raven o'er the Infected House

Programs for civil rights through new legislation also faltered for another reason beyond the control of the movement. For the last two years of Lyndon Johnson's administration, the war in Vietnam (1961–1975) came to dominate American politics to the point that it precluded effective policy-making elsewhere. LBJ deepened and escalated a military commitment to uphold the republican government of South Vietnam— a policy implemented by his predecessor, John Kennedy.

John Kennedy had committed a modicum of troops to support the repressive regime of Ngo Dinh Diem in South Vietnam, engaged in civil war with those of his own people committed to reunion with North Vietnam under the Communist leadership of Ho Chi Minh. Kennedy believed that the war in Vietnam represented a symbolic battle for American security, since any movement of an aligned, or even neutral state in the third world was damaging to American influence. He and his military advisers and, subsequently, LBJ, rejected a neutral solution. By pursuing the elusive goal of a military solution to a political problem and overlooking the human, financial, and domestic consequences, Kennedy ensured the future escalation of the war and the final defeat of American forces.

American war strategy under LBJ was characterized by barbarousness, incompetence, and a debilitating sense of impending defeat. The tactics included wholesale bombings of villages in South Vietnam suspected of hiding Vietcong fighters; the use of toxic chemicals to defoliate large areas of forest; and a concern for the number of dead that superseded concern for territory captured and led to enthusiasm for a body count and special atrocities to achieve it. Thus such small villages as My Lai 4 had their shivering populations of old men, women, and children indiscriminately shot, bayoneted, or machine-gunned. The escalation of the war led to deep divisions of opinion within the United States in which the hard-line hawks, supporters of American involvement, believed that the failure to achieve victory was because the level of violence, especially by bombing, was too low. The doves, opponents of involvement, wondered if the United States was prepared to kill the people of Vietnam and their country in order to save them.

Just as television brought civil rights into the homes of millions of Americans and educated them about the issues, so it did with Vietnam. Once the conflict and slaughter in Vietnam and the protests against these activities at home were brought by television into people's living rooms, the great majority were revolted by what they witnessed and began to take the doves' arguments quite seriously. The result was open division within American society. It was openly recognized that American troops in Vietnam were thoroughly demoralized. The general collapse of discipline and morale was attested to by various forms of corruption, drug abuse, racial brawls, and fragging attacks on officers. Thus in February and March 1968, according to opinion polls, public support for the war in the United States declined from 60 percent to 40 percent and opposition rose from 25 percent to 40 percent.

Of African-American response to the war, historian Richard Polenberg observes, "Vietnam served as a crucible in which racial nationalism hardened and congealed." Very few African-Americans supported the war. A Gallup public opinion poll in Spring 1971 disclosed that 83 percent of African-Americans (compared with 67 percent of whites) believed that America had erred in sending soldiers to Vietnam in the first place. SNCC leaders consistently opposed the war and in January 1966 they delivered a joint condemnation of the draft. African-American leaders were under pressure from their followers to oppose the war, especially on account of the inequalities of the draft. Very few young African-Americans could secure a deferment to complete college. African-American casualties in the war were almost twice those of whites in

The earnest side of Robert Kennedy captured at a press conference. Considered the natural heir apparent of the Kennedy clan and unofficial leader of liberal Democrats after the assassination of JFK, he broke with LBJ, left the administration, and was elected as senator for New York. His belated bid for the 1968 Democratic presidential nomination warmed his admirers but worried detractors, who believed he was unfairly cutting in upon the radical territory carved so successfully by Senator Eugene McCarthy of Wisconsin on an antiwar, civil rights platform. His own assassination immediately after winning the California primary sent the Kennedy dream of power into eclipse. (*U.S. News and World Report;* Library of Congress.)

relation to their respective populations. This particular cause for opposition was reinforced by African-Americans' general suspicion that the war was exhausting resources better needed in America itself.

The National Black Antiwar, Antidraft Union was organized by Gwendolyn Patton, who was perhaps the first significant African-American activist to link the cause of black nationalism to radical white thought, such as Marxist theory. The war seemed an imperialist adventure by whites against nonwhites. Thus it struck a responsive chord of opposition for an ethnic group who had experienced slavery and institutionalized racism. One poster banner angrily displayed at protest rallies read "No Vietnamese Ever Called Me Nigger."

The sense of alienation felt by African-Americans toward the United States grew stronger with the passage of time. In the case of African-American servicemen, experience of Vietnam at first hand only served to intensify their hostility to it. A survey in 1970 discussed by Wallace Terry II in "Bringing the War Home" for *Black Scholar* of November 1970 disclosed that "more than half of the enlisted men objected to taking part in the war because they believe it is a race war pitting whites against non-whites or because they flatly don't want to fight against dark-skinned people."

American involvement in Vietnam produced a cauldron of seething discontent. The whirlwind of protest it aroused began to draw together the implacable resentment of the unfulfilled civil rights movement and the unbridled energy of student disaffection. All these diverse elements profoundly affected the shift in African-American protest from civil rights to black power.

BBC radio producer Daniel Snowman asked if the various protest movements of the 1960s—civil rights, student activism, and antiwar opposition—were in any true sense united left-wing movements? He answered his question with a qualified no. The three forms of protest were not strictly contemporaneous. The African-American and student protest movements came before opposition to the war had coalesced. All sporadic attempts to draw them together failed. However, there was considerable overlap between their personnel and their tactics. The leader of the Berkeley Free Speech Movement, Mario Savio, and his allies, had been educated and radicalized by the civil rights movement, as had Tom Hayden of SDS. For their part, African-American leaders, such as Martin Luther King, were quite outspoken in their opposition to the war. Moreover, it was the war in Vietnam that united various threads in the movement in determination to change the system and thus provided them with a focal point.

Ever greater funds spent on the war meant that there must be fewer resources for domestic reforms. In addition, American involvement in Vietnam was crudely, but widely, characterized as a metaphor of white racial exploitation. As ever more of the violence and slaughter was carried by television into the homes of millions of Americans, viewers, including radicals, were becoming educated about the uses of violence. Thus impoverished African-Americans, returning veterans, and angry students came to appreciate that the more hostile, even violent their reaction, the more likely they were to receive attention.

Bloody Thoughts with Violent Pace

The series of long, hot summers continued the tide of riot and uprising. In 1967 there were uprisings in at least sixty-five cities in some thirty-two states in which eighty-eight people were killed. One of the most serious was in Newark, New Jersey, where the municipal authorities had long been indifferent to such chronic ghetto problems as high unemployment and shortage of housing. Suddenly their plans to demolish about fifty acres of slums in order to construct a new medical school led to five days of rioting from July 12, 1967. The uprising left twenty-five people dead and another 725 injured; 1,462 people were arrested; damage to property was estimated at about $15 million.

Perhaps the worst riot of all occurred in Detroit, beginning on July 23, 1967, when police raided an illegal African-American drinking club in the west side ghetto. The riot lasted five days. Governor George Romney of Michigan could not keep the peace and requested federal troops from the president. It took two airborne divisions to restore order, by which time forty-three people were dead. The press originally discussed the deaths in Detroit as the work of snipers. This was the way police treated those arrested. The *Detroit News* of July 26, 1967, declared that "Negro snipers turned a 169 square block area north of West Grand Boulevard into a bloody battle-ground last night." The truth was that the immediate and essential cause of the Detroit riot was the police. Relations between police and African-Americans had been hostile ever since the white race riot of 1943. Police were used to dealing with African-Americans as potential criminals and certainly as adversaries. The immediate cause of the 1967 riot was police harassment of the illegal speakeasy and local resistance to the police. It spread into a looting riot. The carnival atmosphere turned sour and the first victim was a white looter shot by a Syrian-American store owner. The riot provided a first-class opportunity for African-Americans to retaliate against a law enforcement that seemed inimical to them. Despite orders not to move close in and arrest looters, the police did move in and fired at thieves running away.

Various investigations were conducted into the uprisings and riots. All condemned white society for its racism and perfidy. Thus the investigation into the Watts riot of 1965 conducted on behalf of Governor Edmund G. ("Pat") Brown of California by John McCone, former director of the CIA, led to a report that emphasized despair in the ghetto caused by a vicious spiral of economic failure and the feelings of lassitude and helplessness it generated among African-Americans who had come to Los Angeles since 1945. McCone and his panel criticized white ignorance of, and complacency toward, the abject condition of African-Americans. Since ghetto dwellers could take no pride in home ownership, ghetto arsonists did not regard destruction of homes or stores in the ghetto as self-destruction but, rather, as opportunistic warfare against the camps in which they had been interred by a hostile society. Some ghettos were badly served by public transport and thus ghetto dwellers felt enclosed, literally as well as metaphorically.

The inevitable political repercussion was the so-called white backlash in which the white middle and lower class insisted that African-Americans and their uprisings should be contained and quelled by various restrictive measures. Thus, instead of trying to address the causes of the uprisings, local authorities preferred to spend money on riot control by such means as armored cars and weapons for local police.

President Lyndon Johnson appointed a commission headed by Governor Otto Kerner of Illinois to investigate the causes of riot in 1967. Officially entitled the *Report of the National Advisory Commission on Civil Disorders* but generally known as the Kerner report, it was published on March 3, 1968. It eliminated any conspiracy theories. However, it conceded that certain militant African-American organizations sometimes helped fuel and light flames of disorder. Moreover, it also criticized the lawlessness and violence of the police as contributory factors, stoking the embers of resentment among African-Americans.

The commission had eleven members but only two of them were African-American. Such commissioners as Otto Kerner of Illinois, Mayor

John Lindsay of New York, and the police chief of Atlanta approached their great task with unusual insight and candor but received less acknowledgement than was their due. A Virginia congressman accused the commissioners of trying to shift the blame from "the rioters and on to decent, orderly, tax-paying, church-going people," which, of course, was what their words implied. Moreover, criticism was hurled at the commission's humane recommendations: construction of six million decent homes within five years; establishment of two million industrial and government jobs within three years; the creation of a humane nationwide public relief system providing a minimum income of $3,335 per annum for a family of four, of which 90 percent would be supplied by the federal government. These provisional solutions were less important to the commission than its persistent underlying theme of compassion: "The need is not so much for government to design new programs as it is for the nation to generate new will. Just as Lincoln a century ago put preservation of the Union above all else, so should we put creation of a true union—a single society and a single American identity—as our national goal."

Thus the commission's analysis was familiar. African-Americans were victimized by white society, which excluded them from full and equal participation unless they could attain rewarding employment. They could only achieve better employment through a better, higher form of education than their schools provided. "What white Americans have never fully understood—but what the Negro can never forget—is that white society is deeply implicated in the ghetto. White institutions created it, white institutions maintain it, and white society condones it."

The first riots had erupted before the slogan of black power was rediscovered. Moreover, there was no clear indication that separatists sought African-American political power through riot. Nevertheless, a psychic connection existed between the rhetoric of black power and the tumult of African-American uprising. The Kerner report suggested that the typical rioter was neither a criminal deviant nor the poorest, nor the least educated. The majority of rioters were between fifteen and twenty-four years old and had little respect for authority in their own families. These rioters were likely to be among the most alienated in the African-American community, keenly aware of their deprivation in comparison to whites and other African-Americans. Joe R. Feagin and Harlan Hahn concluded in their *Ghetto Revolt* (1971) that uprisings occurred at least in part because African-Americans had developed a "sense of black consciousness and a desire for a way of life with which they can feel the same pride and sense of potency they now derive from being black."

The Martyrdom of Martin Luther King

The course of violence disrupted the residual momentum of the civil rights movement. In Memphis, Tennessee, Martin Luther King experienced his worst setback in March 1968 when a march turned into a riot. Some young African-Americans threw Molotov cocktails and the police retaliated by firing into the crowd. King said in his sermon on March 31 in the National Cathedral in Washington, D.C., "If nothing else is done to raise ghetto hopes, I feel this summer will not only be as bad but worse than last time." Fearing that the substantive gains of civil rights were being compromised, if not actually subverted, by the riots and white reaction to them, Martin Luther King then embarked on a new strategy. This took the form of a Poor People's Campaign in Washington, D.C., concerned partly to draw the attention of Congress to the condition of the poor, and partly to restore the political credibility of the civil rights movement. King commented how it was no good being allowed to eat in a restaurant if you had no money to pay for a hamburger. His remark summed up his success in persuading white Americans of the rights of African-Americans to enter freely in all places of accommodation and the tragedy of poverty in the inner cities, which hitherto no one had been able to remedy.

Tragically, Martin Luther King was assassinated in Memphis, Tennessee, on April 4, 1968, by James Earl Ray, an escaped white convict. He fled to London, where he was captured in June 1968. In 1969 he was tried and convicted but for many years he would not reveal his motive, nor the source of his money, nor the means of his escape. Twenty years later it was openly alleged that he had been hired by certain agents in the FBI. Not only the deed itself but also the consequences of King's assassination were tragic. Although his murder prompted civic authorities, African-American churches, and civil rights organizations to work together to prevent further conflagrations in the cities, it deepened the white community's puritan horror of tumult and sharpened its determination to prevent further disturbances by purchase of an entire battery of riot-control equipment for troubled cities. Moreover, it removed the one African-American leader who could reconcile different African-American and white constituencies.

The new head of the SCLC, Rev. Ralph D. Abernathy, tried to continue the work of Martin Luther King in a camp beside the Reflecting Pool between the Washington Monument and the Lincoln Memorial. Known as "Resurrection City USA," it was, in essence, a shantytown, housing African-Americans, whites, and American Indians. Although whites sympathetic to their plight demonstrated in support of Resurrection City on June 14, 1968, twelve days later it was closed down by the police.

During his last month Martin Luther King often said how discouraged he was by the deep divisions within the civil rights movement, the overwhelming nature of the problems it was trying to address, and his own "weariness" and "bewilderment." He said that "people expect me to have answers and I don't have any answers." Thus he told one interviewer that he saw his "dream turning into a nightmare." Some historians find there were two different leaders in Martin Luther King: the optimistic crusader seeking full rights of citizenship on grounds of morality and the more mature, pessimistic, controversial, and uncertain politician who had come to realize that civil rights were not enough. This was the antiwar protester who predicted that "the bombs that you are dropping on Vietnam will explode at home in inflation and unemployment." In *The FBI and Martin Luther King, Jr.* (1981) David J. Garrow argues that, in his last years, King was a real, and not just an imaginary threat to the establishment, having become so radical in his views as to be a somewhat revolutionary figure.

The martyrdom of Martin Luther King undoubtedly helped canonize this single-minded advocate of civil rights. Within sixteen years of his death Congress determined that his birthday would be celebrated as a public holiday nationwide—an honor only previously afforded George Washington, the president who was the father of his country, and Abraham Lincoln, the president who had saved the Union. Historian Gary Wills believes that the 1960s Age of Aquarius belonged more truly to Martin Luther King than it did to John Kennedy or Lyndon Johnson. Whatever their continuing difficulties, African-American citizens could now move freely in places of public accommodation and claim their right to vote and to equal, desegregated education—all achievements of the Second American Revolution headed by the remarkable Baptist minister.

Nevertheless, there was a fascinating irony pointed out by the novelist Walker Percy, who commented that Dr. King actually did more to liberate southern whites than blacks. What Walker Percy meant was that desegregation was, in time, more economical, more cost effective than continued segregation. It was obviously cheaper to have one school system, one hospital system, than two, and the scale of economy descended all the way down to drinking fountains. Moreover, when southern whites realized that desegregation had never been a true threat because they still had control of the economy, they could abort their absurd obsession with race and channel their energies into their own interests.

The assassination of Martin Luther King and the riots that ensued in various cities gave momentum to final voting in Congress for the Civil Rights Protection Act of 1968. Originally conceived to provide protection to civil rights workers and people exercising their right to vote, to work, and to use public places, its character was altered by one amendment proposed during congressional discussion. This prohibited discrimination in the sale or rental of housing and the provision was intended to extend to 80 percent of all housing. However, the government's attempts to eliminate discrimination in housing were far more sporadic than had been the case with schooling and voting. Moreover, the Housing and Urban Development Act of 1968 attempted to ban discrimination in the sale or rental of housing by eradicating unfair practices by realtors, landlords, and bankers. Moreover, on the assumption that about six million subsidized units would be constructed over a ten-year period, the federal government required builders who had federal subsidies or mortgage guarantees to establish marketing plans aimed at affirmative-action opportunities. This would have had considerable force since, by 1971, one in every four new domestic units was constructed with government finances whereas twenty years earlier the ratio had been one in twenty.

In 1969 George Romney, secretary of housing, began Operation Breakthrough, an attempt to open the suburbs to people on low incomes, including African-Americans. Thus when Warren, a suburb of Detroit, applied for federal money for urban renewal, Romney made it clear that the availability of federal funds would be directly related to Warren's willingness to accept a low-income project.

However, the powers of the federal government were far more restricted when it came to desegregating houses than had been the case with schools. As Nathan Glazer remarked in *Affirmative Discrimination* (1975), "People are not assigned to housing by central bureaucratic

In contrast to the vocal fireworks and the fisticuffs of the Democrats, the Republican National Convention of August 1968 in Miami was a routine affair in which Richard Nixon (*lower left*) rose without trace to claim the presidential nomination, taking the ultraconservative Spiro Agnew, governor of Maryland, as his running mate. It was not known then that Agnew, most vocal in his denunciation of radical dissent, was defrauding the American people by evading due income tax payments, nor could it have been predicted that Nixon's insatiable lust to retain power would propel his staff into the illegal acts of the Watergate affair that would undermine the fabric of government itself. Federal support for civil rights went into eclipse. Standing above Nixon and Agnew is Congressman Gerald Ford of Michigan, House minority leader and a cautious voice of reason who would, without election, succeed, first, Agnew in 1973, then Nixon in 1974, when public exposure sent the two malefactors into political oblivion. (*U.S. News and World Report;* Library of Congress.)

institutions as they are assigned to schools." Although such institutions as universities and schools, corporations and contractors might depend upon federal funds, suburban communities did not. When the government threatened to cut off funds for constructing water pipes and sewer pipes, citizens called its bluff and remained immovable. Opposition to Romney's strategies reached such a pitch of intensity that the administration of Richard Nixon (1969–1974) felt obligated to renounce policies intended to achieve suburban integration.

Miami and the Siege of Chicago

Few administrations ended with such a loss of popularity as did that of Lyndon Johnson. The inconclusive, enervating, and sordid war in Vietnam, compounded by the administration's blatant deceits about the true state of affairs in Indochina, broke public trust in Johnson. This sorry situation was aggravated by LBJ's incorrigible defensiveness, secretiveness, and resistance to criticism, constructive as well as destructive.

In the primary campaigns for the presidency in 1968 Senator Eugene McCarthy of Wisconsin rallied a group of youthful antiwar protestors and challenged LBJ in the Democratic primary in New Hampshire. In the event he secured a majority of New Hampshire delegates to the Democratic National Convention. His success, coming immediately after the Tet offensive of February 1968, prompted Senator Robert Kennedy of New York to announce his own candidacy and Lyndon Johnson to announce that he would not seek the nomination.

Democratic bosses across the nation were discovering just how widespread was the alienation from the party felt by many Democrats. The traditional economic ties between Democrats and the party had been loosened by their economic prosperity and yet they were increasingly critical of the quality of American life, especially the reluctance of politicians to take effective action on the vexed issues of Vietnam, civil rights, poverty, and law and order. The assassination of Robert Kennedy by Jordanian immigrant Sirhan Sirhan in Los Angeles on the night of June 5, 1968, left Eugene McCarthy the apparent first choice of most Democrats. However, it was Vice President Hubert Humphrey who had the greater number of delegates at the Democratic National Convention in Chicago.

Events inside the convention hall proved of far less interest than the tumult outside. A large crowd of student radicals, advocates of civil rights and black power, hippies, yippies, and antiwar protesters had come to make their opposition to boss politics, the conventional bourgeois wisdom, and establishment rules plain. Police control of the demonstrators deteriorated into riot on the streets as the police used gas, truncheons, and mass arrests to disperse the demonstrators. The upshot of the police riot was widespread concern about the government's ability to maintain law and order. There was also wide dissatisfaction with the nomination of Hubert Humphrey inside the convention hall, and the procedures by which it had been achieved. Moreover, the police riot provided Humphrey with an impossible initial handicap.

By comparison, the Republican National Convention in Miami was dull but orderly. Front runner Richard Nixon managed to deflect a threat from Governor Ronald Reagan of California by enticing Reagan's southern supporters by what was called "the Southern Strategy"—a promise to reverse Supreme Court decisions on civil rights in the South.

The unusual element in the actual presidential campaign was the formation of an American Independent party by renegade southern Democrats around Governor George C. Wallace of Alabama, now widely known for his opposition to civil rights. The platform opposed increasing federal control of states' affairs, desegregation, and greater racial tolerance and it promised to enforce greater law and order. The Republicans decried Wallace on account of his small size and pretentiousness and, in parody of Johnson's initials, LBJ, referred to Wallace as the "little bitty judge." Thus, the presidential election of 1968 offered voters a choice of three political survivors of an earlier period—Democrat Hubert Humphrey, Republican Richard Nixon, and Independent George Wallace. In the narrow election victory of Richard M. Nixon in November it was impossible not to see that the most tumultuous period in American social history since the Civil War was about to draw to a close.

7

Chaos Is Come Again

With the inauguration of Richard Nixon as president in 1969, the sympathy African-American rights had attracted in the Kennedy and Johnson years seemed to evaporate. Nixon's hard-hearted approach to student demonstrations and civil rights activists was designed to exploit the white backlash against violent protests. He made it clear that he would not actively promote the doctrine of racial equality or the programs of the Great Society. Nevertheless, Richard Nixon did promote some advances for civil rights by way of job opportunities, including goals and timetables for all companies doing business with the federal government, as well as continuing to promote the dismantling of dual school systems in the South.

A Silent Majority

While the majority of Americans were profoundly troubled by the war in Vietnam, the vexed state of race relations, urban problems, and poverty, they did not often agree with the remedies proposed by the New Left: immediate withdrawal from Indochina; a system of redistributive taxes; and the busing of school children. The most significant political alliance of the late 1960s and thereafter was the union of the populist "silent majority" of middle Americans from the Protestant South or Catholic ethnic groups in the Northeast and Midwest with the conservative plutocracy of the great corporations. Both were indifferent to social problems. Liberals had erroneously thought they could eradicate segregation in the South without changing American society as a whole, notably its political institutions and social relations. When they became aware of their mistake, they tried to eliminate discrimination and poverty in the North, also without disturbing the status quo. Thus they lost the trust of the white majority. The electoral victories of Republican presidential nominee Richard Nixon in 1968 and 1972 on behalf of a conservative elite were not an aberration from the continuous procession of victories for liberal presidents starting with Franklin Delano Roosevelt in 1932. Kevin Philips argued in *The Emerging Republican Majority* (1969) that the Democratic majority bound by the Great Depression and the New Deal was being transformed into a natural Republican majority. This was partly on account of sociological factors in which a new suburban middle class was developing from new immigrant and working-class stock who had passed from the depression of poverty through the threshold of comfort. It was also partly due to more general geographic and demographic factors, with the development of sunbelt cities and suburbs from Florida and the South across Texas and the Southwest and thence to southern California. The advocates of corporate planning for welfare, argued Kevin Philips, were just as much a self-perpetuating oligarchy as the financiers and industrialists of the 1920s.

Kevin Philips described the confusions of many Americans and their response thus:

They have at least temporarily become conservatives, in the sense of believing that they are more likely to lose than to gain from social change. The economic issues that now concern them most, inflation and high taxes, reinforce their social conservatism. More deeply, they are disturbed by the challenges to the system of values that has guided their lives.

Hippies and black militants, drug addicts, mafiosi, "welfare mothers"—are perceived as transgressors against the moral verities that have always been accepted by most Americans, poor as well as rich, and middle class, black as well as white.

Other analysts differed from Kevin Philips about the precise origins of the new majority but all agreed that it now existed as a potent political force for retrenchment.

One of the prime means by which the American people had been made forcibly aware of great moral issues was extensive television coverage of such tumultuous events as civil rights demonstrations, African-American uprisings, antiwar protests, and, not least, party conventions —on all of which there was extensive coverage in the summer of 1968. In spring 1969 there was a marked shift in news coverage of such events by television networks. This was partly because of the great expense of elaborate news coverage, partly because of a change in atmosphere among television policy makers. They now regretted their earlier emphasis on tumult, knowing that they had moved too far ahead, or to the side of, their viewers' immediate interests. There was also an element of self-censorship in restricting coverage of disorder. Vice President Spiro Agnew's criticisms of the media were intended to persuade them to restrict their coverage of dissent and they succeeded in doing just that.

In federal politics Richard Nixon generally proved unequal to the task of congressional liaison, where his predecessor, Lyndon B. Johnson, had been most successful. Altogether, there were very few concrete legislative proposals from Nixon until January 1971, when the president announced "Six Great Goals," of which only one, revenue sharing between the federal government and the states, was widely accepted, and only then after much modification. Although the Republicans sometimes claimed that it was under one of their own and not a Democratic administration that school segregation was being broken in the South, it was largely despite the efforts of the Nixon administration. Journalist Godfrey Hodgson, referring to the busing controversy and its outcome, observes that "it happened because the Nixon administration lost a battle to prevent its happening, and so failed to keep a pledge to prevent its happening."

Education from Brown to Busing and Bakke

In 1972 Secretary of Health, Education and Welfare Elliot Richardson disclosed statistics that implied, first, that the discredited dual school system in the South existed no longer and, second, that a century of legal segregation was drawing to a close. In 1960 two million, over two-thirds, of African-American school children in the South had attended exclusively African-American schools. In 1972 only three hundred thousand, about 10 percent, did so. Thus the proportion of African-American children who attended schools with a majority of white children rose from below a fifth in 1968 to over two-fifths in 1972. Furthermore, Elliot Richardson noted that in the South fewer African-American chil-

African-American capitalism. Lee Sampson of Alliance Venture, Inc., a prosperous citizen of the African-American middle class, surveys his domain. (Photograph taken for *U.S. News and World Report*, by D. Dornan; November 10, 1970; Library of Congress.)

dren, absolutely and proportionately, attended segregated schools than in the rest of the country. Thus it seemed that the South was accepting and complying with the Supreme Court's ruling in the *Brown* case of 1954.

Although enforced legal school segregation in the South was disappearing, de facto segregation, based on residential distribution, on where African-American and white families actually lived, remained virtually intact. Thus the percentage of African-American school children attending schools that were 80 percent or more African-American in the North and the West fell only marginally, from 69.7 percent in 1968 to 68.3 percent in 1971.

What kept the issue of education to the fore was the consistent and rigorous attitude of the Supreme Court. During the period when civil rights was out of favor, it was the Court that kept the torch of reform aflame. Maintaining its original decision in the *Brown* case, the Supreme Court ruled in the case of *Green* v. *County School Board of New Kent County* (1968) that the school board in New Kent County, Virginia, must assign children to particular schools in the interests of integration rather than continue a policy of allowing parents freedom of choice between two schools—a practice that simply continued de facto segregation. In *Alexander* v. *Holmes County Board of Education* (1969) the Supreme Court ruled further that Mississippi school districts must abolish dual systems at once and, if necessary, defy parental choice and assign students to particular schools to achieve integration. The Court ruled unanimously against further delay. Chief Justice Warren Burger declared that "the obligation of every school district is to terminate dual school systems at once and to operate now and hereafter only unitary schools."

It was in the case of *Swann* v. *Charlotte-Mecklenberg Board of Education,* decided on April 20, 1971, that the Court turned to busing of school children as a legitimate tool to achieve integration. The case concerned a large district in North Carolina extending thirty-six miles long and twenty-two miles wide with 107 schools and eighty-four thousand students. In theory parents could choose where to send their children to school. De facto segregation remained intact in practice because in this locality African-Americans, who accounted for 29 percent of the local population, lived mainly in one particular section of Charlotte. The Court was adamantly opposed to de facto segregation. Therefore, it proposed application of mathematical ratios to determine a suitable balance between the races and the use of buses to achieve this balance despite any expense or inconvenience involved. Busing entailed collective traveling of some white children to schools in "black" localities and of African-American children to "white" localities. The only point at which busing could be considered counterproductive was if it was over such long distances that the schoolchildren's health would suffer.

In 1970 the Detroit Board of Education had devised and adopted a scheme to distribute African-American and white American children more equitably by revising attendance zones. It was blocked by the state. Moreover, members of the school board who supported the scheme were made subject to recall and voted out of office. The NAACP then fielded the case of *Bradley* v. *Milliken* to show that public schools in Detroit were segregated by race. When the case reached the U.S. District Court, Judge Stephen Roth ruled on September 27, 1971, that the Detroit school system was segregated, a result of unconstitutional proceedings by the city school board and by the state. The following March Judge Roth went further. He declared that no plan specifically limited to

Detroit could, in itself, eliminate segregation and that, in order to achieve desegregation, it would be necessary to devise a plan for the three counties surrounding Detroit that would assign students to particular schools and would schedule busing. In June 1972 he instructed a panel to provide plans for integrating the Detroit school system with those of fifty-three suburban districts. The premise of his ruling was upheld by the Court of Appeals, which declared, "Big city school systems for blacks surrounded by suburban school systems for whites cannot represent equal protection of the law." However, because Judge Roth had not heard all the school districts whose fate he decided upon, the Court of Appeals ruled against the practical application of his decision.

The thrust of Supreme Court decisions toward busing to achieve desegregation aroused a momentous tide of opposition from people of many classes. Sometimes the tide of resentment erupted into violence. In fall 1971 opponents of busing in Pontiac, Michigan, seized and burned buses. This came only ten years after buses carrying freedom riders in the South had been set alight. It seemed to the media an ominous sign that racist attitudes once indissolubly associated with the lily-white South had now spread nationwide. Busing proved a potent election issue and undoubtedly contributed to the ease with which presidential aspirant George C. Wallace won the Democratic primary in Florida in early 1972. By fall both House and Senate passed laws against busing and some people even proposed a constitutional amendment against it. In June 1972, exhausted by ceaseless arguments and various forms of political pressure put upon them by their constituents, congressmen decided to compromise. No busing rulings decided by a court would be implemented until 1974, except wherever all subsequent appeals had been exhausted.

Nixon had two strategies towards busing. The first was to appropriate and use it for putative political advantage in 1972, the year he was seeking reelection. The second was to ensure that his pronouncements combined the contrary principles of desegregation in the interests of liberal credibility across the world and of opposition to busing on the grounds of realpolitik at home. In an extensive message to Congress on March 1972 he announced his commitment to "give practical meaning to the concept of equal educational opportunity" while giving less prominence to "busing as a tool for achieving equal educational opportunity." Nixon then proposed an Equal Educational Opportunities Act to establish new criteria for equality of opportunity and a Student Transportation Moratorium Act to bring an end to busing until the issue could be resolved by a due federal law, even by a constitutional amendment.

The public furor against busing was so intense that few politicians could hope to remain unscathed. In Detroit no candidate who supported busing survived the primary elections in August 1972. The South exaggerated the issue and seethed with rage as feverishly as it had during cases of token integration in the early 1950s. Some whites put their children in private schools and some moved to the suburbs. Hence, initially, the percentage of white children in public schools in the cities fell by 10 percent. Nevertheless, although resentment smoldered and occasionally burst into flame, children and parents came to accept busing, albeit most reluctantly.

Busing was so controversial an issue in the early 1970s that it roused academics to reconsider the various other issues associated with the 1960s ideal of integrated education.

At the Harvard School of Education David Armor conducted a study of Project Metro, the plan for busing African-American children from Roxbury, a Boston ghetto, into white schools in the neighboring suburbs. After three years of research David Armor published his findings in "The Evidence on Busing" for *The Public Interest* in 1972. He concluded that busing did not enhance self-esteem and achievement among African-Americans, improve race relations, or expand opportunities for better education. "The available evidence . . . indicates that busing is *not* an effective policy instrument for raising the achievements of blacks or for increasing interracial harmony." Armor went further and implied that liberals were so intent on promoting their own point of view that they did not always heed their own findings. Armor's conclusions were so controversial that he brought down upon himself the ire of the academic world, including four Harvard professors who accused him of distorting evidence.

Not all the criticism of busing was motivated by conservatism or racism. In their study of inequality and the public school system, *Inequality* (1972), written from a radical perspective, Charles Jencks and his coauthors criticized busing on practical and philosophical grounds. They believed busing achieved no discernible improvement in the education of African-American children. Rather, busing suggested how "all black schools are by definition inferior. This position strikes me as both racist and politically untenable over the long haul." Jencks urged abandoning school as the prime access to social equality and substituting other, more direct routes. "As long as egalitarians assume that public policy cannot contribute to economic equality directly, but must proceed by ingenious manipulation of marginal institutions like the schools, progress will remain glacial."

Frederick Mosteller, a professor of math statistics at Harvard, and Daniel Patrick Moynihan were coeditors of a collection of Harvard papers that included contributions from professors Thomas Pettigrew, David Armor, and Christopher Jencks. One conclusion of the Mosteller-Moynihan Report was that because differences in quality among schools across the United States attended by different children were fewer than previously supposed, then the United States was closer to achieving its goal of equality in terms of educational opportunity than anyone had realized.

The nation entered the middle third of the twentieth century bound to the mores of caste and class. The white race was dominant. . . . Education beyond a fairly rudimentary point was largely determined by social status.

In a bare third of a century these circumstances have been extensively changed. *Changed!* Not merely a sequence of events drifting in one direction or another. On the contrary, events have been bent to the national will.

The notion that spending ever greater sums on education was not achieving goals of equality in education was grist to the mill of conservatives who thought federal spending on education generally was, at 7 percent of the cost of schooling, too high anyway. Congressman Albert Quie of Minnesota believed that the arguments against spending to redress inequality were made on dubious grounds because funds intended for compensatory education had been siphoned away to middle-class schools. Nevertheless, the Jencks interpretation was cited by Nixon's team to justify budget cuts in education for 1974.

In the *Rodriguez* case of 1974 the Supreme Court rejected a requirement that educational expenditure should be the same right across different school districts in the same state. The decision was made over the vehement minority dissent of Justice Thurgood Marshall.

However, the Court was obliged to act, and acted decisively, in the case of Alan Bakke, who in 1973 and 1974 had been refused entry to the medical school of the University of California at Davis. At that time the school reserved sixteen out of its total number of a hundred places for those it described as "disadvantaged students"—Chicanos, American Indians, and African-Americans. Bakke claimed, correctly, that he had a better academic record than some of the favored disadvantaged students. Thus he maintained that he had been denied equal protection of the law as guaranteed by the Fourteenth Amendment. This was also the opinion of the Supreme Court of California in 1976 and of the United States Supreme Court, which heard arguments in 1977 and announced its ruling on June 28, 1978. The Court ruled by five votes to four that the application of "explicit racial classification" to situations where there had been no indication of discriminatory behavior in the past was, indeed, a violation of the equal protection clause of the Fourteenth Amendment. Thus it ordered the University of California to admit Bakke to its medical school.

Nevertheless, the Court also ruled (again by five votes to four) that affirmative action procedures in which race was only one element in admissions were not in violation of the Fourteenth Amendment simply because universities had a legitimate right to make a goal of diversity in their student body. The Court's majority decision, written by Justice Lewis Powell, paid full tribute to arguments that affirmative action amounted to discrimination in reverse. Since white Americans comprised a whole variety of ethnic minorities and the majority of these could claim to have been victims of discrimination in the past, there was "no principal basis for deciding which groups would merit 'heightened judicial solicitude' and which would not." Moreover, preferential admissions policies reinforced stereotypes "that certain groups are unable to achieve success without special protection based on a factor having no relation to individual worth." Hence, they might aggravate existing ethnic and racial antagonisms, since "there is a measure of inequity in forcing innocent persons . . . to bear the burden of redressing grievances not of their making." Thus a "consistent application of the Constitution from one generation to the next" was possible only if civil rights were awarded to individual citizens rather than to entire racial groups.

Four justices dissented—William Brennan, Byron White, Thurgood Marshall, and Harry Blackmun. William Brennan spoke for this minority in his opinion that the Constitution had not been color blind in the past and that the United States could not "let color blindness become myopia which masks the reality that many 'created equal' have been treated within our lifetime as inferiors both by the law and by their fellow citizens." Certain racial distinctions were legitimate. When Congress had enacted the Civil Rights Bill of 1964 it had not been intended to stop "all race-conscious efforts to extend the benefits of federally financed programs to minorities who have been historically excluded

H. Rap Brown, militant leader of the SNCC in the late 1960s, caught here in full oratorical flight at a press conference. His confrontational rhetoric of African-American retaliation against whites provoked profound fear among the propertied classes. His teased Afro hairstyle, dark glasses, and coy miniscule bandage may have seemed unnecessary accoutrements of radical camp by the 1990s, but in the 1960s they implied a seductive, dangerous menace. (*U.S. News and World Report;* Library of Congress.)

from the full benefits of American life." It was precisely because the inability of minority students to meet conventional standards of admission "was due principally to the effects of past discrimination" that race-conscious procedures were not only acceptable but also necessary. While it was true that a duly qualified white candidate who was rejected suffered an injury, it was an injury "not distinguishable from disadvantages caused by a wide range of government programs."

The Gary Convention of 1972

While the silent majority of middle America was adopting an increasingly conservative attitude toward civil rights, the loose civil rights coalition was adopting increasingly radical positions, even as it was disintegrating as a coherent political entity.

In 1970 the African-American population was officially accounted 22,580,000, that is, 11.1 percent of the total population of the United States of 207,976,452 on the mainland and all outlying areas, although certain analysts believed that there was a serious underestimate of the black population by about 1.9 million. The African-American population was distributed as follows: 53 percent in the South; 39 percent in the North; and 8 percent in the West. As many as 16.8 million (74 percent) lived in metropolitan areas, of whom 13.1 million (58 percent) lived in central cities.

The cult of black separatism became more pronounced as African-Americans in the inner cities became increasingly disaffected from the white establishment. This alienation reflected a mood of deep pessimism across America about the system. It was reinforced by the emerging conflicts between integrationists and separatists. Nevertheless, a facade that there was still "one movement" survived into the 1970s. The Congressional Black Caucus (CBC), formed of the then nine African-American members of Congress, cooperated with nationalist leaders to initiate meetings in Gary, Indiana, in the early 1970s. Richard Hatcher, newly elected mayor of Gary, Indiana, called a meeting to determine a firm strategy to mobilize African-American voters and influence the Democratic party's leadership. The Northlake Illinois Conference of September 24–25, 1971, was probably the only instance after 1965 when representatives of almost every major wing of the civil rights and African-American movements came together. Delegates at this conference included Julian Bond of SNCC; CBC members Walter Fauntroy of

Washington, D.C., Augustus Hawkins of California, and John Conyers of Detroit; Vernon Jordan, leader of the Urban League; Roy Innes of CORE; and SCLC representative Andrew Young. They discussed and agreed upon a plan by Imamu Amiri Baraka (LeRoi Jones) for holding a major African-American independent political convention in early 1972, election year.

The result was the Gary Convention of March 10–11, 1972, the largest African-American political convention in American history. About three thousand official delegates attended, representing revolutionaries, nationalists, culturalists, integrationists, and religious leaders. About twelve thousand people altogether attended and it was chaired by Baraka, Hatcher, and Congressman Charles Diggs of Detroit. Jesse Jackson, one of Martin Luther King's aides, also attended, fresh from creating his PUSH (People United to Save Humanity) operation. The convention formed a National Black Political Assembly to help elect African-American mayors. Some leaders bitterly attacked the policy statements of the convention. Roy Wilkins did so before the actual convention was held. For the moment, the black nationalist faction was dominant at a time that analyst Manning Marable sees as "the zenith, not only of black nationalism, but of the entire black movement during the Second Reconstruction."

The central document of the National Black Political Assembly was the "Black Agenda," an aggressive, visionary pronouncement to be compared in fervor to the preamble of the Populists' reform platform announced in Omaha, Nebraska, in 1892. It is instructive to compare the statement by African-Americans of 1972 with the plaintive emotional appeal written by Ignatius Donnelly eighty years earlier. Donnelly declared uncompromisingly,

We meet in the midst of a nation brought to the verge of moral, political and material ruin.

The Pan-Africanists announced,

We come to Gary in an hour of great crisis and tremendous promise for Black America. While the white nation hovers on the brink of chaos, while its politicians offer no hope of real change, we stand on the edge of history and are faced with an amazing and frightening choice: we may choose in 1972 to slip back into the decadent white politics of American life, or we may press forward, moving relentlessly from Gary to the creation of our own black life. The choice is large but the time is very short. . . . The crises we face as black people are the crises of the entire society. They go deep, to the very bones and marrow, to the essential nature of America's economic, political, and cultural systems. They are the natural end-product of a society built on the thin foundations of white racism and white capitalism.

Although plenary sessions disclosed major differences on such controversial issues as school desegregation and busing and the liberation of Palestine, there was considerable euphoria at the prospect of black nationalism. Even such apostles of the conventional wisdom of integration as Coretta Scott King and Jesse Jackson joined the throng, calling out, with their hands upstretched, "Nationtime! Nationtime! Nationtime!"

It is possible to take a far more cynical view of the Gary Convention and see it as the final convulsion of a great political upheaval bereft of new ideas. The convention did not lack leaders but it was at war with itself and aware of its own disintegration and impotence.

Black Nationalism and Pan-Africanism

In the 1970s committed black nationalists were shifting allegiance from black power to Pan-Africanism. This was partly because militants were searching for a more precise definition that would tie their political and cultural aspirations to the historical relationship between African-Americans and blacks in Africa and the Caribbean. It was also in part a reaction against a realization that the American political establishment was bending the rhetoric and the ideology of black power to its own ends. After both President Richard Nixon and Edward Brooke, the African-American attorney general of Massachusetts, used and simplified "black power" to mean black capitalism, apparently within the hegemony of white capitalism, militants were determined to resist this most unwelcome appropriation of the term. Robert T. Bowen, founder of the Institute for Black Studies in Los Angeles, declared in his "Letter to Black Americans" for *Black World* of August 1970 how black power had moved "from a verbal dynamic to something short of a uniquely American joke. By now even the most outspoken elements of our people are fatigued with the diluted mystique of 'soul.'" In contrast, Pan-Africanism suggested a continuous struggle for racial equality across a world disturbed by colonialism, apartheid, and segregation.

However, both the Nixon administration and large white commercial companies, such as the Chase Manhattan Bank, genuinely wanted to encourage African-American capitalism. Whereas the number of banks owned by African-Americans doubled in the course of the 1960s, it doubled again from twenty-one to forty-five in the period 1970–1975. Between 1969 and 1972 the number of businesses owned by African-Americans rose from 163,073 to 194,986 and the number of workers they employed rose from an average of four to an average of six. Their gross income increased from $4.5 billion in 1969 to $7.5 billion in 1972. This was hardly on a par with businesses owned by whites since the business income of African-Americans accounted for only 1.7 percent of the gross income of all American businesses.

Manning Marable believes that the economic recession of 1969–1970 allowed employers the opportunity to expel thousands of African-American militants from the industrial work force. However, in the early 1970s many African-American union leaders, who had been conservatives only a few years before, began to voice radical opinions. In September 1972 they formed the Coalition of Black Trade Unionists at a conference in Chicago attended by twelve thousand African-American trade unionists from thirty-seven unions. The principal players were William Lacy, secretary-treasure of the American Federation of State, County, and Municipal Employees; Charles Hayes, vice president of Amalgamated Meatcutters; Cleveland Robinson, president of the National Afro-American Labor Congress; Bill Simons, president of Local 6 of the American Federation of Teachers in Washington, D.C.; and Nelson Jack Edwards, vice president of the United Auto Workers.

New scholarly organizations were founded to promote various forms of black nationalism. They included the National Conference of Black Studies and the African Heritage Studies Association, created in October 1969 at the annual conference of the African Studies Association in Montreal. Also in 1969 Nathan Hare and Robert Chrisman founded the *Black Scholar,* probably the most significant of the various new militant journals.

The most ambitious of the new creations was the Institute of the Black World. It grew from embryonic plans for an Institute for Advanced Afro-American Studies with some association with Atlanta University, conceived in 1967 by Professors Stephen Henderson and Vincent Harding, chairs, respectively, of the departments of English at Morehouse College and of history at Spelman College. After the assassination of Martin Luther King, his widow, Coretta Scott King, invited Vincent Harding to develop a King Library Documentation Center. Harding and his colleagues introduced his original concept of the Institute into the

King Center for a brief time and then created an independent research center, the Institute of the Black World (IBW). By fall 1969 the Institute's senior research staff included, besides Vincent Harding, the sociologist Joyce Ladner, the educator Chester Davis, and the historians Lerone Bennett, Jr., and Sterling Stuckey. Its most original theorist was political scientist William Strickland, who was deeply interested in applying socialist theory to the state of African-American culture and society. The IBW drew on the resources of a wide range of engaged African-American intellectuals to work both in its offices and in the field, notably Mary F. Berry, previously head of the education division of HEW, and Harry Heywood, a former Communist party member.

Advocates of black power did not necessarily lie to the left of the Democratic party. In 1972 Floyd McKissick, former director of CORE and perhaps second only to Stokely Carmichael as a champion of black power, made a tactical move toward support of Richard Nixon and the Republican party, possibly as part of his strategy to secure Nixon's support for his planned African-American community, Soul City in North Carolina. McKissick's newfound Republicanism and that of his associates prompted African-American critic Harold Wise to describe political maneuvering within the black power movement as nothing more or less than "Neo-Booker T. Washingtonism in disguise."

Stokely Carmichael played as crucial a part in the shift from black power to Pan-Africanism as he had in the earlier shift from civil rights to black power. In 1967 he had visited West Africa and in January 1969, abandoning his brief association with the Black Panthers, he moved to Conakry, Guinea. For a few years he studied there with Kwame Nkrumah, the deposed leader of Ghana. He returned to the United States from time to time and founded the All-African People's Revolutionary Party. Historian Charles Hamilton observed in *Pan-Africanism* (1974), a book edited by Robert Chrisman and Nathan Hare, that "Pan-Africanism recognizes that in this period of history—with international alignment of economic, military and political forces being what they are—it behooves all African peoples to effect a rapprochement for our collective survival and development." Manning Marable describes the nucleus of Pan-African thought thus:

The neo-Pan-Africanist movement began by asserting that all blacks throughout the diaspora were "an African People," rather than Afro-Americans, Afro-Brazilians, or simply black. The essential precondition of any political activity was the psychological and cultural affirmation of an ever-encompassing African consciousness. Pan-Africanists argued that all aspects of the dominant culture and values of the United States should be rejected. Traditional philosophical and cultural values from African society were advocated as superior to the white oriented capitalist society.

In terms of world affairs Pan-Africanists urged an ideologically neutral foreign policy, aligned neither with the first world of Europe nor the second world of North America and English-speaking countries. Imamu Amiri Baraka urged the creation of a World Africa party to "provide African people, wherever they are, with *Identity, Purpose,* and *Direction.*"

Some radical nationalists felt most uneasy about the distance between Pan-African rhetoric and the immediate needs of African-American citizens in America's inner cities and the rural South, who resented its generalized, inappropriate, and ineffectual application. Mark Smith opined in an article for *Black Scholar* of January-February 1975 that "some of us were deeply involved in community issues before we became Pan-Africanists. We soon learned to leave our Pan-Africanism at home, because attempts to superimpose it on the real struggles of the masses met with confusion and rejection." There was a world of difference between African-Americans preferring to be called black and aspiring to black power and their wanting to be thought of as Africans and proposing a World African party with the aim of redeeming the cultural reputation of the continent of Africa and reasserting its political independence from residual vestiges of economic and white colonialism.

Yet the domestic politics of Pan-Africanists were indistinguishable from those of black power. Stokely Carmichael, Imamu Amiri Baraka, and Charles Hamilton tried to mobilize Pan-Africanists to take part in registration drives, community organizations, and campaigns to promote greater political awareness among African-Americans. The Congress of African People was persuaded by its most eloquent members, Baraka and Haywood Henry, a Boston activist, to determine five criteria for any African-American candidates seeking its support in an election. They would be expected to be accountable to the African-American electorate; continuously to expose the white system as corrupt and unworkable; to raise controversial issues; to work to augment power through alliances and coalitions; and to support black nationalism and Pan-Africanism. These wide-ranging criteria were so general that African-American Democrats had no difficulty in giving them nominal support.

Economics disrupted the show of unity among Pan-Africanists, with Stokely Carmichael and Muhammad Ahmad arguing that the roots of Marxist theory were planted in the fertile soil of African communalism while Imamu Amiri Baraka and Don L. Lee wanted economics to take third place behind issues of culture and race. They preferred Tanzania as a model for African-American socialism. *Ujamaa,* their word for African socialism, meant "familyhood" in the language of Tanzania. They wanted to believe that the confrontation between capital and labor experienced in the first world was a white phenomenon, irrelevant to Africans. Yet left-wing Pan-Africanists such as Earl Anthony continued to argue that "the only course for the developing states is 'scientific socialism' or Marxism." Thus, whereas some Pan-Africanists wanted to minimize ethnicity and race, others wanted to maximize them at the expense of economics and class.

If the Gary Convention of the National Black Political Assembly of March 10 and 11, 1972, was the highwater mark of African-American assertion, if not African-American confidence, about what could be achieved, the tide in favor of black nationalism thereafter seemed to ebb irreversibly. The following two National Black Political Conventions held in Little Rock, Arkansas, in 1974, and in Cincinnati, Ohio, in 1976 attracted decreasing numbers of delegates and observers. By 1977 the National Black Political Assembly had dwindled to fewer than three hundred members, whether activists or of the rank and file. Those African-American politicians and intellectuals who had never truly forsaken integration as a goal soon disavowed their ties with militant nationalists. Several became acutely critical of African-American studies programs at universities. A few were received into the ill-fated administration of President Jimmy Carter (1977–1981).

One cultural peculiarity of the 1970s has somewhat obscured the political reality. This was the widespread adoption of such cultural attributes of black nationalism as various Afro hairstyles, dashikis, art, and music, as well as African names, into African-American and white American popular culture generally. This confused the very sharp political boundaries between the divergent movements of civil rights and black power.

We can discern some reasons for this confusion in the career of Muhammad Ali. Muhammad Ali (the former Cassius Clay), a great and dexterous heavyweight boxer in the proud tradition of Jack Johnson and Joe Louis, was the only champion to carry the eventual distinction of

Suffer the little children. A photo by Werner Wolfe that presents an idyllic scene of school integration with contented kids, African-American and white, waiting for a school bus in New York in the mid-1960s. (*U.S. News and World Report;* Library of Congress.)

winning the supreme heavyweight title three times. He was taken as a representative of the most conservative strain of black nationalism when he joined the Nation of Islam. He was courageous in refusing to be drafted to fight in Vietnam, a decision that led to his being stripped of the heavyweight title. His adoption of an Islamic name placed him in the center of the black nationalist tradition. By the mid-1970s, perhaps to maintain his flotilla of former wives and their children, he was appearing regularly on television commercials, first by promoting automobile accessories. His association with black nationalism was cultural rather than political.

In the two years between the Gary Convention in 1972 and the next convention in Little Rock, Arkansas, in 1974, various African-American leaders who favored integration far more than nationalism withdrew their support. The Congressional Black Caucus propounded a gentle alternative of its own to the NBPA's Black Agenda. This was the Black Bill of Rights. Congresswoman Shirley Chisholm ran as an Independent in some Democratic primaries but would neither attend the NBPA convention nor endorse any nationalist position. Other leaders gave their support to different Democratic aspirants for the presidency. The most conspicuous delegates at Little Rock were not widely known faces but little-known nationalists who happened to be intellectuals, students, and community organizers.

In the short run, the NBPA had no chance of competing for African-American allegiance with the two principal parties. This was especially true while it lacked sufficient funds, a full-time staff, clear ideology, and a political strategy to touch working-class African-Americans and non-racist white organizations. On the level of popular consciousness most working-class African-Americans identified profoundly both with the Democratic party and Democratic presidents, who seemed to offer better economic prospects, affirmative action, and a range of social programs intended to help them. Their disaffection with the Republicans increased on account of the covert but discernible racism of the Nixon administration.

As party politics unfolded in the period 1972–1976, it became clear that neither was the Democratic party going into permanent eclipse following the debacle of presidential nominee George McGovern's ignominious defeat in 1972, nor would it serve as the primary vehicle for equality for African-Americans. Moreover, the time for widespread continuous agitation, which had characterized the politics and subculture of various radical movements in the 1960s, had passed by the mid-1970s. Black nationalists compounded their difficulties by failing to initiate practical strategy in these changed times. Worse, they began to quarrel among themselves. The sinews of black nationalism among African-American working- and middle-class members withered and activists allowed minor differences between one another to assume the absurd proportion of parricide of the black race. Cultural nationalists turned on Marxist theory as yet another exemplar of white supremacy.

Marxism did not erupt in African-American politics like a volcano that had been sleeping for many years. It was prompted by the systematic and considered study of Marxist theory among civil rights workers since the 1960s. Some members of SNCC had been attuned to Marxism ever since the inception of their organization in the early 1960s. From the mid-1960s the Revolutionary Action Movement led by Max Stanford had introduced ideas of Marx and Lenin to civil rights activists. The most significant contribution in the attempt to relate black nationalism to Marxist theory was provided by husband and wife James and

Grace Lee Boggs. From Detroit these accomplished polemicists led a nationalist group, the Advocators, who wanted the pragmatic application of Marxism, shorn of its old left rhetoric, to black nationalism. James Boggs's *Revolution and Evolution in the Twentieth Century* (1973) was the most accessible attempt to introduce the ideas of Marx and Lenin to a readership committed to black nationalism. It was about this time that Baraka also became a Marxist. He reckoned that if the struggle against racism were ever to succeed, then it was first necessary to seize political power and overthrow white capitalism.

The Sixth Pan-African Conference

The divisions, exacerbated by accusations and recriminations, burst into the open and disfigured a major international forum, the Sixth Pan-African Conference held at the University College in Dar-es-Salaam in the summer of 1974. This conference was one in an occasional series of meetings since 1919 that had drawn together various black activists and intellectuals from Africa, the United States, and the West Indies to discuss politics, economics, and culture. The 230 delegates from the United States were considered the most divided and unruly of all the delegations. Black American nationalists discovered at Six-PAC that African leaders had little sympathy for their hemispheric approach to the ideal of Pan-Africanism. The cumulative effect of the PAC proceedings was to deepen the divisions between left- and right-wing nationalists. Kalamu ya Salaam surveyed this process disconsolately in a series of debate articles, collectively entitled "A Response to Haki Madhubuti," for *Black Scholar* of January-February 1975. He criticized cultural nationalists for neglecting culture and class at the expense of race and he criticized Marxist nationalists for rejecting blackness.

The National Black Political Assembly was now in fragments. Ronald Daniels and Mtangulizi Sanyika (the former Haywood Henry) launched a dramatic and successful strategy to remove Baraka as secretary general of the NBPA at a tense session in Dayton, Ohio, in November 1975. Bereft of its few elected officials and of its most charismatic leader and now deep in debt, it was unable to mount its planned '76 campaign strategy, devised by Mtangulizi Sanyika, to field an independent African-American candidate in the election. By 1977 membership of the NBPA had dwindled to a few hundred.

Its demise completed the elimination of various institutions of black nationalism. In March 1977 Johnson Publications of Chicago fired editor Hoyt Fuller and the entire staff of *Black World* before closing down the journal the following month. Cut by accusations of undue Marxist bias, Nathan Hare precipitately left the magazine *Black Scholar*. Between 1971 and 1976 the number of black studies departments at universities across the country was reduced by half. Some duly qualified but militant African-American professors found they could not secure permanent full-time employment.

Older black nationalist organizations also suffered in this period. In the Nation of Islam the death of Elijah Muhammad in 1975 and the religious reformation imposed by his son and successor Wallace Deen Muhammad, including the adoption of Sunni Islam and a new name, the World Community of Al-Islam in the West, further weakened an organization that had suffered a profound loss of credibility following the departure of Malcolm X in 1964.

Neither the left nor the right wings of black nationalism were able to recruit or build support beyond their extremely narrow bases, despite the significant education provided by Martin Luther King and the civil rights movement and the inspirational rhetoric of Malcolm X. They had neither the organization, funds, nor special aptitude for cultivating the great majority of African-American workers, students, and the unemployed.

The Professional Elite

In fact, what was happening was not simply the maintenance of two unequal nations, one African-American and one white, but the evolution of two clearly distinct communities within black America. One, comprising between 5 and 10 percent of the African-American population, was the professional elite, an African-American bourgeoisie, privileged to enter the white-dominated world and enjoy limited but accruing wealth following a good education and training. The remaining African-American population also enjoyed increasing prosperity while it was in work but continued to fall behind in terms of accumulated wealth, to fall

The civil rights movement in the United States attracted admiration from nonwhite peoples right across the world, including polemicists in the People's Republic of China, who issued this poster in support of the African-American civil rights movement as part of their own Cultural Revolution of continuing protest and foment in 1964. (Library of Congress.)

决支持美国黑人的正义斗争

坚对种族歧视

¡Oponerse a la discriminación racial!

OR – SE AO
PERIALISMO

لتقديم الاحتقار

ttons contre
impérialisme!

OPPOSE RACIAL

DISCRIMINATION!

万恶的殖民主义、帝国
度是随着奴役和贩卖黑人而
来的，它也必将随着黑色人
底解放而告终。

victim to unemployment, and to have less confidence in the beneficence of American capitalism and, indeed, democracy. Nevertheless, the economic ascendancy of a privileged elite among African-Americans in the late 1970s encouraged the moderates' hopes of upward mobility for African-Americans through the natural workings of the American economy.

The new elite comprised entrepreneurs, professional workers, and, also, politicians such as Benjamin Hooks, Vernon Jordan, and Jesse Jackson. The term *entrepreneurs* encompassed a range of occupations established at the turn of the century. It also included such comparatively new occupations as professional athletes (who numbered around seven hundred in 1978) and businessmen in the worlds of recording and entertainment. However, most African-American businesses were still family concerns with no extra paid employees and gross annual receipts of less than twenty thousand dollars. The category of professional workers included judges, lawyers, and clergy; college professors and administrators; and corporate executives, managers, and accountants. In 1970, when the total African-American workforce was 7.24 million, 148,000 African-Americans (2 percent) were categorized as administrators or managers and 593,000 (8 percent) were categorized as professional or technical employees. The number of African-American elected officials rose from 103 in 1964 to 1,469 in 1970 and 4,311 in 1977. As to politicians, between 1970 and 1977 the number of African-American mayors rose from 48 to 178. The Joint Center for Political Studies publication *Profiles of Black Mayors in America* (1977) disclosed that they were usually college graduates, political moderates, married, and over fifty years old—significantly older than the militants of the same period. Most did not owe their election to nationalist organizations. Ronald Walters, commenting on their middle-of-the-road politics for *Black Scholar* of October 1973, noted how such officials "fear the disapproval of the apparatus, the personal loss of status and opportunity" provided them by the Democratic party. By comparison, when committed left-wing nationalists ran for political office, as did Ronald Daniels for mayor of Youngstown, Ohio, in 1977, they were usually defeated. In an article for the *Review of Black Political Economy* of summer 1978, P. T. Stone noted how most of the African-American elected officials "were never leaders in their own communities." In comparison, African-American aspirants to office who "are female, not highly educated, who have low status occupation or are not involved in conventional political activities are at a decisive disadvantage in the political arena."

Manning Marable believes that the new African-American elite was distinguished by five characteristics.

First, the new bourgeoisie was characterized by reasonable but modest income. In 1964 the top 5 percent of African-Americans earned, on average, $11,400; by 1979 that top 5 percent was earning, on average, $34,000—about three-quarters of the average earnings of the highest paid 5 percent of whites. The highest paid 20 percent of African-American wage earners received almost 45 percent of the aggregate income of all African-American families. The highest 5 percent of aggregate income among African-Americans was 15.9 percent.

Second, as to employment stability, while the ratio of unemployment between African-Americans and whites was about two to one throughout the 1970s, the African-American bourgeoisie suffered far lower rates of unemployment than other African-Americans. In 1975 the total rate of unemployment among African-Americans was 14.7 percent for men and 14.8 percent for women (compared with 7.2 percent for white men and 8.6 percent for white women). However, for African-Americans in professional or technical positions the rates were 6.7 percent for men and 4.2 percent for women; for those who were managers or administrators (except in farming), the rates were 4.7 percent for men and 5.9 percent for women. However, African-Americans who worked as artisans, operatives, and laborers had unemployment rates of 19.2 percent for men and 21.9 percent for women. The average unemployment rates for African-American workers in blue collar jobs was 16 percent for men and 20.9 percent for women.

Third, as to education, in the 1970s about 6 percent of all African-Americans twenty-five years of age or older—about 650,000 people in all—had completed undergraduate or graduate degrees at colleges and universities. The majority of the increase in the number of African-Americans who were college graduates was accounted for by the desegregation of previously all-white colleges and universities in the South and the dramatic increase in African-American enrollment encouraged by various affirmative action programs at universities in the North and West.

The fourth feature of the new African-American elite was the creation of African-American professional organizations. For instance, in December 1969 nine accountants in New York created the National Association of Black Accountants. Within a decade it had organized chapters (several on university campuses) into four regions, with their national headquarters in New York. In November 1972 African-American police officers across the country founded their own separate nonprofit organization. In 1973 the National Association of Black School Educators (NABSE) was organized by politically moderate and conservative schoolteachers with the aim of raising the level of academic attainment among African-American students.

African-American entrepreneurs also formed their own support groups. In April 1971 executives from thirty-six corporations owned by African-Americans founded the National Association of Black Manufacturers (NABM). African-American executives, government workers, and entrepreneurs in the media in the tristate area of New York, New Jersey, and Connecticut established EDGES Incorporated, a nonprofit association that provided community groups with speakers on education and economics. By the mid-1970s these and other African-American associations had superseded organizations created by black power groups.

Last, as to consumer aspirations, the most influential African-American publication was *Ebony*, published from Chicago by an African-American entrepreneur with a circulation in excess of 1.28 million. Of a sample issue of 172 pages, 147 pages carried enticing advertisements from African-American and white corporations. Another national publication promoting consumer culture was *Black Enterprise*, with an average circulation of two hundred thousand. There was an African-American version of *Playboy*, entitled *Players*, that had a circulation of three hundred thousand. The principal organ of the civil rights movement was still the *Crisis*, the journal founded by the NAACP and by W. E. B. Du Bois in 1910. It had a circulation of one hundred thousand. (This information was provided by the "Review of Black Periodicals" for *Confrontation/Change Review* of Winter 1977–1978.)

The sum total of these factors was that the African-American elite was encouraged to become staunch advocates of American capitalism, whose beneficiaries they had become since American capitalism had made significant concessions to them on such issues as affirmative action. Thus their philosophy might be expressed in the aphorism coined by Whitney Young, director of the Urban League—"Equal Opportunity." They wanted the chance to enter the privileged world of capitalistic opportunities on a similar basis to whites of appropriate qualifications. They did not want a restructuring of American economics and politics lest this should endanger their new, hard-won advantages. The undoubted prosperity of certain privileged sectors among the fortunate African-American elite seemed to hide the apparently irreversible drift of numerous African-Americans toward the nation's poor. Commenting that in 1978 African-American households accounted for 28 percent of those with an annual income of less than five thousand dollars, rather than 22 percent, the figure for 1970, Andrew Hacker declared in a review essay for the *New York Review of Books* of March 20, 1980, "Insofar as this pattern continues . . . we will continue to see a substantial income gap separating the races."

PART THREE

After

Leontyne Price, the most lustrous soprano of the 1960s. Born into a modest family in Laurel, Mississippi, where her father worked in a sawmill and her mother worked as a midwife, she established herself as a preeminent artist in the most elite art form, opera, which she made more accessible to millions by the warmth and vibrancy of her vocal presence and the nobility and compassion of her demeanor.

After training at the Juilliard School, appearing as Gershwin's Bess, and earning accolades in European opera houses, she made a sensational debut at the old Metropolitan Opera, New York, in January 1961. Greatly admired for her interpretations of Verdi's heroines, especially Aida and his Leonoras, where her vocal sheen and sensitive phrasing were heard to best advantage, by her success she opened the doors of the world's opera houses to two generations of African-American classical singers. In 1965, when she was awarded the Medal of Freedom, LBJ commented on how "her singing has brought light to her land." (Photograph of Leontyne Price as Bess by Carl Van Vechten, 1954; Library of Congress.)

8

Political Access

In the 1970s and 1980s the civil rights movement still had a considerable role to play in American politics—southern, northern, and federal. Many of its bases of support were the same as in the days when it first emerged to the fore in the political arena.

Whereas the loss of momentum after 1968 can be interpreted as a loosening of the fabric of the civil rights movement, with many historians, such as Harvard Sitkoff in *The Struggle for Black Equality* (1981), seeing the death of Martin Luther King as the death of hopes for the movement, its main achievement had been the Voting Rights Act of 1965. The rights to vote and to hold public office were the most visible changes in African-American life since the 1950s. Andrew Young, an African-American mayor of Atlanta, observed, "Anyone looking for the civil rights movement in the streets is fooling himself. Politics is the civil rights movement of the 1970s." Accordingly, whereas in 1954 only one in four African-Americans could register to vote, by 1970 over two-thirds were on the voting registers. The number of African-American elected officials in the South rose from fewer than one hundred in 1965, five hundred in 1970, and sixteen hundred in 1975 to nearly twenty-five hundred in 1980. The national total rose dramatically from three hundred in 1965, fourteen hundred in 1970, three thousand in 1975, to forty-seven hundred in 1980, and over seven thousand in 1989. In the late 1970s African-Americans held eighteen seats in Congress. (They had held none between 1901 and 1928 and only two between 1945 and 1954.) As Mayor Andrew Young claimed, "You don't have to demonstrate when you can pick up the phone and call someone." In other words, political access through conventional channels, rather than mass demonstrations, was now the appropriate route for civil rights reform.

Moreover, by the late 1980s the expanded civil rights movement represented many different groups, including twenty-nine million African-Americans, nearly nineteen million Hispanics, over 123 million women and girls, twenty-nine million elderly people, and thirty-five million people handicapped with mental or physical disabilities. These groups had formed a national coalition, the Leadership Conference on Civil Rights, which represented 185 different national groups.

Not only had the civil rights movement on behalf of African-Americans raised public consciousness in the United States about the concerns of other significant groups, whether these groups were defined by ethnicity, sex, or age, but it had also made people across the world far more aware of human rights in general, whether political or social. Thus it heightened respect for President Jimmy Carter's human rights speeches in the late 1970s.

Another index of changed sensibilities and an indication that civil rights on behalf of African-Americans had become central to politics was provided by city hall politics in Chicago in the late 1980s. Bobby Rush, alderman of the second ward, had been a member of the Black Panthers. Helen Shiller, who had once worked for the white auxiliary of the Black Panthers, in 1988 represented a northside ward. Don Rose, who had organized some of the protest demonstrations in 1968, had gone on to manage the successful mayoral campaigns of a woman, Jane Byrne, in 1979, and an African-American, Harold Washington, in 1983. The former protesters claimed that city government in Chicago had improved greatly following the Democratic National Convention of 1968. Although Richard Daley, who died in 1976, was reelected mayor twice after the notorious police riot outside the convention, there was no doubt that the disaster encouraged disaffection among middle-class residents of highrise apartments on the shores of Lake Michigan, the so-called lakefront liberals, who had helped elect Jane Byrne and Harold Washington. The rising tide of opposition was just as critical as the growing political power of the African-American electorate in the city. When Harold Washington won the mayoral election in 1983, he required their votes as well as those of his African-American constituency.

Muhammad Ali, the only boxer to win the world heavyweight championship three times, in a relaxed smile between takes of his screen biography, entitled *The Greatest,* in 1977. One of the most charismatic of all sports stars, he was also one of the most controversial, partly because he was a defensive boxer of great ability, partly because his refusal to serve in the U.S. Army in Vietnam led to his being stripped of his heavyweight title, partly because of his conversion to Islam, and partly because of his boundless conceit, which led him to boast that he could float like a butterfly and sting like a bee. (Columbia Pictures Industries, Inc.; Museum of Modern Art Film Stills Archives.)

His 18 percent of the white vote came disproportionately from the lakefront liberals. Moreover, once in office, he would not have been able to hold a working majority in the city council without the crucial support of certain white aldermen from the lakefront wards. Despite Harold Washington's premature death in 1987 and the succession of Eugene Sawyer, an African-American politician associated with the old guard, who was then appointed acting mayor by the city council, the restructuring of power politics in city hall that Washington had achieved and the greater voting power of the African-American electorate (about half the total) suggested for a time that the former outsiders would continue to control the reins of power in Chicago in the 1990s. Here was another instance of the way the movement of civil rights had penetrated the conventional political structure. Nevertheless, Daley's son, another Richard Daley, eventually won Democratic mayoral primary elections over Sawyer and became mayor.

Another example was provided in 1989 when Coleman A. Young won his fifth consecutive term as mayor of Detroit.

The way African-American politicians were becoming more closely bonded within the mainstream of American politics was also suggested by the controversies that swirled around Marion S. Barry, Washington's mayor during the 1980s. During his twelve years in office, Marion S. Barry, a former SNCC worker, helped guide and nurture Washington's maturation as a major center for business and for the arts. Downtown Pennsylvania Avenue, once a row of flophouses, pornographic shops, and pawnbrokers, was rebuilt with fashionable hotels and office buildings. Businesses certainly benefited during the Barry years, notably property developers, who provided funds for Barry's three mayoral campaigns. This provoked accusations that he was a tool of business interests who was, according to a long-time civil rights worker, Roger Wilkins, "a symbol for white people of black incompetence and self-indulgence."

Three-quarters of the city's population were African-Americans. For many of these, in the words of R. W. Apple, Jr., in an article for the *New York Times* of January 21, 1990, "The Democratic mayor's ability to speak their language, to identify himself with their troubles, to win the allegiance of their clergymen and to take on the white news media with seeming impunity, was enough, even when he was accused, again and again, of infidelity and of drug use." Rumors had abounded of the mayor's drinking and drug problems, especially after Charles Lewis, an old friend, was sentenced in 1989 to prison for fifteen months after being found guilty of possessing cocaine and distributing it. As part of a plea bargain with prosecutors, Charles Lewis said that both he and the mayor had used drugs together several times. The rumors about Barry's use of drugs came to a head with his arrest by police in the Vista Hotel, Washington, on January 18, 1990, for possession of crack—cocaine. This was a personal tragedy for Barry, his family, and his supporters. Barry's arrest provoked a media sensation. It was exactly the sort of incident that all responsible politicians, African-American and white, wanted to avoid since it implied a weakening of the social fiber the higher any of them rose in office.

R. W. Apple commented further how the mayor's arrest, compounding several years of negative television and press reports, had cemented for Washington a reputation as unsavory as that of Chicago during the heydey of gangster Al Capone in the era of national prohibition of alcohol. In January 1990 the *Washington Monthly* magazine ran an article exposing inefficiency, neglect, and squalor during Marion S. Barry's tenure as mayor. Under the headline "The Worst City Government in America," several stories concerned injustices to the old, the chronically ill, and the dying, who had expired as a result of delays and inefficiency. The mayor's arrest resulted in a profound setback, and, perhaps, made impossible his goal of achieving statehood for the District of Columbia. It undermined support for home rule legislation of 1974 that had ended a hundred years of absolute congressional control of the city.

After an anticlimactic trial in which the jury found the mayor guilty on only one count, he was sentenced to six months in prison.

The Truly Disadvantaged

Despite outer trappings of political access, the 1980s was not a period in which other traditional and fundamental objectives of civil rights could advance significantly, although the needs of millions of African-American citizens were as pressing as before. These statements were especially true of the years in which the Republican Ronald Reagan, former Hollywood actor and governor of California, served as the fortieth president (1981–1989). In fact, the political climate of the 1980s was indifferent, not to say hostile, to major social reform. Proposals for welfare reform, national health insurance, and programs of public employment fell victim to a new form of liberal sophistry. It claimed, quite rightly, that economic progress in the 1960s had lessened poverty and that social welfare was increasingly disproportionate, compared with other expenditures. It also asserted, rather more dubiously, that poor people really did know their rights and that they not only applied for aid as never before but also received it.

In 1981, declaring, "Government is not the solution to our problem; it is the problem," President Ronald Reagan proposed to limit the size and scope of government in the interests of lowering inflation, interest rates, and unemployment. He proposed to abolish unnecessary regulations, close posts of federal officers who resigned, and insist upon a "consistent" monetary policy by the Federal Reserve Board. He requested Congress to cut $41.4 billion from federal social spending.

Nevertheless, he also pledged himself to protect social security and medicare, which mainly benefited the middle classes. Furthermore, he wanted Congress to reduce federal income tax by 30 percent and reduce the marginal tax from 75 percent to 50 percent.

In the sphere of civil rights, Ronald Reagan declared his opposition to affirmative action. His administration contended that such policies had as many harmful as positive effects. The administration said that reverse discrimination was unfair discrimination and reduced efficiency by encouraging the hiring of unqualified applicants. It proposed that proof of intention to discriminate must be established prior to any federal intervention and that such devices as quotas and timetables must be rejected as ways of compensation for past discrimination.

Moreover, in the period 1981–1983 the administration reduced the budget of the Equal Opportunity Commission (EOC) by 10 percent, the budget of the Office of Federal Contract Compliance Programs (OFCCP) by 24 percent, and the budget of the civil rights division of the Department of Justice by 13 percent. The number of complaints about discrimination by governmental contractors in employment decreased from fifty-three in 1980 to eighteen in 1983. The Civil Rights Division of the Justice Department now changed its strategy and rejected any coercive means of achieving school desegregation. By 1983 it had filed only one case for school desegregation.

For the first time since the New Deal programs aimed at reducing poverty were substantially reduced on the premise that excessive dependence of the poor on federal welfare encouraged the growth rather then the reduction of poverty. Analyst James Patterson concludes, "Certainly, in the conservative mood of the early 1980s, middle class attitudes traditionally hostile to public welfare seemed as strong as ever, and no new rediscovery of poverty—or liberal reform of welfare—appeared in sight."

However, the problems for African-Americans in white society did not disappear simply because they were dismissed by certain politicians. In his *The Truly Disadvantaged: The Inner City, the Underclass, and Public Policy* (1988), William Julius Wilson, a University of Chicago professor and sociologist, explained how, despite the victories of civil rights and the achievements of the Great Society of the 1960s, an African-American underclass really had emerged and conditions in the inner cities had gradually worsened in the 1970s and 1980s.

In the twenty years from 1968 to 1988, the percentage of households,

Former actor Ronald Reagan hit his true form as a popular Republican governor of California representing the rising tide of right-wing sentiment that became identified with the emerging Republican majority. After this continuously aspiring presidential candidate eventually took the Republican nomination and then the election in 1980, his presidency (1981–1989) introduced the concepts of monetarism and Reaganomics into the federal administration, with considerable reductions in social welfare spending that weakened the life support of a massive underclass that was developing in America's cities. (*U.S. News and World Report;* Library of Congress.)

both African-American and white, headed by women rose dramatically. The percentage of African-American households headed by women rose from 27.7 percent in 1968 to 44.3 percent in 1985. In the same period the percentage of white households headed by women rose from 8.9 percent in 1968 to 25.7 percent in 1985. The unemployment rate rose far more precipitously for African-Americans than for whites, rising from 6.7 percent in 1968 to 13 percent in 1987. This was compared with a rise for whites of from 3.2 percent in 1968 to 5.3 percent in 1987.

The median family income rose for African-Americans and whites in about the same proportion. Thus the median family income for African-Americans was $5,360 in 1968 and $17,604 in 1986. This was compared with a white median family income of $8,937 in 1968 and $30,809 in 1986. Whereas the official percentage of the population below the official poverty line fell for African-Americans and rose for whites, it was clearly African-Americans who remained most disadvantaged. In 1968 34.7 percent of African-Americans were below the poverty line (compared with 10 percent of whites). In 1986 31.3 percent of African-Americans were below the poverty line (compared with 11 percent of whites).

William Julius Wilson believed that committed zealots of the Great Society agencies in the 1960s had treated such problems as poverty, race, and class as though significant programs in the spheres of education, job training, and community development could reduce poverty, eliminate racism, and eradicate class rivalries by themselves, independent of fundamental economic and demographic trends. Since then, through good times and bad, poverty got worse. This applied not only to periods in which wages fell and unemployment rose but also to those years when the economy improved. Moreover, when the economy worsened, it was African-Americans who suffered most.

While racism still existed, it alone could not explain the fact that conditions in the inner cities and unemployment among African-Americans both deteriorated over thirty years. Employment rates for young African-American men were far higher in the late 1980s than in the early 1950s, when racism was far more prevalent. Moreover, the dramatic rise of an African-American middle class would not have been possible if residual racism had remained a potent force with a decisive veto on employment. While affirmative action programs served a most useful function in trying to redress problems caused by decades of discrimination, they succeeded most in helping educated and skilled African-Americans while ignoring the equally significant claims of poor African-Americans without skills and without much education. Thus civil rights activists whose strategies were aimed at affirmative action and against discrimination were, quite unintentionally, lessening the horizon of the growing underclass.

Commenting on the close relationship established by earlier research between prospects of employment and marriage rates, William Julius Wilson connected the declining number of marriages by African-American women to the faltering economic fortunes and diminishing rates of employment among young African-American men. He constructed an index of marriageable African-American men—the number of African-American men who were employed for every hundred African-American women of the same age group—and his index showed a dramatic decline after the 1960s. In 1960 there were about seventy employed African-American men between twenty and twenty-four years of age for every hundred African-American women of the same age group. However, in the early 1980s there were fewer than fifty such men for every one hundred such women in that age group. The pattern was similar for other age groups. The increasing formation of African-American families headed by women accompanied the steady decline in marriageable African-Americans over the years.

Why did employment among young African-American men decline so dramatically? At first, in the 1950s and 1960s, rates of employment among African-American teenagers fell primarily because of the increasing mechanization of southern agriculture. In 1950 about half the African-American teenagers in the South were working as farm laborers. By 1970 their jobs had disappeared. The pattern for African-American men over twenty years old was somewhat different. Employment opportunities for this age group declined after 1970. It was after 1970 that white women and the expanded white class of the baby boom generation entered the labor market in significant numbers and took precedence (in employers' eyes at least) over African-Americans with less education and fewer skills. As significant were the shifts in the economy from manufacturing to service industries. These entailed a mass exodus of manufacturing industries from northern cities to northern suburbs, which dealt a devastating blow to the employment prospects of African-Americans in the inner city. Hitherto, African-American men represented a most significant proportion in such central manufacturing industries as automobile, rubber, and steel, in which the need for their skills and labor subsequently declined owing to declines in the industries themselves. Moreover, after 1970 the number of jobs requiring employees with anything less than a complete high school education also fell owing to a decline in the manufacturing of goods. At the same time, the number of jobs requiring employees to have more education—white collar, professional, and highly skilled jobs—rose. These were not open to African-Americans (or whites) who had not completed high school.

The Great Migration of African-Americans from south to north in search of work in industry was, briefly, intensified by the decline in opportunities in agriculture in the South. However, in the 1970s and 1980s those very opportunities they sought in northern industry also disappeared as manufacturers and industrialists chose to relocate their plants in areas where they could pay less, such as the South or overseas.

At the same time, a considerable number of low-skilled jobs were relocated to the suburbs. Cities became primarily centers for financial and professional services, for which undereducated African-Americans and whites were not qualified. However, well-educated African-Americans were duly qualified and prospered in these changing circumstances, as did duly qualified whites. This economic trend supported the expansion of the African-American middle class while less educated and skilled African-Americans fell behind.

Moreover, African-American middle-class families and African-American working-class families nurtured by stable employment took advantage of new job opportunities and the opportunity of less discrimination in housing to leave the inner city for the suburbs in large numbers. Whereas previously African-Americans of all classes had lived near one another in the cities when society was far more segregated, the exodus of middle-class African-Americans to the suburbs served to intensify problems of inner-city decay. Inner-city ghettos became the domain of African-Americans who were poor, unemployed, and from single-parent families. William Julius Wilson also argued that poverty intensified in certain inner cities in the 1980s. These various factors undermined community institutions maintained previously by stable middle- and working-class African-Americans; removed positive role models for African-American children; and eliminated earlier social networks based on employment because in earlier decades most urban African-American adults had been employed.

Thus in the 1970s and 1980s such major cities as Chicago, Cleveland, and Detroit were all experiencing profound social difficulties. Middle-class whites were taking themselves, their investments, and their tax revenues to the suburbs, thereby leaving declining city centers to cope with aggravated problems of poverty, slums, and bad schools without anything like adequate resources.

Among the most crucial problems of the inner city were adverse patterns of behavior, such as a general decline in family loyalties, the drug subculture, the failure of children to complete high school, and the peer pressure of juvenile gangs. Conservative economist Glenn C. Lowry of Harvard contended that certain African-American leaders exploited what he called the "victim status" of African-Americans as a "political asset"—a convenient but superficial explanation to obscure more fundamental reasons for the situation in which many inner-city African-Americans found themselves.

Across the nation white liberals had hoped that renewed economic development would provide funds to address these and other social problems in the inner cities. Yet this was impossible when the actual growth was in one place and the problems were in another. Having analyzed what went wrong on the national scene, William Julius Wilson recommended various remedies. He wanted the introduction of full employment policies with the precise aim of reducing the huge underclass of inner cities and providing a new percolation of wealth to help rejuvenate dying city centers. Thus he argued against Democratic and Republican policies in the 1980s of high unemployment to produce low inflation. Seven consecutive years of high unemployment in the period 1980–1986, when the rate was 7 percent or more (the longest such period since the 1930s), had resulted in particularly high rates of unemployment among African-Americans. Thus, in the same period of 1980–1986, the average rate of unemployment among African-American men was almost 17 percent. This factor alone had a devastating impact on the problems of the inner cities.

In his book William Julius Wilson also advocated new initiatives in education and professional training to enhance the skills of young African-Americans and help relate them to real opportunities for employment in a continuously changing labor market. For poor families he argued for more and better child assistance and more adequate levels of family assistance.

Not all the changes between the mid-1960s and the late 1980s were for the worse. Far from it. The percentage of African-Americans and whites who completed high school (or its equivalent) between the ages of eighteen and twenty-one also rose—from 78 percent of whites and 55.9 percent of African-Americans in 1967 to 83.6 percent of whites and 75.6 percent of African-Americans in 1985. The percentage of African-American and white students between the ages of eighteen and twenty-one enrolled in college also rose for African-Americans, from 17.2 percent in 1967 to 24.8 percent in 1985. This was greater than the rise for whites, from 35.7 percent in 1967 to 38.8 percent in 1985.

Southern Politics in the 1980s

Twenty years after the great victories of the civil rights movement the South came under renewed political scrutiny. The more obvious policies of race had yielded to the newer policies of gain and the development of huge metropolitan areas in the so-called sunshine belt had brought prosperity to many.

The proportion of African-Americans to whites in the South continued to decline, partly because of the continued exodus of southern African-Americans to the North, partly because of the influx of whites to the South. Having already made certain inroads into Democratic party territory in the South, the Republican party began to grow ever more assertively in the South after the defeat of Barry Goldwater by Lyndon Johnson in 1964. From 1964 onward rural insurgents began to appropriate the Republican party from its original proprietors in the region—the white upper middle class and African-Americans from all classes. In time it came to be dominated by people from affluent families with a long tradition of wealth. Thus in "Politics and Society in the South," Earl and Merle Black opined that "Southern Republicanism is the party of *Southern Living.*" *Southern Living,* a magazine about houses, gardens, and food in the New South of sunbelt cities and suburbs, was published from 1966 onward by the Southern Progress Corporation from its headquarters in Birmingham, Alabama. Since its emphasis was on the creature comforts of bourgeois lifestyle, it did much to redress the South's backward image and thereby counter some of the adverse publicity acquired during the peak years of civil rights protests. The monthly magazine quickly attained a circulation of three million copies. Again we can see the point made by novelist Walker Percy that Martin Luther King had done more to free southern whites than African-Americans. Once whites could see beyond their obsession with race, they recognized that desegregation had never been a threat because it was they who still controlled the economy. Thus they could concentrate their energies on more productive pursuits. Accordingly, the great conservative landowners who once dominated state governments and held sway over key congressional committees had been superseded by metropolitan moderates. The other significant force for moderation was, of course, the enfranchisement of African-Americans, which had made politics more receptive to African-American needs.

Moreover, Republicans actively campaigned to entice Democrats in the South to their ranks. Mark Braden, chief counsel of the Republican National Committee in the late 1980s, found that Republicans could turn civil rights laws to their distinct advantage. Thus they helped African-Amercans challenge gerrymandering and various electoral practices

TABLE 3

Party identification among white adult Southerners, 1952–1984

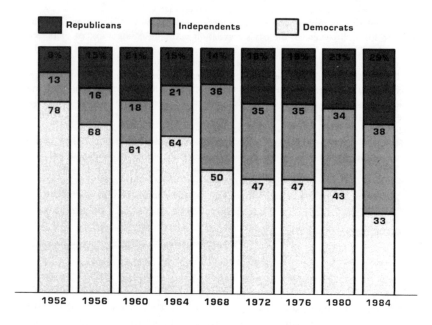

that had helped white Democrats maintain their oligarchy in power in the South.

Table 3 suggests the rate of Republican encroachment into white Democratic territory in the South. The upshot was that although the Democrats were commanding a solid South in 1952, claiming as much as 78 percent of eligible white southerners, by 1968 they had only a bare majority, with 50 percent, and by 1984 they had actually become a minority party, with 33 percent, while the Republicans were ahead of them with 38 percent.

Furthermore, over the years there was a dramatic decline of southern support for Democratic presidential candidates, from 78.2 percent for Franklin Roosevelt in 1940 to only slightly more than a third or less than a half for Hubert Humphrey in 1968, George McGovern in 1972, and Walter Mondale in 1984. Even the apparent exceptions to this rule —the southerners Lyndon Johnson in 1964 and Jimmy Carter in 1976 and 1980—were less assured of overwhelming support than might have

The 1990 census disclosed that of the total American population of 249.6 million about 30.0 million (or 12.1 percent) were African-Americans, an increase of 13.2 percent since 1980 but fewer by 650,000 than previous official estimates.

The highest concentration of African-Americans remained in Washington, D.C., accounting for 65.8 percent of the city's population but representing a loss of 11 percent since 1980. The states with the highest concentration of African-Americans were Mississippi (with 35.6 percent of the state population); Louisiana (30.8 percent); South Carolina (29.8 percent); and Georgia (27.0 percent). Whereas in four of these states the concentration was partly accounted for by a modest rise in the African-American population of between 3.1 percent (Mississippi) and 9.6 percent (Louisiana), in Georgia there had been a staggering increase of 19.2 percent to a total of 1.74 million African-Americans in the ten years between 1980 and 1990.

However, the largest increases were in five states with modest populations overall and minuscule African-American populations: New Hampshire (an increase of 80.4 percent but only 0.6 percent of the total); Minnesota (78.0 percent but only 2.2 percent of the total); Vermont (71.9 percent and 0.3 percent of the total); Alaska (64.6 percent and 4.1 percent of the total); and Maine (64.3 percent and 0.4 percent of the total).

been expected. The Republicans were building a coalition sufficient to give Ronald Reagan first 52 percent in 1980, then 62.3 percent in 1984. The fundamentalist right survived and resurfaced to help remold politics in its image. Moreover, its religious views were reinforced by a profusion of leaders such as Pat Robertson, former television evangelist of Virginia and eventually a minor presidential candidate in 1988.

An instance of various developments in southern politics in the 1980s is provided by Mississippi. The state that had once said "Never!" to change in the great period of civil rights elected a reform governor in 1987. This was Ray Mabus, then aged thirty-nine and a Harvard-trained lawyer from Sargent Shriver's law firm in Washington (Fried, Frank, Harris, Shriver, and Kampelman). His platform proclaimed "basic, drastic change." He was elected in the very same week that Ross Barnett, the obdurate governor who had blocked James Meredith's entrance to the University of Mississippi at Oxford in 1962, died peacefully in the hospital, aged eighty-nine. Thus, after an unparalleled record as the emblem of southern racism and continuously last in the nation in per capita income, employment, and literacy, it seemed that voters had agreed that "Mississippi will never be last again." The electorate also elected a group of young reform-minded legislators and administrators alongside Mabus who were determined to introduce a new progressive state constitution. Inauguration celebrations for Mabus were extensive, elegant, and youthful affairs. Dr. James G. Wilson, a research physician who had left Harvard medical school to live and work in his native state, remarked, in mock homage to the Kennedys, "Camelot has come to Mississippi."

Mississippi had benefited from the enfranchisement of African-Americans, who, in the late 1980s, accounted for about 30 percent of the state's registered voters. It had also benefited from the coming to maturity of the baby boom generation during and just after the height of civil rights agitation. They were especially receptive to change, the change of affluence and a change of consciousness. They had been revolted by the state's treatment of James Meredith in 1962 and outraged by the murders of the civil rights martyrs in 1964. This was especially so because these events had humiliated Mississippi not only in the United States but also across the world.

Mabus believed that Mississippi must follow the route to change already trodden by such states as North Carolina and Tennessee, although his critics—and two out of three white electors had voted against him in 1987—believed that his reforms, including higher salaries for teachers, would cost more than the state could afford. Mabus had originally been enticed back to his home state by Governor William F. Winter, who wanted to get the state's first compulsory education law passed and wanted Mabus to help write it. After numerous difficulties, the Education Reform Act was passed by the state legislature in a special session in 1982. Mabus was subsequently elected state auditor and used the latent power of his office to gain $1.7 million in reimbursements from numerous county supervisors who had customarily dispensed county labor and equipment in return for political allegiance. This was traditional boss politics. Mabus's campaign attracted the attention of the FBI to investigate public officials, leading to over forty indictments for various forms of malpractice. Mabus's reputation as a reformer prompted the Washington media consultancy firm of Doak, Shrunk, and Associates, who advised him in his gubernatorial campaign, to undertake analysis of electoral expectations in 1987. They concluded that Mabus's own preferred strategy of drastic change would be very favorably received. Doak, Shrunk received $1.4 million of the Mabus record campaign chest of $2.9 million. Although whites voted for Republican candidate Jack Reed by about two votes in every three, Mabus garnered the African-American vote nine times out of ten and, then, enough additional white votes to win.

In the *New York Times* of February 28, 1988, Peter J. Boyer expressed his belief that

the enfranchisement of the heavy black population has created in Mississippi, as it has elsewhere in the South, a new sort of politician, one who is necessarily adept at building black-white coalitions. The profile is socially progressive and fiscally conservative, and, because of the relative lack of resources with which to fund programs, there is an emphasis on innovation. This profile is fetching to the national Democratic party trying to fight the southern realignment of the Reagan era, and Southern politicians who fit the profile have near-instant national politics.

This situation was repeated elsewhere where a younger generation unscarred by past racist attitudes, such as Governors Bill Clinton of Arkansas and Charles E. ("Buddy") Roemer of Louisiana, came to power. Moreover, in 1986 Mississippi elected its first African-American congressman this century—Mike Espy, a graduate of Howard University who later took a law degree in California and then became assistant secretary of state in Mississippi at age twenty-five. Espy recognized that it was the very backwardness of Mississippi that allowed young educated African-Americans opportunities they would not get in more prosperous states.

Mabus and his allies came to power in a period in Mississippi politics when the issues had shifted from race to funds and taxes in the interest of dismantling the establishment, including an outmoded constitution written by a planter class in reaction to the First Reconstruction of 1865–1877.

Jesse Jackson, Ronald Brown, and the Elections of 1988 and 1989

There could be no clearer indication that "politics is the civil rights movement of the 1970s" and, more crucially, of the 1980s than the political rise of Jesse Jackson, a powerful African-American orator whom some saw as heir to Martin Luther King.

It was, perhaps, inevitable that the Republicans would choose to field Vice President George Bush as presidential successor to Ronald Reagan in the election of 1988. During that election various problems within the Reagan administration helped concentrate attention on the Democrats' array of presidential aspirants. Governor Michael S. Dukakis of Massachusetts soon built an impressive lead in the primaries. Nevertheless, it was the Reverend Jesse Jackson who captured the attention of the mass media and managed to assemble enough support to enter the Democratic National Convention in Atlanta in July 1988 with twelve hundred delegates, the second highest number.

He was born Jesse Burns in Greenville, South Carolina, in 1941, the son of Helen Burns, a high school student, and Noah Robinson, her next door neighbor, married and aged thirty-three. When Jesse was about a year old his mother married Charles Henry Jackson, a post office maintenance worker, who later adopted him. His half brother, Noah Ryan Robinson, raised next door, recalled how "Jesse has an insatiable urge —which is an asset when you consider it as a fuel—to achieve, to be respected and recognized. I think being born out of wedlock bothered him disproportionately to the way it did anyone else we grew up with. The thing that drives him is a subliminal longing for respect and recognition that he is somebody." He was educated first at the University of Illinois, where he had a football scholarship, and then at North Carolina Agricultural and Technical College in Greensboro, where he became involved in civil rights activities and whence he graduated in 1964 with a bachelor's degree in sociology. He decided to become a minister because he recognized that the men who were changing American politics, such as Martin Luther King and Ralph Abernathy, were from a new school of activist clergymen. Although he entered Chicago Theological Seminary on a scholarship, he never graduated. He left to work with Martin Luther King and was subsequently ordained by another minister in Chicago. Impressed by the vigor and organizational skills of his new recruit, Martin Luther King made him director of Operation Breadbasket, the economic section of the SCLC. His style offended, amused, and galvanized his coworkers, and also King, who, it was said at the last, found his recruit's omnivorous desire for self-promotion somewhat exasperating.

In 1971 Jackson left the SCLC and created Operation PUSH—People United to Save Humanity. The title was subsequently changed to People United to Serve Humanity. He acted as PUSH president until his 1984 campaign for the Democratic presidential nomination. The center of

PUSH was a former synagogue on the South Side of Chicago. Its aim was to use boycotts of white-owned companies to win franchises, provide contracts, and offer jobs to African-Americans. The group achieved agreements with such corporations as Burger King, Coca-Cola, Seven-Up, and Henblein. However, PUSH had its failures. The National Institute of Education, a federal organization that reported on educational programs, disclosed in a report of 1982 how students were disappointed with a lack of concrete results in their program, PUSH-Excel. Joseph A. Califano, who served as secretary of health, education, and welfare in the Carter administration and helped PUSH secure federal funds, opined in his *Governing America* (1981) that "the problem with Jackson's program is his inability to sustain its momentum when he was not present, its dependence on his charisma." Moreover, PUSH was criticized for benefiting only a select group of African-American businessmen rather than the African-American community at large. The recipients of corporation business included Noah Ryan Robinson, Jesse's half-brother, who secured business from Coca-Cola and Henblein after successful boycotts.

In 1986 and 1987 PUSH was boycotting Revlon, the cosmetics company, after one of its executives told *Newsweek* that its competitor African-American cosmetics companies—whose customers it was trying to entice with a range of hair products—made inferior products and would soon be acquired by white companies. The PUSH boycott was aimed at persuading Revlon to employ more African-Americans in management and to cease trading with South Africa. Once Revlon had conceded, it expected the boycott to be ended. Instead, it found that Jesse Jackson shifted his terms. Critics believed this was part of a strategy to bolster several African-American-owned cosmetic companies who were among Jesse Jackson's contributors.

After earlier campaigns in which he concentrated on racial issues, Jesse Jackson attempted to capture the political mainstream in the campaign of 1988 by widening his political horizons and seeking a new era of reforms in the tradition of the New Deal and the Great Society. Thus he called for increased federal spending on such social programs as farm and housing subsidies and a foreign policy more interested in the peoples of South America and South Africa than in their governments. Moreover, he argued for the establishment of a Palestinian homeland. He called for direct involvement by the federal government in industrial management through the creation of an American investment bank that

An unusually reflective Jesse Jackson pauses before addressing a question at a press conference. While his attempts at sustaining a political momentum for social change for dispossessed people across America were periodic and subject to dissension, his reputation as the most powerful and charismatic orator since the 1960s was confirmed by his inspired use of rhetoric during his campaigns for the Democratic presidential nomination in 1984 and 1988 and led to speculation and some expectation that one day he would enter government. (*U.S. News and World Report*; Library of Congress.)

would draw upon public pension funds (protected by federal guarantees) to find monies for improving roads, bridges, and systems of public transportation.

Jesse Jackson came closer to the Democratic nomination in 1988 than many thought possible and far closer than would have been conceivable even ten years earlier. However, a few days before the convention Michael Dukakis, knowing he would win on the first ballot, chose Senator Lloyd Bentsen of Texas as his running mate. The party refused to incorporate all but one of Jackson's proposals in its platform, including his demands for a higher tax on the rich and powerful and for recognition of a Palestinian state. They only agreed to incorporate his proposal to denounce South Africa as a terrorist state.

Jesse Jackson was the first national figure in two decades capable of raising African-American hopes, opening discussion of racism and poverty while attempting to raise consciousness about other social problems charged with racial overtones, and he was able to do so in nonracial terms. Nevertheless, Jackson stood in marked contrast to an emerging generation of African-American politicians. By the early 1990s he had still not held elective office. The final verdict of history may well be that he was a transitional figure, one whom Mayor Andrew Young of Atlanta described as "America's prophet in residence."

Despite their role in local office, many African-American politicians felt that they were pressing against a glass ceiling—especially in the South—when it came to elections for statewide office. Congressman John Lewis, the former civil rights activist who became a representative for the Democrats in Georgia, explained in 1989, "There are only so many black majority congressional districts, only so many black majority towns and cities. To move up and out, people must be able to build broad coalitions." It was the very power of Jesse Jackson's campaign as a mighty emblem of African-Americans' attaining political status that led to the emergence of Ronald Harmon Brown as Democratic national chairman.

In the three successive presidential elections of the 1980s the Democrats' presidential nominees compromised their rhetoric and failed to convince strong voters or hold together traditional Democrats. As Robert Kuttner observed in an article for the *New York Times* of December 3, 1989, "Afraid to run on ideology, the Democrats ran as technicians; and they were beaten by better technicians who were clearer about their own ideology and thus better able to manipulate powerful political symbols. For more than a decade, the national Democratic party has been out-spent, out-organized and out-strategized by the Republicans while its electoral base has eroded." It was, therefore, most ironic that the task of reconciling liberals, conservatives, and technocrats in the interest of building up the Democratic party should fall to an African-American. By dint of circumstances and political talent, Ron Brown was able to move comfortably between the ranks of poor people thrilled by Jackson's rhetoric and the middle class of ever rising expectations.

Ronald Harmon Brown was elected national chairman of the Democratic party in 1988, supported by Democrats as diverse as liberals Mario Cuomo of New York and Senator Edward Kennedy of Massachusetts, moderate Senator Bill Bradley, and the conservative former governor of Arizona, Bruce Babbitt. Among their reasons for supporting Ron Brown for chairman was their sense that he would serve as a moderate complement to Jesse Jackson, whose combination of fiery rhetoric and lack of practical experience troubled many. David Price, congressman from North Carolina, remarked, "He is such a very different guy from Jesse Jackson. He doesn't have the same inner demons. He doesn't have that bottomless thirst for respect."

Ron Brown was raised in Harlem. His father, Bill Brown, was manager of the Theresa Hotel on 125th Street, a center of the Harlem Renaissance. Bill Brown was later one of the first African-American officials of the New Deal's Federal Housing and Finance Agency. Both parents were college graduates and they determined that their son should have good schooling. Ron Brown attended Hunter College Day School, the Walden School, and the Rhodes School in Manhattan before going to Middlebury College. When his fraternity, Sigma Phi Epsilon, decided to waive its whites-only clause to receive him, the chapter was disaffiliated from the national organization. Ron Brown majored in political science and graduated in 1962. His success at college and, later, in the military made more biting his subsequent discovery as a civilian of social segregation in the South. This convinced him that he must play a most active role as a social worker in the Lower East Side and as a civil rights worker with the National Urban League, which he joined in 1967. He became a Washington lobbyist and eventually director of the Washington office.

In 1979 he became a member of Senator Edward Kennedy's staff but, following various troubles in the Democratic party, he left to join the law firm of Patton, Boggs, and Blow. (He had earned a law degree from St. John's University, New York, during his period as a social worker.) After considerable hesitation, he decided in April 1988 to become Jesse Jackson's convention manager, having previously declined to manage Jackson's presidential campaign. It was his skill there that made him a leading candidate for the position of party chairman.

As chairman, Ron Brown proved his credentials in 1988 and 1989 to the most skeptical of traditional Democrats by building and repairing an effective party machine, winning a series of elections, and building up considerable financial resources. Bill Crotty, a Florida developer and prominent party fundraiser who had been initially somewhat wary of Ron Brown remarked how "Ron has gone out of his way to reach out to people who felt maybe they weren't welcome." There was considerable irony in the situation in which the crucial test of the first African-American to become chairman of a national party, and that a party of the common man, should be his ability to entice millionaires. Ron Brown's predecessor, Paul E. Kirk, Jr., had also suffered problems of association with prominent liberals, including Edward Kennedy, and with the AFL-CIO. He had tried to defuse criticisms by using compromising language and moving to the political center. However, Ron Brown could only do so in terms of rhetoric. He could not compromise by becoming more white. Thus he encountered residual, but potent, embers of racism.

David Dunn, one of Ron Brown's law partners, claimed that "some people call themselves Democrats because in many rural counties there was no Republican party and the local establishment always controlled the Democratic party. An event like Ron Brown's election forces a reckoning." In Florida, the Republicans exploited the issue of Ron Brown's color and his liberal credentials to accelerate a wave of defections of sheriffs, clerks of the court, and county commissioners from the Democratic party. Many Democrats who were not troubled by Brown's liberalism were disturbed by his aristocratic style of dress, his wearing of elegant suits—hallmarks of the establishment—at the very same time that he was to be taken as a symbol of minority rights.

Brown intended to fuse the disparate Democratic state parties and the Democratic National Committee with a duly coordinated and cohesive campaign organization. In 1989 he persuaded the party in the neighboring states to send money and party workers to assist the campaigns in two special by-elections in Indiana and Alabama. He withheld money from the gubernatorial campaign of Douglas Wilder of Virginia until the various factions agreed to collaborate together.

Faced with clear instances of increasing conservatism, Ron Brown, delivering his first address as chairman of the Democratic Leadership Council in March 1988, made remarks that might have been shrewdly calculated to synthesize liberal sentiments with conservative prudence when he declared, "There is no one tougher than Democrats when it comes to protecting our children against drugs, our cities against crime," while calling for "a new ethic which links right with responsibilities in the context of physical prudence."

The victory of African-American candidate Douglas Wilder as governor of Virginia in 1989 in traditionally white conservative territory was widely considered a powerful signal to African-American politicians in the South. Wilder's victory on the same day that Democrat David Dinkins was elected mayor of New York was interpreted by Ronald H. Brown as emblematic of the success of crossover politicians who could transcend local racial loyalties. Ronald Brown observed, "You get black voices speaking for the whole party, not just for black Americans." Indeed, while Douglas Wilder campaigned on a series of controversial issues—crime, development, and women's rights to abortion—he did not campaign on the issue of race or racial solidarity. Similarly, David Dinkins presented himeslf as a peacemaker able to move across ethnic lines. This was important because David Dinkins's mayoral campaign in 1989 was set against a particularly somber backdrop—accusations and counteraccusations following the brutal and senseless murder of Yusuf Hawkins in the Bensonhurst section of Brooklyn in September 1989. Yusuf Hawkins was an African-American teenager assaulted and killed when he wandered into a predominantly Italian-American neighborhood.

The Democrats' election victories in November 1989 were satisfying to all those within the party who wanted to see it emerge as a true multiracial coalition. Liberal Democrats hoped that this coalition would have the courage to take and sustain a liberal stand on such controversial issues as abortion while maintaining a traditional posture of activist government—meaning a government that would actively work to strengthen people's economic prospects while staying out of their personal lives. This was, after all, a period when Republicanism held the White House.

Ain't No Court Supreme Enough to Keep Me from My Dream

In a budget address in February 1989, three months after his election, President George Bush gave his pledge to work "to knock down the barriers left by past discrimination." Nevertheless, it was likely that the civil rights policies of his administration would depend substantially on the administration's own interpretation of what those particular barriers were. In 1989 there were literally hundreds of court cases from the Reagan years that awaited judicial rulings. On the whole, the rulings of the Reagan years had reflected a view of school desegregation as supervised by the Court that affirmative action was no longer necessary in hiring municipal workers. It seemed that official rhetoric declared that it was wrong to remedy discrimination against African-Americans by adopting measures that might, in turn, discriminate against white Americans.

Nor did informed African-American commentators support affirmative action strategies—even if they were, themselves, committed advocates of civil rights. The essayist Shelby Steele, a professor of English at San Jose State University, argued in the *New York Times Magazine* of May 13, 1990, that the strategy of preferential treatment placed a burden of implied inferiority upon African-Americans. This led to their experiencing "an expanded realm of debilitating doubt, so that the doubt itself becomes an unrecognized preoccupation that undermines their ability to perform. . . ." Thomas Sowell, the conservative economist, argued in *Preferential Policies: An International Perspective* (1990) that affirmative action programs at colleges and universities failed to advance disadvantaged or poor African-Americans and that their failure was being attributed—incorrectly—to the inadequacies of the students rather than to faults in the programs. Those who argued for the continuation of affirmative action, despite its manifest problems, included Drew S. Days, a professor of law at Yale who had served the Carter administration as assistant attorney general for civil rights.

Nevertheless, in the later 1980s the Supreme Court delivered a series of decisions that ensured that civil rights cases, some involving affirmative action, would once again become a subject of political debate. By this time, the political atmosphere was no longer pregnant with change and its possibilities. The Court's gradual but resolute shift to the right was received with relief by a substantial element of public opinion responsive to the new conservatism of Ronald Reagan.

This does not mean that the liberal spirit had died. The Supreme Court's 1984 ruling on discrimination by institutions that received federal funds in the case of *Grove City College* v. *Bell* was immediately challenged by liberals and civil rights groups who put pressure on Congress to overturn it by new legislation. The issue was whether institutions in receipt of federal funds could be coaxed or coerced away from discriminatory practices by the threat or actuality of having those funds withdrawn. Conservatives said no; liberals argued yes. The result of pressure upon Congress was the Civil Rights Restoration Act that was passed into law over President Reagan's veto in 1988. However, it took advocates of the new law four years to achieve their aim and for a long time the campaign was bogged down in controversy over its possible impact on abortion rights—a controversy that opened new wounds in the broad coalition of the civil rights movement of the 1980s.

In a two-week period in early June 1989 the Supreme Court delivered four major decisions on various civil rights cases that were essentially conservative. In three of these cases a new conservative majority of five overruled the remaining four liberals and thereby rewrote long-established rules on proof and procedure. This new conservative majority comprised three justices appointed by Ronald Reagan—Justices Sandra Day O'Connor, Antonin Scalia, and Anthony M. Kennedy—as well as William M. Rehnquist, whom he had elevated to chief justice, and Byron R. White, who had maintained a conservative response to civil rights issues through the 1980s.

Hitherto, the Supreme Court under Earl Warren and Warren Burger had acted as an insistent conscience upon Congress, upon leading administrators, and upon the nation in general. Under Chief Justice William H. Rehnquist, the Court followed the values of the already emerged Republican majority. The series of decisions prompted Richard Cohen to opine in his column for the *Washington Post* on June 16, 1989, that, by these decisions, the Court itself was deliberately drawing the long period of reform since the *Brown* decision of 1954 to an end. "The Second Reconstruction period has ended," he declared. The tactic of this new conservative majority was to rearrange details of process while leaving the general picture of the law untouched—at least at first glance. For its part, Congress was far more comfortable in devising laws of general application—"discrimination is forbidden"—than in prescribing specific details. It was this crucial difference between the two branches— the legislature's concern with the sweep of laws and the judiciary's obsession with practice and process—that allowed conservatives to gain much while admitting little. By concentrating on the letter of the law, they could mute its spirit.

Each of the decisions of June 1989 upset the superstructure of judicial interpretations. For instance, Title VII of the Civil Rights Act of 1964 forbade discrimination in employment on the basis of race, sex, and certain other categories. Because the language was spare, it was the Supreme Court that provided depth, definition, and force to these words. Thus, in the case of *Griggs* v. *Duke Power* of 1971 the Court had decided unanimously that Title VII not only prohibited purposeful discrimination but also job requirements and practices that had a discriminatory effect. The Court ruled in the 1971 *Griggs* case that employers had to justify the necessity for such practices. Chief Justice Warren Burger wrote in that case how the Civil Rights Act of 1964

proscribes not only overt discrimination but also practices that are fair in form, but discriminatory in operation. . . . Congress directed the thrust of the Act to the consequences of employment practices, not simply their motivation.

However, in the 1989 case of *Wards Cove Packing* v. *Atobio*, the decision written by Byron White shifted the onus of proof from employers to employees, who had to prove that the challenged practices were not necessary: "The plaintiff bears the burden of disproving an employer's assertion that the adverse employment action or practice was based solely on a legitimate neutral consideration." Lawyers representing African-Americans and women in suits over job discrimination said that the *Wards Cove* decision imposed an onerous burden upon plaintiffs. For their part, employer groups greeted the result as a welcome, long overdue relief from rules they considered hostile.

Civil rights activists and those sympathetic to them were well aware that it was difficult and hazardous to challenge civil rights rulings by the Supreme Court and seek new legislation to reverse it. Thus, a brief filed on behalf of sixty-six senators and 145 congressmen in one of the cases of June 1989, *Patterson* v. *McLean Credit Union*, making a plea to the

Court not to upset precedent, noted that "any congressional effort to change a decision of the Court could prove divisive" and could "confront grave difficulties in addressing the nuances that have arisen from case-by-case elaboration of the statute."

However, in the case of *Patterson* v. *McLean Credit Union* the Court unanimously decided on June 15, 1989, to follow the advice of the 211 congressmen and abide by a decision of 1976. This was *Runyon* v. *McCary,* which had interpreted a civil rights law of the First Reconstruction of 1865–1877, known as Section 1981, to bar private, as well as official, acts of racial discrimination. However, the conservative majority ruled in an opinion written by Justice Anthony M. Kennedy that Section 1981 covered discrimination in the initial hiring process but not subsequent discrimination in the workplace. Civil rights leaders reacted by saying that this parsing of the old law would severely weaken it as a tool against job discrimination.

In the case of *Martin v. Wilks,* decided by five votes to four on June 12, 1989, the Court ruled that white firefighters in Birmingham, Alabama, had the right to sue to reopen an affirmative-action settlement approved by the Federal District Court in Birmingham in 1981. The settlement had intended to redress discrimination that had prevented African-Americans from gaining senior positions in the department. In 1989 the Supreme Court decided that whites affected by the affirmative action plan ordered by the Court could sue to reopen the case. Chief Justice William Rehnquist ruled that "a voluntary settlement in the form of a consent decree between one group of employees and their employer cannot possibly 'settle,' voluntarily or otherwise, the conflicting claims of . . . employees who do not join in the agreement." The decision was based on rules of procedure that govern federal courts rather than on the laws themselves. Thus it could allow the reopening of cases believed long settled.

Accordingly, supporters of civil rights measures in Congress devised a Civil Rights Act of 1990. Its underlying intention was to protect employees against discrimination both before and after they had been hired. Moreover, the framers of the bill wanted to return the burden of proof to the employer to show the need for a practice once the employee had proved in court that discrimination did exist. This particular civil rights proposal made it clear that it was always illegal to use race, ethnicity, gender, or religion as a factor in any employment decisions. Employees would be enjoined to preserve the stability and certainty of court-approved plans designed to remedy discrimination. In addition, the bill was an attempt to reestablish fair rules for determining when victims of discrimination should file their claims.

A fourth contrast in Supreme Court decisions of the 1980s is provided by decisions in *Fullilove* v. *Klutznick* of 1980 and *Richmond* v. *Croson* of 1989. In 1980 in the case of *Fullilove* v. *Klutznick* the Court had approved the practice of setting aside certain funds designated for public works for minority contractors.

In 1989 in *Richmond* v. *Croson* the Court set limits on such arrangements. Justice Sandra Day O'Connor wrote the majority opinion that "while there is no doubt that the sorry history of both private and public discrimination in this court has contributed to a lack of opportunities for black entrepreneurs, this observation, standing alone, cannot justify a rigid racial quota in the awarding of public contracts in Richmond, Va."

Changes in other laws allowed the Bush administration to take a more active role on behalf of people who believed they were victims of discrimination in housing. Under the Fair Housing Amendments Act of 1988, plaintiffs were permitted to seek relief through administrative law or in a trial by jury. If they opted for trial by jury, then the Department of Justice had to provide lawyers to represent them. Nevertheless, it was expected that any distinction in civil rights enforcement between the Bush administration and that of its predecessor was more likely to be in style than in substance.

Once in office, President George Bush announced a new program for African-American colleges in May 1989. His administration was pledged to undertake the following reforms. It would strengthen a previous executive order to federal agencies, who would be authorized to award more grant and contract money to African-American institutions. The administration pledged itself to create the president's board of advisors on historically African-American colleges and universities. The board members, to be appointed by the president, were to include college presidents, business leaders, and officials of elementary and secondary schools. In addition, the board was to assist Secretary of Education Lauro F. Cavazos in monitoring the various federal agencies' commitment to African-American colleges and to advise the secretary on ways in which these colleges could be strengthened.

The Bush administration also committed itself to cooperate with businesses in order to encourage private support toward African-American colleges. For this, the White House Office of National Service was to ask businesses to offer matching grants to colleges and to help them develop more effective ways of managing their finances, housing their faculties, and widening and deepening the range of their course offerings.

By the close of the 1980s the pattern of school desegregation across the country was a patchwork of strategic compromises in the service of local realpolitik. What was crystal clear, however, was that efforts at desegregation were most successful when they avoided compulsory busing and when they also included such features as enriched academic programs and so-called magnet schools. Magnet schools were schools specially funded and with distinctive academic or recreational features —features intended to make them very desirable from the point of view of parents and children. Busing had first been introduced because resistance to significant school integration was so intense. Yet the furor that busing itself provoked, especially in the 1970s, was so continuous and fierce that local officials across the country had decided to shift strategies. Their solutions were varied programs of remedies. These included the new, crucial elements of choice for parents in terms of specialized schools and many academic and vocational programs.

Boston provides an interesting instance of this varied strategy. In 1987 Boston schools were released from federal jurisdiction—thirteen years after violence toward busing had produced a crisis reported across the world. In 1989 Boston introduced a new strategy, creating three zones in the city for elementary and middle schools. Thus, parents were allowed to choose their children's schools within these zones, provided the choices, taken together, resulted in an overall racial balance both within each zone and in individual schools. In order to ensure the balance, it was necessary for school officials to monitor parents' choices. However, school officials said that in 1989 80 percent of children in grades one through six were able to attend the school of their parents' first choice.

Another variant on the theme of mixed strategies was provided by Kansas City, Missouri. Kansas City adopted a complex desegregation of magnet schools, enriched academic programs, and improved school buildings in order to entice white children from the suburbs to schools in the city center. This was a costly plan to be financed by new taxes amounting to several millions of dollars. However, school officials reported that the initial response in fall 1989 was encouraging, with 980 white students from the suburbs transferring to both elementary and high schools in the city. In fall in 1989 Seattle, where African-Americans made up less than 10 percent of the population, voters approved an initiative calling for an end to busing to achieve racial balance by the narrow margin of twelve hundred votes out of 140,000 cast. It was tied to a pledge that city sales tax revenues be used for magnet schools and voluntary desegregation.

In 1989 the Little Rock School District, an area then predominantly African-American, sued the state of Arkansas and two mainly white suburban districts on the grounds of discrimination in allocation of resources and won its case. In December 1989 a federal district judge approved a $129 million settlement providing money over ten years for desegregation programs. Yet in major cities with heavy African-American and Hispanic populations, such as New York, Chicago, Los Angeles, Washington, and Philadephia, desegregation was virtually dead as an issue.

Hue and Cry

Just as the civil rights movement helped stimulate public awareness in the 1950s and 1960s of the social and political rights of human beings across the world and thus, incidentally, fostered expectation of the human rights campaigns of the 1970s, so did the accession to political office in America of the new generation of African-American politicians provide a domestic complement to momentous shifts in the Communist bloc of Eastern Europe.

The burst in the dam of uniform Communist solidarity occurred swiftly and with overwhelming force in 1989 and 1990 after the accumulation of many years of intense political frustration and pent-up energies was released. In 1985 Mikhail Gorbachev came to supreme power in the Soviet Union, eventually as president, and, by proclaiming his commitment to Glasnost and Perestroika, terms usually applied to openness and restructuring, he seemed to invite ever more vocal cries of protest against totalitarian communism and the professing of options to it. Calls for more representative government outside the domination of the Communist party led to various measures of political reform in East Germany, Poland, Czechoslovakia, Hungary, and Bulgaria that were achieved by comparatively peaceful means in 1989. However, mass protest in Romania in December 1989 provoked Nicolae Ceausescu, dictator for twenty-four years, into unleashing the army on civilians, with considerable loss of life. Many soldiers changed sides and their desertion led to the overthrow, capture, and execution of Ceausescu. Perhaps the most important symbolically of all the cracks came with the dismantling of the Berlin Wall around the Brandenburg Gate, a hideous scar dividing West Berlin from East Germany and the frightful symbol of the Cold War for almost thirty years.

The excitement generated cries for independence in some of the Soviet republics of the USSR. The Baltic States sought autonomy, and divisions in Azerbaijan between Christians and Moslems resulted in civil war. By February 1990 there were demonstrations on the very streets of Moscow calling for an end to totalitarian domination by the Communist party in Russia itself. These continued and the traditional May Day parade of military forces in Red Square was punctuated by truculent civilian protests. Monolithic communism was collapsing under the weight of its own inefficiency. There were also diplomatic moves toward the reunification of Germany, leading to a merger of currencies and economic systems in July 1990 and full unification in October.

All of this was seen in sharp, dramatic, and ironic contrast to a tumultuous uprising in Tiananmen Square, Beijing, during the summer of 1989, when mass demonstrations by Chinese people, many of them students and other young people, against totalitarian domination were quelled by brutal and ugly use of force by the Chinese authorities, ending in massive loss of life.

Of course, it would be an exaggeration and somewhat absurd to claim that the cries of protest within the Communist world were in any way directly linked to the American civil rights movement. However, in one very particular and emblematic way they had a common root—the desperate plea of individual, oppressed people for their own freedom and sense of lightness away from domination by the forces of government. The civil rights movement had played an instrumental role in making people right across the world conscious that individuals, no matter how oppressed, could, by demonstrations and arguments based on moral persuasion, change their fate. It was the people of the deep South in the United States who throughout the 1950s and 1960s had done so by taking on the tradition of Mohandas Ghandi in India and deliberately enduring more suffering—though they were the very people who had suffered most.

A clear indication that the protest by African-Americans had sent a powerful message across the world that all oppressed people could rise was conveyed with stark force on February 11, 1990, when Nelson Mandela, relentless foe of apartheid in South Africa and a symbol of the determination of black and colored peoples across the third world to claim due civil rights and dignity for themselves, was released by the government of South Africa, having been a political prisoner of the government for no less than twenty-seven years. His release was a symbol that the dignity of the individual can never be extinguished—no matter how brutal the forces of the state.

9

The Moving Finger

Whatever the final verdict of history on the achievements of civil rights and black power, there is little question that the civil rights and black power movements helped stimulate another renaissance of African-American stories and novels. This was partly because a new generation of writers was encouraged by the extent and inventiveness of African-American protest and was gaining confidence that its novels would excite and entertain a new generation of readers. It was partly because, from the commercial viewpoint of publishers, African-American writing became ever more fashionable. As Chester Himes observed in his autobiography *The Quality of Hurt* (1972), "The American black is a new race of man, the only new race of man to come into being in modern times."

The Renaissance of Postwar African-American Fiction

African-American fiction after 1965 continued to command attention because of its immense power in fielding anew various forms that owed much to black culture in freedom in Africa and slavery in America. This is what English commentator A. Robert Lee refers to as "those habits of language and folklore which have been passed on by generations of black family elders." Other influences included the urban Jewish prose style and preoccupations of such novelists as Saul Bellow (b. 1925) and

Bernard Malamud (b. 1914); the ultramodern fantasies of Thomas Pynchon (b. 1937) and Kurt Vonnegut (b. 1922); and, most notably, the great civil rights movement and its various achievements and vicissitudes, especially in the 1960s when the momentum for changes in racial awareness, discrimination, and political equality were at their greatest. As Ishmael Reed explains in his novel *Yellow Back Radio Broke-Down* (1969), "No-one says the novel has to be any one thing. It can be anything it wants to be, a vaudeville show, the six o'clock news, the mumblings of wild men saddled by demons." Thus, as he suggested in *19 Necromances from Now* (1970), various new forms represented "Fantasy, Nationalism, the Supernatural, Hoo Dooism, Realism, Science Fiction, Autobiography, Satire, Scent, Erotica, Blues, International Intrigue, Jazz. . . ." A. Robert Lee is a persuasive guide in his extended essay and this account follows his observations closely.

Chester Himes (b. 1909), Ann Petry (b. 1911), and Willard Motley (1912–1965) forged, independently, a clear, distinctive style of stark, declaratory prose splattered with tortuous images of chase and conquest as a form of protest.

Closest to pioneer novelist Richard Wright among this select group was Chester Himes, who knew Wright in Paris. Of Himes's early novels, the most compelling is *The Primitive* (1955), with its conventional story of a black writer and his white mistress whose lost weekend of alcoholic oblivion ends in violence and murder, told with biting humor and deployed to expose traditional ambiguities in interracial love affairs. In the 1960s Himes moved directly into crime thrillers in which his African-American detectives Coffin Ed Johnson and Grave Digger Jones explore Harlem as an apocalyptic world of exotic culture, debasing poverty, and heated emotions among Bible-thumping evangelists, hustlers, drug pushers, pimps, and Muslims in such works as *Cotton Comes to Harlem* (1965) and *Blind Man with a Pistol* (1969). The series of nine stories about the detectives was originally published in French. It provided a classic instance of a plebeian genre transcending its outer conventions of detailed scene-setting, ghetto slang, and streetwise insights to evoke a mythic, surreal world of characters who are literary prototypes of the humble overcoming adversity. In this respect, Chester Himes's novels are in the European tradition of Prosper Merimée's novella, *Carmen*.

Critics claimed that in *The Street* (1946) Ann Petry did for New York what Richard Wright had done for Chicago with *Native Son*, mixing fast-paced action, circumstantial detail, and protest commentary in the tragedy of Lutie Johnson, a well-intentioned maid driven to murder by degrading circumstances. Willard Motley used white rather than African-American protagonists to establish different ethnic versions of Bigger Thomas, such as the Italian-American Nick Romano of *Knock on Any Door* (1947), the victim of a mean city who becomes enmeshed in a vortex of drugs and vice, leading to murder and, eventually, to his trial and execution.

Other writers in this tradition included Willard Savoy, who told a familiar story in *Alien Land* (1949) of an African-American light enough in color to pass for white; Julian Mayfield, who unmasked the tawdriness behind the million dollar dream of winning the numbers racket; Herbert Simmons, who set *Corner Boy* (1957) in St. Louis, Missouri, with its own particular brew of drugs in the ghetto and a story about wrongful imprisonment; and William Gardner Smith, who used a European setting for *The Last of the Conquerors* (1948), about life in the army, and *The Stone Face* (1963), set in Paris in the aftermath of the Algerian War and drawing parallels between European imperialism and American racism.

Whereas Ralph Ellison, following the success of *Invisible Man,* remained a withdrawn author content to let his written words speak for him, James Baldwin (1924–1987) was often most ready to speak to the mass media. Yet his body of work included six novels, many short stories, and essays. Indeed, it was as the essayist of *Notes of a Native Son* (1955) that he first attracted attention, thereafter becoming a frequently heard commentator and debater upon black America despite lengthy periods of self-imposed exile in France. He had fought personal battles for due recognition well before the 1960s taunts from Muslims and radicals alike that his adherence to traditional American liberalism was outdated. Yet few, if any, of his critics could equal his command of language and rhetoric, perhaps a legacy of his youth, learning to be a preacher in Harlem.

Go Tell it on the Mountain (1953) reworks the biblical story of Ishmael in Genesis to show how a youth, John Grimes, can outgrow and outdistance himself from the psychological sinews of his family living in Harlem. His mother yearns for his dead father, who was harried to suicide by the police. His stepfather, Gabriel, a preacher, is tortured by his Calvinism and his own responsibility for the violent end of his own child, Royal. Baldwin's later novels lack the sensitive evocation of setting and delicate psychological balance of *Go Tell it on the Mountain,* being more self-conscious and strident. Thus *Another Country* (1962), set in Greenwich Village, echoes its title, taken from Christopher Marlowe's play *The Jew of Malta* with its dubious sexual pun, in the recollections of sister, mistress, companions, and lover of the late jazzman Rufus Brown.

James Baldwin's literary response to the policies of African-American radicals in the 1960s was *Tell Me How Long the Train's Been Gone* (1968), about an actor broken by a heart attack but given an extra lease on life by the proselytizing influence of Black Christopher, who draws him into militant politics. The message of this tract for the times is clear: traditional assumptions about race and liberal politics have been eroded and must be replaced by more assertive, more militant views. *If Beale Street Could Talk* (1974) reasserted the values of community in an elegiac story of a black Romeo and Juliet victimized by the police. In his expressive family saga, *Just above My Head* (1979), James Baldwin returned to the torrid brew of religion and sex associated in his mind with the worlds of evangelism, gospel singing, and creative black artists. The evocation of place in a novel that moves from Harlem to London to Paris is as masterly as is his ability to conjure up the deepest and most intimate human aspirations and needs.

The most prolific writer—and the one who probably sold the most books—was Frank Yerby (b. 1916). He turned briefly away from his commercially successful pulp fiction of white romances to subjects with a pronounced racial theme, such as *Speak Now* (1969), about a love affair between black and white set against the backdrop of the abortive student revolution in Paris in 1968, and *The Dahomean* (1971), a saga of an African family.

With the passing of time African-American writing became ever more diverse. In fact, it was freedom of form that distinguished the generation of African-American writers who came to maturity in the 1960s and 1970s from those of Ralph Ellison's generation. Among the most prominent was LeRoi Jones (b. 1934), who took the African name Imamu Amiri Baraka and became widely known for his militancy. By the early 1960s he had established himself as a rising young playwright for his dramas *The Dutchman* and *The Slave* and as an accomplished essayist for *Blues People* and *Black Music*. He was the founder of the Spirit House in "New Ark," an African-American school for adults exploring new horizons in politics and culture. He also wrote such revolutionary dramas as *The Death of Malcolm X, Home on the Range,* and *Columbia*

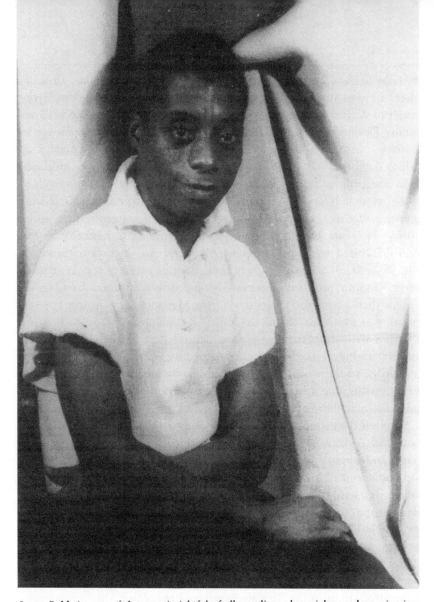

James Baldwin, one of the most insightful of all novelists, playwrights, and essayists into the dilemmas of African-Americans in an age of rising expectations. While his early works of the 1950s were ahead of their time and many radicals considered him too conservative and suspect in the 1960s, his potent sense of inner anguish in his best works has stood the test of time while more volcanic voices of protest have spent their force. His themes included indictment of racial tyranny; the struggle for sexual stability; and the redemptive power of love. (Photo by Carl Van Vechten; Library of Congress.)

the Gem of the Ocean. In 1967 he taught at San Francisco State College, where he was influenced by Maulana Ron Karenga and adopted the model of Karenga's U.S. organization as a matrix for the Black Community Development and Defense Organization founded in Newark in January 1968. This became a base whence, with such associates as Balozi Zayd and Mfundishi Maasi, he could exert a decisive influence upon the politics of black nationalism. *The System of Dante's Hell* (1965) is an odyssey through the Newark ghetto to be compared with Dante's *Inferno. Tales* (1967) is a collection of sixteen expressionist stories about an African-American youth's coming to maturity and is clearly inspired by James Joyce's *Dubliners.* An important theme of Imamu Amiri Baraka's work was that American society was composed of two separate racial cultures employing distinctly different languages.

This theme was also dear to William Melvin Kelley in *dem* (1967), referring to whites as "them" or "dem." It compares and contrasts white suburbia with the African-American city center ghetto in a screwball comedy about a perplexed white executive, Mitchell Pierce, whose knowledge of the world has been supplied by television. His wife gives birth to twins, one white, one black. This is a comedy of racial confusion used as a metaphor for deeper human confusions.

Whether the theme was blues, folklore, or slave narrative, the realistic strains of African-American writing included the South as well as the North and a South imbued with rustic attractions and respect for hearth and home as well as a place of racial oppression. In his novels John O. Killens (b. 1916) moved from pleas for liberal accommodation in *Youngblood* (1954) to black militancy in *And Then We Heard Thunder* (1963) and *Black Man's Burden* (1965). In *'Sippi* (1967), about the civil rights movement in the deep South, he compared and contrasted the strategies of gradual reform with those of black power. However, in *Cotillion: or, One Good Bull Is Worth Half the Herd* (1971) he moved to gentle satire at the affectations of the African-American bourgeoisie.

Ernest Gaines (b. 1933) based much of his work in the Cajun country of Louisiana and explored the mix of Cajuns (descendants of the French settlers of Nova Scotia, or Acadia, expelled by the British in 1755), Creoles (white descendants of the early French settlers), African-Americans, and people from mixed backgrounds. His early Cajun fiction was overshadowed by the critical and commercial success of *The Autobiography of Miss Jane Pittman* (1971). This was a folk novel in the form of the autobiography of a woman who began her life as a cotton slave and lived to be a hundred and ten and take part in the civil rights movement. In *My Father's House* (1978) Ernest Gaines also pitted past against present in his account of an African-American minister in the rural South obliged to try to come to terms with the protest of his radical son.

Albert Murray (b. 1916) of Alabama transposed his idiomatic knowledge of southern music and blues to the urban North in *The Hero and the Blues* (1973) and *Stomping the Blues* (1974). His finest novel was *Train Whistle Guitar* (1974), a folk tale set in a pastoral landscape with a nurturing family that shows why blues has been a central part of African-American culture.

In comparison, William Demby (b. 1922) is more serious minded about the author's debt to realism and his obligation to invent new forms. *Beetlecreek* (1950) followed the tribulations of an African-American adolescent guided by an eccentric white mentor. The claustrophobic setting is a one-horse hill town in Virginia from which the youth is only released at the very end by a fire in which his kindly mentor is immolated. After a period in Italy where, among other things, he worked as a screenplay writer for Michelangelo Antonioni and Roberto Rossellini, he drew from a wider horizon in *The Catacombs* (1965). In the best tradition of cinema crosscutting, it takes the form of a diary and describes a civilization entrapped by its dependence upon electronics and the mass media. The focal point is Doris, a black extra in Rome slated to appear in the Joseph Makiewicz version of *Cleopatra* with Elizabeth Taylor. When Doris becomes pregnant, the diarist does not know if he or an Italian count is the father of her child. Yet when he follows her into the catacombs, the ancient underground sanctuaries of the early Christians, he interprets her coming childbirth as a symbol of unexpected regeneration. *Love Story Black* (1978), set in Manhattan, is less remarkable and its significance lies in its emphasis on literary collage.

African-American History

The movements of civil rights and black power also had a profound impact upon the writing and reading of African-American and black history. Attempts to introduce and popularize African-American history for America in the 1960s included a CBS series in seven parts, *Of Black America,* a public television series of thirty lectures collectively entitled *Americans from Africa: A History,* and John Hope Franklin's four weekly installments for *Life* magazine, *Search for a Black Past.* In the 1980s they included two elaborate six-part serials on the civil rights movement from the 1950s onward, *Eyes on the Prize,* mixing newsreel coverage, personal reminiscences, and commentary.

In August 1968 the National Endowment for the Humanities sponsored seven conferences at colleges across the country to discuss the creation of courses on African-American studies. Various states, notably California, Connecticut, Michigan, New Jersey, and Oklahoma, introduced requirements to have African-American history taught in public schools. Congressional subcommittee hearings on an unsuccessful bill to create a national commission on Negro history and culture made people more conscious of the significance of African-American history. Publishers printed or reissued scores of books about African-Americans and had their history textbooks revised to emphasize the contributions of African-Americans to the history of the United States.

In terms of historiography, the age of the civil rights movement itself has sometimes been described as a Second Reconstruction complementary to the official period of Reconstruction of 1865–1877. Both were periods of effort by a few to draw African-Americans more fully into American society. This was certainly the intention of authors such as Carl M. Brauer in his *John F. Kennedy and the Second Reconstruction* (1977) and underlying such articles as George S. Bruson, Jr.'s "The Second Reconstruction" for the *Journal of Negro History* of October 1974. Young African-American historians were intent on showing the distinctiveness of African-American history and culture and tracing its roots in both African and American history, rather than presenting the history of African-Americans as some sort of subculture in the United States. In this respect their writing developed from newly awakened African-American consciousness.

Slavery became a central candidate for reinterpretation by historians following publication of Stanley Elkins's controversial *Slavery* (1959). It was one of many new interpretations by white scholars who, having rejected stereotypes of racial inferiority, were seeking newer interpretations to account for the position of social inferiority in which many African-Americans found themselves. Stanley Elkins probed this interpretation to compare the African-American experience under slavery to the experience of victims of the Nazis in concentration camps during World War II. He concluded that both groups were inmates and that their incarceration had encouraged in them a form of infantile behavior.

In the 1960s work by African-American historians was essentially revisionist in reaction to the prevalent arguments set by white historians. Thus Kenneth Stampp had begun his *The Peculiar Institution* (1956) with the premise that "innately Negroes are, after all, only white men with black skins, nothing more, nothing less." Work by African-American historians that followed was in reaction to such assertions. Robert Fogel and Stanley Engerman in *Time on the Cross* (1974) used statistical analysis to try to show how slaves held such middle-class values as responsibility, hard work, and, ironically, a sense of upward mobility. Thus these historians tried to imply that men and women retained powers of rational analysis within a coercive system. In *Roll, Jordan, Roll,* (1974) Eugene Genovese discussed the traditionalist paternalism model of slaveowners while eliminating any tinge of racism from it. However, he failed to dissect anything but white society's view of slavery as part of its own development to democratic freedom and equality of economic opportunity. Yet a sincere sustained attempt to penetrate the history of American slavery from the point of view of the slaves and to describe a distinctive African-American culture was begun by such African-American historians as John Blassingame in *The Slave Community* (1972); Vincent Harding in "Religion and Resistance Among Antebellum Negroes, 1800–1860" for August Meier and Elliott Rudwick's *The Making of Black America* (1969); Nathan I. Hughes in *Black Odyssey* (1977); Leslie H. Owens in *This Species of Property* (1978); Albert Raboteau in *Slave Religion* (1978); and Sterling Stuckey in "Through the Prism of Folklore" for the *Massachusetts Review* of Summer 1968.

The cumulative impact of these histories was to dispel—at least in academic circles—any residual myth that the primary explanation of inequality among African-Americans is the legacy of slavery. These historians, in various diverse ways, showed how, against all odds, African-Americans had developed a culture to cope with slavery while retaining their courage and resilience. African-Americans succeeded in maintaining a culture distinctive for its African origins by way of familial relationships, institutions, religious observance, and world views.

Their work was complemented by greater understanding among such white historians as Herbert G. Gutman in *The Black Family in Slavery and Freedom* (1977); Lawrence W. Levine in *Black Culture and Black Consciousness* (1977); Thomas L. Webber in *Deep like the Rivers* (1978); and Peter Wood in *Black Majority* (1974). Similar sensitivity about the

African-American contribution to Reconstruction was shown by Eric Foner in his *Reconstruction: America's Unfinished Revolution, 1863–1877* (1988).

One of the trends underlying African-American historians' continuous search for the truth has been their abandoning traditional liberal interpretations of history as a progressive movement toward equality. Thus, instead of focusing on racial inequality alone, they have diversified their criticism to encompass structural faults in the American system that have fostered racism. Mary F. Berry in *Black Resistance, White Law* (1971) and A. Leon Higginbotham in *The Matter of Color* (1978) turned their attacks upon the judicial system that encouraged racism. Lerone Bennett, Jr., in *The Shaping of Black America* (1974), considered the structural obstacles to equality for African-Americans in the very founding of the American nation. Sterling Stuckey in "Twilight of Our Past: Reflections on the Origins of Black History" in John A. Williams and Charles Harris's *Amistad II* (1971) said, "It is the whole system itself which needs to be investigated, the system whose jails and prisons are almost bursting at the seams with black prisoners." Thus, "it is not the victim who is the most in need of study—it is the executioner." Nell I. Painter in *Exodusters* (1977) and Leon Litwack in *Been in the Storm So Long* (1979) disclosed the dynamics by which blacks from Africa and from slavery became American citizens and the contradictions between the freed people's expectations and those of southern whites. These three historians insisted upon, and provided, a method of investigation that was responsible toward African-American sensitivities. In their *Long Memory: The Black Experience in America* (1982) Mary F. Berry and John Blassingame did not provide a chronological account but a series of essays on certain aspects affecting and shaping the black experience in America. They offered sharp and incisive analyses of various subjects such as black nationalism and managed to integrate cultural, artistic, and sociological trends in an impressive way.

The new emphasis on education for African-Americans and education about African-Americans for readers, both African-American and white,

One of the most sensitive and charismatic screen actors, Sidney Poitier (*standing*) was, for three decades, Hollywood's leading African-American star, often cast as a stalwart champion of right against white racism, as in this, one of his most famous roles, Virgil Tibbs, the lone, plainclothes and northern cop who is wrongfully but briefly suspected of murder in a bigoted southern town in Norman Jewison's award-winning film, *In the Heat of the Night* (1967). (Museum of Modern Art Film Sills Archive.)

resulted in the creation of several hundred political and cultural organizations across the country and the emergence of a new generation of
African-American intellectuals that was highly articulate about black
nationalism. It included the poet Don L. Lee (Haki Madhubuti), founder
of the Institute of Positive Education, based in Chicago; the poets Ted
Jones, Sonia Sanchez, Nikki Giovanni, and Etheridge Knight; and writer
Kalamu ya Salaam. Prominent among the political analysts were Profes-
sors Ron Walters of Howard University and William Strickland of the
University of Massachusetts at Amherst; among the historians, Vincent
Harding and John Hendrik Clarke; among the social scientists, James
Turner of the Africana Studies and Research Center at Cornell Univer-
sity; and among the psychiatrists, Frances Cress Welsung. When the
African Studies Association met in Montreal in October 1969 African-
American scholars, much disturbed by the domineering and arrogance
of white historians, decided to organize a separate group, the African
Heritage Studies Association, for "the reconstruction of African history
and cultural studies along Afro-centric lines."

Contemporary African-American Fiction

The rise of African-Americans in politics in the 1970s and 1980s was
complemented by the ever-growing fecundity and popularity of African-
American writers, whether the form was novels or short stories. They
were revealing imaginative reservoirs of talent among a new, gifted
generation whose works were read avidly by a growing readership.
African-American writers began to expand the novel as an art form by
exploring the examples of autobiographies, prison recollections, new
vocabulary, and the lyrics to songs. They were thus abandoning an
unwritten rule that African-American fiction must perforce express social realism and protest. In this respect, such novelists were continuing
the experimental tradition of Richard Wright.

Ishmael Reed (b. 1938) was among the most imaginative of the new
school of African-American writers. He tried to create a new form of
satire that he called Hoo-Doo tales, Hoo-Doo referring to those aspects
of African-American life that could be traced beyond America to Africa
as well as to the American accents of African-American English and
urban blues. In his anthology *19 Necromancers from Now* (1970) Ishmael Reed said,

Sometimes I feel that the condition of the Afro-American writer in this country is so strange that one has to go to the supernatural for an analogy. Manipulation of the word has always been related in the mind to the manipulation of nature. One utters a few words and stories roll aside, the dead are raised and the river beds emptied of their content.

This is writing as incantation, hallucination, and exorcism.

The obvious precedent for his *The Free-Lance Pallbearers* (1967) was the easel art of Hieronymous Bosch. In this novel America has become HARRY SAM and is ruled by a president obsessed with toilets. The African-American hero, Bukka Doopeyduk, discovers a culture distorted by racial madness and eventually appropriated by Martians who speak Chinese. *Yellow Back Radio Broke-Down* (1969) depicts a Hoo-Doo old West in which the rancher Drag Gibson fights the sheriff Loop Garoo Kid in actions inspired by the satires of Western movies. *The Last Days of the Louisiana Kid* (1974) takes the form of a thriller to unfold the differences between African-American culture and white American culture. *Flight to Canada* (1976) is part fantasy, part slave narrative, part satire of Harriet Beecher Stowe, Byron, and Poe.

John A. Williams (b. 1925) continued the vein of political realism in African-American writing, first mined by Richard Wright. In Williams's hands this vein became one that exploited compulsive plots in an easily accessible style that avoided experimental forms. His apprentice works, *The Angry Ones* (1960), about racism in publishing, *Night Song* (1961), based on the career of jazzman Charlie ("Bird") Parker, and *Sissie* (1963), about a brother and sister who work, respectively, as dramatist and singer, expressed Williams's clear-sighted perceptions on the interrelationship between public and private worlds as they impinge upon race. The fast-paced political thriller *The Man Who Cried I Am* (1967) is about the exploitation of African-American artists and intellectuals by white intelligence agencies such as the CIA and the FBI. *Sons of Darkness, Sons of Light* (1969) was more straightforward and probed the question, What if?—in this case, What would happen if New York were taken over by revolutionary black militants? Politics were equally to the fore in the more experimental, even hallucinatory, novel about Abraham Blackman, who fights anew in all America's major wars from the Revolutionary War to the war in Vietnam. Thus John A. Williams unfolds social history as a serial of repeating episodes. *Mothersill and the Foxes* (1975) was a folk comedy of manners. *The Junior Bachelor Society*

(1976) contrasted the present reality of a group of high school friends reunited to honor their former coach against their aspirations as students.

The work of John Wideman (b. 1941) was resolutely within the tradition of Ralph Ellison. Wideman explored the various ways that memory works, notably in *Hurry Home* (1970), a novel of remembrance in which a janitor working in Philadelphia recalls his past traveling in Europe and considers the Africa of myth that he has never seen. In *There Is a Tree More Ancient Than Eden* (1973) Leon Forrest wove a delicate skein of jazz-inspired images to conjure up a black and Creole cast in five separate sequences. His *Bloodworth Orphans* (1977) showed the United States as a "land of racial orphans," all descended from an archetypal slave-owning family, the Bloodworths. Other young writers with abrasive imaginations included Barry Beckman (b. 1944), Cecil Brown (b. 1943), and Charles Johnson (b. 1948).

Certain writers delved into the demonic obscene vocabulary of urban ghettos to expose the nether world of crime and drugs and the challenge of white stereotypes of African-Americans. Thus in *Lord of the Dark Places* (1970) Hal Bennett used language to disrupt conventional attitudes to the white world that had disordered African-American lives. In *S.R.O.* (1971), Robert Deane Pharr unfolded the dirty linen of a Harlem rooming house—the single room occupancy of the title. The plot of *The Hippodrome* (1973), by Cyrus Colter, is about a fleeing murderer who takes refuge in a black sex circus pandering to affluent whites. It has the hallucinogenic quality of a drug-induced nightmare. Other writers of nightmare fantasies include Ronald L. Fair, Nathan Heard, and David Bradley.

The Wig (1966), by Charles Wright, provided a latter-day African-American Candide with the delights of an innocent girl with an outrageous wig and accommodating behavior. It was intended as a parody of the American dream and the Wasp tradition of self-help. in *NO* (1973) and *Reflex and Bone Structure* (1975), Clarence Major (b. 1937) used the crime thriller to disclose complements between the work of a fictional detective unraveling mystery and actual novelists unfolding the meaning of life by adroit use of language to describe its trials and tribulations.

In *Curling* (1968) Robert Boles used his story of an African-American engineer raised by white parents whose mad weekend in Boston ends in a murder and the sudden disclosure of his origins. Al Young (b. 1939) assumed the voice of an exotic everyman narrator for *Sitting Pretty* (1976).

African-American women writers who have come to maturity since the 1960s demonstrated that the world of women had different aspects from the world of men and that they could capture it with authentic voices. Some chose to emphasize being female, others being African-American. Their impact on the literary world has been considerable, notably on account of their evocation of urban life and their penchant for literary experimentation.

Toni Morrison (b. 1931) established herself with *The Bluest Eye* (1970), about Pecola Breedlove, victim not only of incest but also of society's prevailing standards of pulchritude as represented by Shirley Temple. The weight of sexual and racial social stereotyping proves too burdensome and Pecola slides into the isolation of madness. Search for identity and fulfillment was also the subject of *Sula* (1974), in which the career of a wife and mother, Nel Wright, is contrasted over forty years with the freewheeling lifestyle of Sula Peace in the provincial town of Bottom, Ohio. *Song of Solomon* (1977) was a blues-like celebration of adventurer Macon ("Milkman") Dead, set in the context of an African-American community that is creative with slender resources. *Tar Baby* (1981), set in the Caribbean, explored white wealth patronizing blacks' needs in a story of an educated young black woman's coming to terms with her love for an undereducated but streetwise lover.

Alice Walker (b. 1944) and Gayle Jones (b. 1948) treated the sexual encounters of African-American women quite specifically and commemorated what was often a continuous cycle of violation, loss, and survival. Alice Walker's *The Third Life of Grange Copeland* (1970) celebrated the way the hero, having endured slavery in the South, ghetto life in the North, and rural contentment in Georgia is able to pass on his lifetime's experience to his granddaughter, Ruth, who attains maturity in the period of civil rights. In *Meridian* (1976) Alice Walker provided a portrait of a woman whose early life is blemished. She survives as a participant in the civil rights movement and yet remains, at the close, unsatisfied emotionally and materially.

Gayle Jones dissected sexual violence in her accounts of women as mothers, slaves, sexual playthings, and predators bent on vengeance. *Corregidora* (1975) explores the self-discovery by a blues singer from Kentucky of a diary of abused women extending to a cruel white ancestor who owned slaves in Brazil. We are made to understand that this dynasty serves as a metaphor for African-American women across the generations who were exploited but who survived. After a lifetime of abuse, the heroine of *Eva's Man* (1976) deteriorates into madness and feels compelled to take revenge by murder. A collection of short stories, *White Rat* (1977), also explored the way African-American women can assume control of their sex lives.

A recurrent theme in novels by African-American women writers was the role of African-American women as purveyors of authority and tradition, matrilineal purpose set in a world of feckless men. This is the role of Merle Kimbora in *The Chosen Place, the Timeless People* (1969), by Paule Marshall (b. 1929). It takes place in the Caribbean, where white technology is set against the tribal values of a black community. In *The Salt Eaters* (1980), by Toni Cade Bambara (b. 1939), Velma Henry survives her own attempted suicide, recovers her spiritual strength, and leads a black community's radical attack on the pollution and corrupt politics of a chemical corporation.

Childhood is another focal point of such writers as Rosa Guy (b. 1925), Kristin Hunter (b. 1931), and Louise Meriwether. *The Survivors* (1975), by Kristin Hunter, follows a friendship between a streetwise youth and a genteel dressmaker. In *Daddy Was a Numbers Runner* (1970), by Louise Meriwether, a girl growing up in Harlem describes the mores of whites.

Intimate relations as seen from the woman's point of view is the theme of Carlene Hatcher Polite (b. 1932) in *The Flagellants* (1967), in which a consuming sexual passion binds a couple who argue over the best way to work in a white world. Some writers turn to comedy, as in *Sister X and the Victims of Foul Play* (1975), by Carlene Hatcher Polite, set in the world of dance; and *The Landlord,* by Kristin Hunter, in which a landlord, Elgar Endres, buys a block of tenements wherein resides a motley crew, including the confidence man Eldridge DuBois. In *The Lakeside Rebellion* (1978), also by Kristin Hunter, the story of an African-American community's attempt to prevent the building of a new highway that will destroy their town is used to show how African-American citizens have for years systematically undermined white society.

Among writers of short stories James Alan McPherson (b. 1943) established himself in the forefront with *Hue and Cry* (1969) and *Elbow Room* (1977). The freshness of vision in McPherson is revealed by his narrator in "Elbow Room" (1977), from the collection of the same title, when he says, "A narrator cannot function without new angles of vision. I need new eyes, regeneration, fresh forms. . . ." Thus in "I Am an American," McPherson tells of African-Americans in London who find themselves aliens there. "A Matter of Vocabulary" in *Hue and Cry* (1969) is about two brothers who work in a grocery store in Georgia and who are allowed a tragic glimpse into an isolated, impoverished future in the symbol of an abandoned, shoeless woman who stalks the funeral parlor close by. "On Trains" and "A Solo Sung for Dot" conjure up the remembrance of bygone days by black Pullman porters. "Cabbages and Kings" is a tragedy in miniature—the story of a civil rights worker in the 1960s who becomes disillusioned with the course of events and cannot sustain her love for her white coworker, nor, after he leaves, for his black replacements. McPherson discloses details at exactly the most opportune moment in his stories to expose the irony of a society that promises more to its inhabitants that it delivers.

Among the distinctive voices contemporary with these novelists and writers of short stories was playwright August Wilson (b. 1945). Like many, he was concerned with improving the lot of African-Americans in the United States, whom he believed, even in the 1980s and 1990s, had a culture that was very different from that of whites. During the 1980s he wrote a series of plays about the life of African-Americans in the twentieth century, each set in a different decade. The first of the plays, *Jitney,* was set in the 1970s. Then came *Ma Rainey's Black Bottom,* set in the 1920s, *Fences* (the 1950s), *Joe Turner's Come and Gone* (1911), *The Piano Lesson* (the 1930s), and *Two Trains Running* (1968). Some of these plays were shaped and altered as a result of experiences of early performances mounted at the Yale School of Drama, where they were directed by the dean, Lloyd Richards. All the plays attend to August Wilson's superb ability to evoke the language and sentiments of African-Americans in a particular context of time and place and to make them highly articulate. Two of the plays, *Joe Turner* and *The Piano Lesson,* were inspired by artist Romare Bearden's paintings of black America.

Art from Anguish to Realization and Light

New assertion of African-American artistic achievement was also found in painting and sculpture. Critic Michael Brenson explained in his article "Black Artists: A Place in the Sun" for the *New York Times* of March 12, 1989, how, after years of neglect, the work of African-American artists was being considered an essential part of the future of American art. Among previous African-American artists to achieve national recognition were Bob Thompson and Jean Michael Basquiat, famous in the 1960s. However, both died before they were thirty. Another distinguished artist was Aaron Douglas.

One of the most prolific artists was Romare Bearden (1911–1988), who moved through many styles, from social realist gouaches in the 1940s to splattered elemental abstraction in the 1960s. Toward the end of his life he returned to collages that recall his childhood memories of Mecklenburg County in North Carolina. Michael Brenson wrote of Bearden's work in the *New York Times* of June 9, 1989, that his dogs and cats

are not so much pets as witnesses. These are the cocks of sacrifice and the birds emblematic of the rituals and secrets of the natural human world. There are black families and black women—as mysterious and enchanting as sky and dawn. There are instruments that play musicians and lamps and chairs that decide how life around them will be lived. And there are those locomotives, halfway in and halfway out of stations, metaphors for a body of work in which stopping can be only momentary before the journey begins again.

If Ishmael Reed or Charles Wright had ever wanted their satirical and lyrical novels illustrated, then Romare Bearden would have been a natural choice. However, Bearden's later pictures also mix such fantastic elements as Persian miniatures, Greek vases, and Italian gothic painting. Fully aware of the dysfunction of contemporary life, he never lost his sense of excitement about variety and the need for artists to attempt to capture a wide spectrum of that variety.

The 1980s witnessed acclaim for a whole generation of African-American artists. Among them was Michael Puryear, who was selected to represent the United States at the 1989 Sao Paulo Biennale and was thus the first African-American artist to be the sole representative of his country at a major international exhibition. The work of a young photographer, Lorna Simpson, was included in "The Bi-National: American Art of the Late '80s," an exhibition that moved from Boston in fall 1988 to a tour of West Germany in 1989. Lorna Simpson's work was significant because her photographs exposed all sorts of commonly held assumptions about body language and gestures.

Other indications of a new awareness and esteem for art by African-Americans came in three exhibitions devoted to them in 1989: "Tradition and Transformation: Contemporary Afro-American Sculpture" at the Bronx Museum; "The Appropriate Object" at the Albright-Knox Art Gallery in Buffalo; and "Pillar to Post" at Kenkeleba House on New York's Lower East Side. In early 1990, first the Corcoran Gallery in Washington and then the Brooklyn Museum played host to a major art exhibition, "Facing History: The Black Image in American Art, 1710–1914, organized by Guy C. McElroy, an African-American art historian. While a first glance might suggest that the show simply disclosed restrictive white stereotypes of African-Americans, in fact, the paintings and sculptures, seen as a whole and including works by African-American as well as white artists, revealed political and racial conflict on a profound psychological level. Guy C. McElroy told Grace Glueck of the *New York Times* for the issue of January 7, 1990,

All art is by nature a political statement. It represents a way of life in society primarily as seen by the majority culture, and in the case of blacks, influenced by the subject's lack of access to money, education and social power. So the show is clearly a statement about the politics of black life in American society.

Not only had the civil rights movement conferred increased dignity on African-American artists, writers, and musicians, but also African-American artists and sculptors themselves were, by now, sufficiently confident to resurrect the terrors of the past, and by their art, to transcend the original meanings of those terrors. A parallel comes to mind. During the 1980s some artists and art salesmen came to believe that West German art was the best art in the world because West German painters had been able to face the most painful subjects in German history, the terrors of the Third Reich and the Holocaust. One of the most painful facts of American history was the violence visited upon African-Americans, first in the period of slavery, later in the period when African-American citizens were seeking their due civil rights. In the 1980s various African-American artists recalled these terrors, such as the sculptor Melvin Edwards and the painter Robert Colescott.

Abstract expressionism, a dominant form of American art of the 1940s, 1950s, and 1960s, was a crucial form for African-American artists, providing enough space for everyone to enter, drawing upon improvisation and gesture as a means of expressing basic emotions and energies. However, throughout the 1950s and 1960s the preferred style of commercial paintings and sculpture was immaculate, flat surfaces. In contrast to this glossy look, African-American artists preferred to show the effort that went into their work, and thus they revealed the pressures of the African-American experience. Michael Brenson explains how

in the course of recognizing and encouraging art in which the present and future seemed to be everything, something was always left behind. The tradition of the new is about possibility but it is also about erasure. Part of what was erased was just about every artist for whom memory, history and roots were indispensable.

In paintings of contrived disorder Robert Colescott was best known for parody, inserting African-Americans into unexpected locales. Thus he replaced the pregnant Dutch wife in the famous wedding portrait by Flemish artist Jan Van Eyck with a black woman in a version that he called *Natural Rhythm: Thank You Jan Van Eyck*. Similarly, he replaced Georges Manet's white nude in *Dejeuner sur l'Herbe* with another black woman and painted a black George Washington in his version of the German painter Emanuel Leutze's *Washington Crossing the Delaware*.

Melvin Edwards's preferred form was welded steel structures. His work was eloquent about the sort of imagination that African-American artists brought to painting and sculpture. Born in Houston in 1937, educated in school at California, much-traveled in Africa, Europe, and the Caribbean, a noted teacher at various universities, and a recipient of various fellowships, he was not widely known. This was ironic because many of his works were most provocative, with their use of chains as tall as people and with arches and post lintels reminiscent of preindustrial architecture. His *Lynch Fragments*—a hundred separate works completed in three periods (1963–1966, 1977, and since 1978)—include chains, hammers, and vises—all implements associated with violence done to slaves in the old South.

Many of Edwards's individual sculptures bear African titles. Some of the tools in the sculptures, such as horseshoes, links, nails, and stakes, were found; some were created. Not only did these sculptures reflect an interest in welded steel that had begun during the civil rights years, but they also reflected a determination to take images that had debased African-Americans and use them in a defiant way that was confrontational. As Michael Brenson explains, "You cannot look at these almost indestructible forms without feeling the weight of the history branded into them." Hence, Melvin Edwards used dark emblems of personal racial history and transformed them into positive statements of remembrance and as an affirmation of the vibrancy of the struggle to overcome the past.

Among the shifts in sensibility and perception by public and artists was a recognition of the colors black and white as part of the entire spectrum of colors and their ever-greater use by artists. This was especially true of the abstract expressionism of John L. Moore, who emphasized the way the color black could negotiate a myriad of other colors, and the work of Maren Hasinger, whose vibrant black cable trees manage to take root and thrive out of sterile minimal blocks of white cement. These artists seemed to be making a personal and historical statement about the resilience of African-Americans through adversity.

In the 1980s some African-American photographers mixed painting with their photographs. Christian Walker sometimes sliced his pictures in half and painted on them. The photographs of Carrie Mae Weems often had words embedded in or surrounding them. Pat Ward Williams was, like contemporary African-American writers, deeply committed to the struggles of African-Americans and willing to refer to historical precedents in order to make her case. This was particularly true of her sculptural installation for an exhibition of 1989 at the Williams College Museum of Art entitled "Black Photographers Bear Witness: One Hundred Years of Social Protest." The centerpiece of the installation was a box made up of frames in whose panes were reflected the image of an African-American. This was Henry Brown, a slave who in 1856 had had himself shipped to Philadelphia and freedom in such a case. The title of the sculpture, "Thirty-two Hours in a Box . . . Still Counting (Homage to Henry Box Brown)" was ambiguous, as were its surroundings—four free-standing columns upon which were hung photographs of a violin, a rose, a skyscraper, and the eye of a doll.

While the past continued to cast a dark shadow over the present, African-American authors and artists were able to face its unalterable terrors with a confidence born of social progress and psychological perception. As Ralph Ellison had foretold, African-Americans had become identified with the struggle of the individual for liberation despite alienation from society. Moreover, the metamorphosis of African-Americans in society was largely owing to the remarkable sense of purpose and stamina that they, themselves, had demonstrated in the social and political transformation of the United States in the momentous years of civil rights.

Bibliography

General

Bennett, Lerone, Jr. *Before the Mayflower: A History of Black America*. Chicago, 1961. 2d ed. Chicago, 1969.

Berry, Mary Frances, and John W. Blassingame. *Long Memory: The Black Experience in America*. New York, 1982.

Foner, Philip S. *Organized Labor and the Black Worker, 1619–1973*. New York, 1974.

U.S. Bureau of the Census. *The Social and Economic Status of the Black Population in the United States: An Historical View, 1790–1978*. Washington, D.C.: U.S. Department of Commerce, 1979.

Walker, Robert H. *The Reform Spirit in America: A Demonstration of the Pattern of Reform in the American Republic*. New York, 1976.

White, John. *Black Leadership in America, 1895–1968*. London and New York, 1985.

Williamson, Joel. *The Crucible of Race: Black-White Relations in the American South since Emancipation*. New York, 1984.

Woodward, C. Vann. *The Strange Career of Jim Crow*. New York, 1955. 2d, rev. ed. New York, 1966.

1. Southern Efficiency and Northern Charm

THE PROGRESSIVE ERA

Barbeau, A. E., and Florence Henri. *The Unknown Soldiers: Black Troops in World War I*. Philadelphia, 1974.

Du Bois, W. E. B. *The Souls of Black Folks*. 1903. Reprint. New York, 1961.

Logan, Rayford. *The Betrayal of the Negro: From Rutherford B. Hayes to Woodrow Wilson.* New York, 1965. Originally published as *The Negro in American Life and Thought: The Nadir, 1877–1901.* (New York, 1954).

Meier, August. *Negro Thought in America, 1880–1915.* Ann Arbor, Mich., 1963.

BOOKER T. WASHINGTON AND HIS CRITICS

Harlan, Louis R. *Booker T. Washington: The Making of a Black Leader, 1865–1901.* New York and Oxford, 1972.

———. *Booker T. Washington: The Wizard of Tuskegee, 1901–1915.* New York and Oxford, 1983.

Hawkins, Hugh, ed. *Booker T. Washington and His Critics.* 1962. Reprint. Boston, 1974.

Weisberger, Bernard A. *Booker T. Washington.* New York, 1972.

W. E. B. DU BOIS

Broderick, Francis L. *W. E. B. Du Bois: Negro Leader in a Time of Crisis.* 1959. Reprint. Stanford, Calif., 1966.

Logan, Rayford W. *W. E. B. Du Bois: A Profile.* New York, 1971.

Rampersad, Arnold. *The Art and Imagination of W. E. B. Du Bois.* London, 1976.

Rudwick, Elliott. *W. E. B. Du Bois: Propagandist of the Negro Protest.* New York, 1969.

AFRICAN-AMERICAN CULTURE IN THE NORTH

Anderson, Jervis. *Harlem: The Great Black Way, 1900–1950.* London, 1982. Also published as *This Was Harlem: A Cultural Portrait, 1900–1950.* New York, 1983.

Huggins, Nathan I. *Harlem Renaissance.* New York, 1971.

McKay, Claude. *Harlem: Negro Metropolis.* 1940. Reprint. New York, 1968.

Osofsky, Gilbert. *Harlem: The Making of a Ghetto, 1880–1930.* New York, 1963.

2. *Not in the Mood*

AFRICAN-AMERICANS AND THE NEW DEAL

Bunche, Ralph. *The Political Status of the Negro in the Age of FDR.* Chicago, 1973.

Kirby, John B. *Black Americans in the Roosevelt Era: Liberalism and Race.* Knoxville, Tenn., 1980.

Weiss, Nancy J. *Farewell to the Party of Lincoln: Black Politics in the Age of FDR.* Princeton, 1983.

WHITE OVER BLACK

Carter, Dan T. *Scottsboro: A Tragedy of the American South.* Baton Rouge, La. 1969. Johnson, Charles S. *Patterns of Negro Segregation.* New York, 1943.
Myrdal, Gunnar. *An American Dilemma.* New York, 1944.
Sosna, Morton. *In Search of the Silent South.* New York, 1977.
Zargrando, Robert L. *The NAACP Crusade against Lynching, 1909 -1950.* Philadelphia, 1980.

AFRICAN-AMERICANS IN THE 1940S

Capeci, Dominic J., Jr. *The Harlem Riot of 1943.* Philadelphia, 1977.
Dalfiume, Richard M. *Desegregation of the U.S. Armed Forces: Fighting on Two Fronts, 1939–1953.* Columbia, Mo., 1969.
Lee, Ulysses. *The Employment of Negro Troops.* Washington, D.C., 1966.
Shogan, Robert, and Tom Craig. *The Detroit Race Riot.* Philadelphia, 1964.
Wynn, Neil A. *The Afro-American and the Second World War.* London, 1976.

3. Made Visible

AMERICA, BLACK AND WHITE, AFTER 1945

Bracey, John H., August Meier, and Elliott Rudwick. *Black Nationalism in America.* New York, 1970.
Branch, Taylor. *Parting the Waters: America in the King Years, 1954–1963.* New York, 1988.
Hodgson, Godfrey. *America in Our Time.* Garden City, N.Y., and London, 1976.
Levin, Sam A., et al. *Still a Dream: The Changing Status of Blacks since 1960.* Cambridge, Mass., 1975.
Manchester, William. *The Glory and the Dream: A Narrative History of America, 1932–1972.* Boston, 1973; London, 1974.
Marable, Manning. *Race, Reform, and Rebellion: The Second Reconstruction in Black America, 1945–1982.* New York and London, 1984.
———. *Race, Politics and Power: Comparative Movements in the Black Diaspora.* New York and London, 1985.
Meier, August, Elliott Rudwick, and Francis L. Broderick, eds. *Black Protest Thought in the Twentieth Century.* 2d ed. New York, 1971.
Muse, Benjamin. *American Negro Revolution.* New York, 1970.
Newman, Dorothy K., et al. *Protest, Politics, and Prosperity: Black Americans and White Institutions, 1940–1975.* New York, 1978.
Parson, Talcott, and Kenneth B. Clark, eds. *The Negro American.* Boston, 1967.
Polenberg, Richard. *One Nation Divisible: Class, Race, and Ethnicity in the United States since 1938.* New York and Harmondsworth, Middlesex, 1980.
Sitkoff, Harvard. *The Struggle for Black Equality, 1954–1980.* New York, 1981.

TRUMAN, THE COLD WAR, AND BLACK AMERICA

Berman, William. *The Politics of Civil Rights in the Truman Administration.* Columbus, Ohio, 1970; Lawrence, Kans., 1973.

Bernstein, Barton J., ed. *Politics and Policies of the Truman Administration.* Chicago, 1970.

Du Bois, W. E. B. *The Autobiography of W. E. B. Du Bois: A Soliloquy on Viewing My Life from the Last Decade of Its First Century.* New York, 1968.

McCoy, Donald R., and Richard T. Ruytten. *Quest and Response: Minority Rights and the Truman Administration.* Lawrence, Kans., 1973.

Meier, August, and Elliott Rudwick. *CORE: A Study in the Civil Rights Movement, 1942–1968.* New York, 1973.

Record, Wilson. *Race and Radicalism.* Ithaca, N.Y., 1964.

EISENHOWER AND THE 1950S

Ambrose, Stephen. *Eisenhower, the President.* New York and London, 1985).

Lawson, Steven F. *Black Ballots: Voting Rights in the South, 1944– 1969.* New York, 1976.

Rowan, Carl T., and Jackie Robinson. *Wait till Next Year.* New York, 1976.

HOUSING

Danielson, Michael N. *The Politics of Exclusion.* New York, 1976.

Haar, Charles M., and Demetrius S. Iatridis. *Housing the Poor in Suburbia.* Cambridge, 1974.

Schnore, Leo F. *Class and Race in Cities and Suburbs.* Chicago, 1972.

U.S. Housing and Home Finance Agency. *Our Non-White Population and Its Housing: The Changes Between 1950 and 1960.* Washington, D.C., 1963.

EDUCATION AND THE BROWN CASE

Graglia, Lino A. *Disaster by Decree: The Supreme Court Decisions on Race and the Schools.* Ithaca, N.Y., 1976.

Kluger, Richard. *Simple Justice: The History of Brown v. Board of Education and Black America's Struggle for Equality.* New York, 1976.

Wilkinson, J. Harvie, III. *From Brown to Bakke: The Supreme Court and School Integration, 1954–1978.* New York, 1979.

4. Martin Luther King and the Emergence of the Civil Rights Movement

THE AFRICAN-AMERICAN CHURCH, THE SCLC, AND CIVIL RIGHTS

Bartley, Numan V. *The Rise of Massive Resistance: Race and Politics in the South during the 1950s.* Baton Rouge, La., 1969.

Frazier, E. Franklin. *The Negro Church in America*. New York, 1963.

Garrow, David J. *Bearing the Cross: Martin Luther King, Jr., and the Southern Christian Leadership Conference*. New York, 1986.

Morris, Aldon G. *The Origins of the Civil Rights Movement: Black Communities Organizing for Change*. New York, 1984.

Nelson, Hart M., Raytha Yokley, and Anne K. Nelson, eds. *The Black Church in America*. New York, 1971.

Stevenson, Janet. *The Montgomery Bus Boycott*. New York, 1971.

MARTIN LUTHER KING, JR.

Bennett, Lerone, Jr. *What Manner of Man: A Biography of Martin Luther King, Jr.* New York, 1968.

Garrow, David J. *The FBI and Martin Luther King, Jr.: From Solo to Memphis*. London, 1981.

King, Martin Luther, Jr. *Stride toward Freedom: The Montgomery Story*. New York and London, 1959.

———. *Why We Can't Wait*. New York, 1964.

Lewis, David L. *King: A Critical Biography*. New York and London, 1970.

Lincoln, C. Eric. *Martin Luther King, Jr.: A Profile*. New York, 1970.

Oates, Stephen B. *Let the Trumpet Sound: The Life of Martin Luther King, Jr.* New York and London, 1982.

CIVIL RIGHTS IN THE LATER 1950S

Bates, Daisy. *The Long Shadow of Little Rock*. New York, 1962.

Dulles, Foster Rhea. *The Civil Rights Commission, 1957–1965*. Lansing, Mich., 1968.

"THE WHITE NEGRO"

Mailer, Norman. "The White Negro." *Independent* (March 1957). Repr. in *Advertisements for Myself* (New York, 1964).

SNCC

Carson, Clayborne. *In Struggle: SNCC and the Black Awakening of the 1960s*. Cambridge, Mass., 1981.

Zinn, Howard. *SNCC: The New Abolitionists*. Boston, 1964.

5. A Dream beyond the New Frontier

JOHN F. KENNEDY AND THE NEW FRONTIER

Brauer, Carl M. *John F. Kennedy and the Second Reconstruction*. New York, 1977.

Fairlie, Henry. *The Kennedy Promise*. Garden City, N.Y., 1973.
Knapp, David, and Kenneth Polk. *Scouting the War on Poverty: Social Reform Politics in the Kennedy Administration*. Lexington, Mass., 1971.

CIVIL RIGHTS IN THE EARLY 1960S

Barnes, Catherine A. *Journey from Jim Crow: The Desegregation of Southern Transit*. New York, 1983.
Lewis, Anthony. *Portrait of a Decade: The Second American Revolution*. New York, 1964.
Peck, James. *Freedom Ride*. New York, 1962.
Record, Wilson. *Race and Radicalism*. Ithaca, N.Y., 1964.
Silberman, Charles. *Crisis in Black and White*. New York, 1964.
Sitkoff, Harvard. *The Struggle for Black Equality, 1954–1980*. 1981. Reprint. New York, 1983.
Viorst, Milton. *Fire in the Streets*. New York, 1981.
Zinn, Howard. *The Southern Mystique*. New York, 1964.

THE WARREN COURT

Bickel, Alexander M. *The Supreme Court and the Idea of Progress*. New York, 1970.
Cox, Archibald. *The Warren Court: Constitutional Decision as an Instrument of Reform*. Cambridge, Mass., 1968.
Furston, Richard. *Constitutional Counterrevolution? The Warren Court and the Burger Court: Judicial Policy Making in Modern America*. Cambridge, Mass., 1977.
Kurland, Philip B. *Politics, the Constitution, and the Warren Court*. Chicago and London, 1970.
Mitan, G. Theodore. *Decade of Decision: The Supreme Court and the Constitutional Revolution*. New York, 1967.

MALCOLM X

Breitman, George. *The Last Year of Malcolm X*. New York, 1970.
Clarke, John Hendrik, ed. *Malcolm X: The Man and His Times*. New York, 1969.
Goldman, Peter. *The Death and Life of Malcolm X*. London, 1975.
Haley, Alex. *The Autobiography of Malcolm X*. New York, 1965.
Malcolm X. *The Speeches of Malcolm X at Harvard*. Edited by Archie Epps. New York, 1969.

BLACK MUSLIMS

Essien-Udom, E. U. *Black Nationalism: The Rise of Black Muslims in the USA*. Harmondsworth, Middlesex, 1966.

Lincoln, C. Eric. *The Black Muslims in America.* 1959. Rev. ed. Boston, 1973.
Lomax, Louis E. *When the Word Is Given: A Report on Elijah Muhammad, Malcolm X, and the Black Muslim World.* New York, 1964.

LYNDON JOHNSON AND THE GREAT SOCIETY

Lawson, Steven F. *Black Ballots: Voting Rights in the South, 1944–1969.* New York, 1976.
Marmer, Theodore R. *The Politics of Medicare.* Chicago, 1973.
Morgan, Ruth P. *The President and Civil Rights.* New York, 1970.
Rainwater, Lee, and William L. Yancey. *The Moynihan Report and the Problems of Controversy.* Cambridge, Mass., 1967.

WAR ON POVERTY

Donovan, John C. *The Politics of Poverty.* New York, 1967.
Harrington, Michael. *The Other America.* New York, 1962.
Kershaw, Joseph A. *Government against Poverty.* Washington, D.C., 1970.
Leacock, Eleanor Burke, ed. *The Culture of Poverty: A Critique.* New York, 1971.
Patterson, James T. *The Welfare State in America, 1930–1980: The Struggle against Poverty in America, 1930–1980.* British Association for American Studies; Pamphlets in American Studies 7. Cambridge, 1981.

6. Civil Rights and Black Power

CIVIL RIGHTS IN THE MID-1960S

Belfrage, Sally. *Freedom Summer.* New York, 1965.
Garrow, David J. *Protest at Selma.* New Haven, Conn., 1978.
Huie, William Bradford. *Three Lives for Mississippi.* New York, 1968.
Raines, Howell. *My Soul Is Rested: Movement Days in the Deep South Remembered.* New York, 1977.
Sugarman, Tracy. *Stranger at the Gates: A Summer in Mississippi.* New York, 1960.
Sutherland, Elizabeth, ed. *Letters from Mississippi.* New York, 1965.

LEADERS

Anderson, Jervis. *A. Philip Randolph: A Biographical Portrait.* New York, 1973.
Brink, William, and Louis Harris. *The Negro Revolution in America.* New York, 1964.
Dubofsky, Melvyn, and Warren Van Tine. *John L. Lewis: A Biography.* New York, 1977.
Hudson, Theodore R. *From LeRoi Jones to Imamu Amiri Baraka.* Durham, N.C., 1973.
Rustin, Bayard. *Down the Line.* Chicago, 1971.

SUMMER AND SMOKE

Boesel, David, and Peter H. Rossi, eds. *Cities under Siege: An Anatomy of the Ghetto Riots, 1964–1968.* New York, 1971.

Cohen, Jerry, and William S. Murphy. *Burn, Baby, Burn!* New York, 1966.

Fogelson, Robert M. *Violence as Protest: A Study of Riots and Ghettos.* Garden City, N.Y., 1971.

———, ed. *The Los Angeles Riots.* New York, 1969.

Moynihan, Daniel P. *Maximum Feasible Misunderstandings: Community Action in the War on Poverty.* New York, 1970.

The National Advisory Commission on Civil Disorders (Kerner Report). New York, 1968.

National Association of Social Workers, eds. *Riots in the City: An Addendum to the McCone Commission Report.* Los Angeles, 1967.

Porambo, Ron. *No Cause for Indictment: An Autopsy of Newark.* New York, 1971.

Rose, Stephen M. *The Betrayal of the Poor: The Transformation of Community Action.* Cambridge, Mass., 1972.

Violence in the City: An End or a Beginning? A Report by the Governer's Commission on the Los Angeles Riots. Los Angeles, 1965.

BLACK POWER

Allen, Robert. *Black Awakening in Capitalist America.* Garden City, N.Y., 1969.

Carmichael, Stokely. *Stokely Speaks.* New York, 1971.

Carmichael, Stokely, and Charles V. Hamilton. *Black Power: The Politics of Liberation in America.* New York, 1967.

Cruse, Harold. *The Crisis of the Negro Intellectual.* New York, 1967.

Foner, Philip S., ed. *The Black Panthers Speak.* Philadelphia, 1970.

Forman, James. *The Making of Black Revolutionaries.* New York, 1972.

Grier, William H., and Price M. Cobbs. *Black Rage.* New York, 1968.

Haskins, James. *Profiles in Black Power.* Garden City, N.Y., 1972.

Wright, Nathan, Jr. *Black Power and Urban Unrest.* New York, 1967.

7. *Chaos Is Come Again*

THE SILENT MAJORITY

Phillips, Kevin. *The Emerging Republican Majority.* New Rochelle, N.Y., 1969.

EDUCATION AND THE *BAKKE* CASE

Sindler, Allan P. *Bakke, DeFunis, and Minority Admissions: The Quest for Equal Opportunity.* New York, 1978.

Wilkinson, J. Harvie, III. *From Brown to Bakke: The Supreme Court and School Integration, 1954–1978.* New York, 1979.

BLACK NATIONALISM AND PAN-AFRICANISM

Chrisman, Robert, and Nathan Hare, eds. *Pan-Africanism.* Indianapolis and New York, 1974. The contributions are by Adolph Reed, Charles V. Hamilton, Earl Anthony, Imamu Amiri Baraka, Muhammad Ahmad, and Stokely Charmichael.

Harding, Vincent, and Lerone Bennett. *IBW and Education for Liberation.* Chicago, 1973.

McGinnis, James. "Crisis and Contradiction in Black Studies." *Black World* 22 (March 1973): 27–35.

Smith, Mark. "A Response to Haki Madhubuti." *Black Scholar* 6 (January-February 1975): 32.

Strickland, William. "Black Intellectuals and the American Social Scene." *Black World* 7 (October 1975): 4–10.

———. "Whatever Happened to the Politics of Liberation?" *Black Scholar* 7 (October 1975): 20–26.

Walters, Ronald. "Strategy for 1976: A Black Political Party." *Black Scholar* 7 (October 1975): 13.

Welsung, Frances Cress. "The Cress Theory of Color-Confrontation." *Black Scholar* 5 (May 1974): 32–40.

SIXTH PAN-AFRICAN CONGRESS OF 1974

Clarke, John Henrik. "Beyond Pan-Africanism: An African World Union." *Black Books Bulletin* 2 (Fall 1974): 14–16.

Madhubuti, Haki R. "Sixth Pan-African Congress: What Is Done to Save the Black Race." *Black Books Bulletin* 2 (Fall 1974): 50–51.

Turner, James. "Historical Perspectives: Sixth Pan-African Congress, 1974." *Black World* 23 (March 1974): 17.

8. *Political Access*

THE TRULY DISADVANTAGED

Glazer, Nathan. *Affirmative Discrimination.* New York, 1975.

Jencks, Christopher, et al. *Inequality.* New York, 1972.

Wilson, William Julius. *The Declining Significance of Race: Blacks and Changing American Institutions.* 1977. 2d ed. Chicago, 1980.

———. *The Truly Disadvantaged: The Inner City, the Underclass, and Public Policy.* Chicago, 1988.

RISING AFRICAN-AMERICAN CLASSES

"America's Rising Black Middle Class." *Time,* 17 June 1974, 19–28.

Featherman, David L., and Robert N. Hanser. "Changes in the Socioeconomic Stratification of the Races, 1962–1973." *American Journal of Sociology* (1976–1977): 621–51.

Hacker, Andrew. "Creating American Inequality." Review essay. *New York Review of Books,* 20 March 1980, 23.

Joint Center for Political Studies. *Profiles of Black Mayors in America.* Chicago, 1977.

9. The Moving Finger

AFRICAN-AMERICAN LITERATURE

Butterfield, Stephen J. *Black Autobiography in America.* Boston, 1975.

Gayle, Addison, Jr. *The Way of the New World: The Black Novel in America.* New York, 1976.

Lee, Robert A. *Black Fiction since Richard Wright.* British Association for American Studies; Pamphlets in American Studies 14. Cambridge, 1984.

Margolies, Edward. *Native Sons: A Critical Study of Twentieth Century Black American Authors.* New York, 1968.

Index